from testament to torah: an introduction to judaism in its formative age

JACOB NEUSNER
Brown University

DIANE APOSTOLOS–CAPPADONA, art editor
Georgetown University

PRENTICE HALL, ENGLEWOOD CLIFFS, NEW JERSEY 07632

Library of Congress Cataloging-in-Publication Data

Neusner, Jacob.
  From Testament to Torah.

  Bibliography.
  Includes index.
  1. Judaism—History—Post-exilic period, 586 B.C.–210 A.D. 2. Judaism—History—Talmudic period, 10-425.
I. Title.
BM176.N48 1988   296'.09'015   87–17463
ISBN 0–13–331620–3

Editorial/production supervision and interior design: Marjorie Shustak
Cover design: 20/20 Services, Inc.
Manufacturing buyer: Margaret Rizzi

For Stuart S. Kaufman, a friend from grade six to the present day; a token of affection and esteem after more than forty years of friendship

©1988 by Prentice Hall
A Division of Simon & Schuster
Englewood Cliffs, New Jersey 07632

Printed in the United States of America

10 9 8 7 6 5 4 3 2 1

ISBN 0-13-331620-3   01

Prentice-Hall International (UK) Limited, *London*
Prentice-Hall of Australia Pty. Limited, *Sydney*
Prentice-Hall Canada Inc., *Toronto*
Prentice-Hall Hispanoamericana, S.A., *Mexico*
Prentice-Hall of India Private Limited, *New Delhi*
Prentice-Hall of Japan, Inc., *Tokyo*
Simon & Schuster Asia Pte. Ltd., *Singapore*
Editora Prentice-Hall do Brasil, Ltda., *Rio de Janeiro*

contents

preface

Western civilization as we know it came into being in the centuries between the destruction of the First Temple of Jerusalem in 586 B.C., when the Hebrew Scriptures of ancient Israel reached the form in which we have them, and the rise of Islam to power in the Middle East, North Africa, and southern Europe in the seventh century A.D. The form of Judaism that would flourish in Christian Europe and the Muslim Middle East and North Africa, Christianity in most of its important forms, Roman law, Greco-Roman philosophy—these and other enduring and paramount components of the civilization of the West took shape. If we North Americans want to understand our past as women and men of the West, we turn to late antiquity and ask how those lasting institutions and ideas that make the West what it is came into being. This book introduces an important component, an influential and successful one, Judaism in its formative age.

You will learn two things in this book—one specific, the other general. The one attends to the *what* of a specific religion and its history, the other to the *how* of studying religion in general. The two go together.

The specific lesson is how, when, where, and why Judaism came into being, and, more important, the reason for its remarkable success in the civilization of the West—and of the world. For the Jews were never a large group, nor a strong or popular one, and yet their religion sustained

Judaism, and Judaism provided for them the purpose of their life, the ideal and the pattern of everyday living, turning them into a holy people, God's people, they maintained. Judaism, in other words, answered urgent questions with self-evidently valid truths.

The general lesson is *how* we study the history of a religion, at least in its initial and formative stages: the method. In the Epilogue I articulate the methods I illustrate in the shank of the book, so students become aware of what they have done after they have done it—and so can do the same thing on their own. The value of learning about any subject is measured by whether it helps you learn about other subjects of the same sort. If this book teaches not only the *what* of the history of Judaism, but the *how* of the history of religion, then it will help you to understand worlds remote from Judaism (and Christianity) and to frame questions that will produce understanding of the world at large. When we know the question that the Judaism under discussion answered, then we can explain why that Judaism came into being, why it enjoyed the standing of self-evident truth for as long as it did, and why, in modern times, it met competition from other Judaisms, which asked other questions and answered them with other (to participants, equally self-evidently valid) truths. And when we can explain the birth of a successful Judaism, then we can account for the success and influence of other religious systems as well. That is one important goal of the history of religion, and a principal concern of the Epilogue of this book.

I emphasize these matters of the *what* and the *how* at the outset so that the reader will know what I promise to accomplish, and also what I do not claim to contribute. I am a historian of religion, specializing in Judaism, with particular interest in the formative age of the Judaism that has predominated. I wish to trace the history of the formation of one Judaism—that alone. In so doing, I hope to present a useful model of how to write the history of a religion—that alone. I do not promise to write a general history of all the Judaisms of late antiquity, let alone of all the Jews. Nor do I claim to provide a history of Judaism(s) from ancient times to this morning. These are separate tasks. I think that students of religion may find enlightening an exercise in tracing the beginning, in the full light of day, of one of the great religious systems of the West, the Judaism of the dual Torah.

The history of a religion is not a problem of historical and linear narrative—first came this, then came that. Quite the contrary, within a given family of similar religions—for example, the family of Judaisms or of Christianities—a number of religious systems will compete. Each will write for itself a history that exhibits three traits. It will claim unitary status—that is, to represent the whole, to be *Judaism*, not just *a Judaism*. It will place itself in a linear relationship to all that has gone before and that is to come. It will allege that it forms the increment, the accumulation of all truth, in the historical tradition in which it stands. These three modes of self-understanding, the unitary, linear, and incremental view, ordinarily characterize the inner-looking view of religious systems. But these claims testify to their opposite: diversity within the religious family at hand, plurality of lines of development out of the past, and, it follows, not a single development or increment, but a multiplicity of possibilities, all of them realized somewhere and somehow. The historian of religion must make sense of the claims of unity and linear and incremental development, but need not entertain their validity in the face of contrary facts of plurality, diversity, and multiplicity. There have been many Judaisms and many Christianities and many Islams. True, there also is one Judaism, orthodox ("right doctrine") and normative, one Christianity ("The Church's one foundation is Jesus Christ the Lord"), and, most assuredly, one nation of Islam. And it is the task of theology of Judaism, Christianity, and Islam to tell us precisely what that one Judaism, one Christianity, one Islam is.

But as a historian of religion addressing the facts of society and system, I see things otherwise. For in describing, analyzing, and interpreting Judaic systems, I cannot make choices among the evidence and declare one system to be orthodox and normative—unless I also pretend that other evidence simply does not exist. In the period under discussion, we identify social groups within Israel that clearly regarded themselves as representing the whole of Israel, that obviously set forth a distinctive world view, and that certainly lived out a way of life different from that of others who also regarded themselves as "Israel." Israel, the nation, produced many Israels, distinct groups, each with its world view and its way of life. As a theologian looking backward, I may well settle questions of truth and error. But as a historian, sifting the evidence of the time, I cannot declare not to have existed groups that, in their day, flourished and exercised considerable influence. Evidence for the historian of religion and evidence for the theologian constitute two distinct, though interrelated, worlds of data. We cannot confuse the one with the other, or the kind of insight sought by the one with the truth provided by the other.

As a religious Jew, I cherish the truth of the Torah as it is taught by the theology of Judaism. As a historian of religion working on Judaism, I cherish the insight into the human condition contributed by the case of Judaism, the example of what it means to be a human being under this circumstance, in this particular setting: humanity in the Judaic condition. The one endows me with truth, the other grants me insight, and both tell me about me—and about the world. And so, I hope, it will be for others.

The history of religion defines the task of description, analysis, and interpretation—making sense of the whole, all together and all at once. If this book does its work well, then students will gain two things. First, they will understand how, out of the diversity of Judaisms before 70 A.D., a single Judaism took shape and became normative for a long time. Second, they will have in mind a model of how other diverse religious situations may be described, analyzed, and interpreted. By doing the history of one religion in its formative age, students may acquire a useful model of how to do a history of religion. That is my ambition.

My hope is that this book will serve a variety of courses in general education, as well as in the study of Bible and religion, the origins and formative history of Western civilization. I realize that the approach is somewhat different from what is familiar. My basic theory of education is simple: *Don't ask; discover!* I hope that in the pages of this book students may discover not only the *what* of things they did not know, but more especially, the *how* of the search for understanding.

Teachers in those courses will enjoy my genuine thanks if they can point to ways in which I may make this book in later editions a still more effective instrument of instruction in the history of religion and in the study of the formative centuries of Western civilization as defined by the biblical religions of Judaism and Christianity.

Jacob Neusner
Brown University
Providence, Rhode Island 02912

ACKNOWLEDGMENTS

I wish to thank the custodians of the works of art for supplying photographs and granting permission to use them. Diane Apostolos–Cappadona, art editor, wishes to thank Susan B. Matheson, Curator of Ancient Art, Yale University Art Gallery, and Erella Hadar, Consulate General of Israel, New York, for their assistance.

sIGNIfICANt Dates

B.C.

586   Destruction of the First Temple in Jerusalem and exile of Judeans (Jews) to Babylonia

ca. 500   Return of a small number of the exiles to the land of Israel/Palestine, and first efforts to rebuild the Temple.

ca. 450   Nehemiah and Ezra return to Jerusalem and restore the Temple.

ca. 450   Formation of the Pentateuch, the Five Books of Moses, out of received materials of the period before 586 by the Temple priesthood; Pentateuch adopted as the constitution of Jerusalem and Judea.

ca. 330   Alexander's conquest of the Near and Middle East brings Hellenistic government, language, and culture to the region. Jerusalem and Judea incorporated into world-empire.

ca. 300   After Alexander's death, the land of Israel falls under the rule of an inheritor-general based in Egypt. Country remains essentially autonomous.

ca. 200   Land of Israel falls under the rule of an inheritor-general based in Syria. Country still autonomous.

ca. 175–140	After Syrian-Greek government encourages Hellenization of the Temple and the people of Israel, a revolt led by the dynasty of the Hasmonean family—the Maccabees—reestablishes the Jewish kingdom as a free state.
140	Alliance with Rome.
ca. 60 B.C.–10 A.D.	Rome takes over the Near East and becomes the dominant power, ruling the land of Israel through its allies and friends, in particular the family of Herod.

A.D.

67–73	Revolt against Rome leads to the destruction of the Second Temple of Jerusalem in August 70. Most of the Jews retain their lands.
132–135	Major revolt, led by a general, Ben Koziba, or Bar Kokhba ("son of the star"), briefly reestablishes Israel's freedom, but is repressed. Jews are forbidden to enter Jerusalem. Repression afterward for a time prohibits practice of the faith, study of the Torah. By 145, country returns to normal. Jews lose their paramount presence in the southern part of the land of Israel, but remain the dominant population in Galilee and other parts of the north.
ca. 200	Publication of the Mishnah.
ca. 250	Publication of Mishnah tractate Avot, the Fathers.
ca. 300	Possible point of closure of the Tosefta, Sifra (to Leviticus), Sifré to Numbers and to Deuteronomy, and other important documents containing sayings attributed to the authorities of the Mishnah.
312	Constantine declares Christianity a licit religion.
361–362	Emperor Julian, as part of effort to embarrass and harass Christianity, allows the rebuilding of the Temple in Jerusalem. Project fails and Julian dies within the year.
387	John Chrysostom tells the Jewish community of Antioch that the failure to rebuild the Temple in 361–362 proves that Jewish worship is no longer valid, and the only way to serve God is through Christian churches.
ca. 400–450	Closure of the Talmud of the land of Israel, systematic commentary to the Mishnah; Genesis Rabbah, commentary to the book of Genesis; Leviticus Rabbah, commentary to the book of Leviticus.
ca. 450–500	Closure of Pesiqta de Rab Kahana, propositions on salvation of Israel associated with the various holy days and seasons of Judaism.
ca. 600	Closure of the Talmud of Babylonia, systematic commentary to the Mishnah, with large tracts devoted, also, to systematic commentary to passages of Scripture.
ca. 640	Muslim conquest of the Middle East, including the Jewish communities of both Babylonia and the land of Israel.

pROLOGUE

Judaism as we know it—that type of Judaism built upon the doctrine of the dual Torah, oral and written, revealed to Moses by God at Sinai—took shape between the first and the seventh century. It drew heavily on Judaisms of the 500 years before the first century, when the Old Testament was written. During that long period of time—a longer span than separates us from Columbus—the great structure rose in stages, not all at once. In this book we take up three important stages in the formative history of Judaism:

1. *The first stage*, the formation, in response to the destruction of the First Temple in 586 B.C. and the return to Zion three generations later, of the Judaism of the Five Books of Moses, in the time of the building of the second Temple in ca. 500 B.C., in Chapter 1;
2. *The second stage* in the formation of Judaism, in response to the destruction of the Second Temple in A.D. 70, in Chapters 2 and 3;
3. *The third and final stage* in the formation of Judaism, in response to the Christianization of the Roman Empire beginning in 312, in Chapters 4, 5, and 6.

The Epilogue on Method will discuss in more general terms how we have reached the conclusions laid out in those six chapters in order to help the student use the lessons learned here in the study of other religious systems.

This book introduces Judaism, with an emphasis on its formative and classical age and literature. We take up the formative millennium in the history of Judaism, from 500 B.C. to A.D. 500. What we want to know is how that particular Judaism developed that defined the Judaic component of Western civilization from antiquity to the present day: the formative age of Judaism in the West. Our interest is not in all the Judaisms of the period beyond the destruction of the First Temple in 586, and we recognize at the outset that the Judaism that emerged from late antiquity explored only one among the many potentialities of the biblical literature that reached closure as (what would later be known as) the Hebrew Scriptures, or "the Old Testament." This is not a history of all Judaisms of the age, but of only one among them. I tell the story of how one strand of the scriptural heritage was spun out and woven with other strands, ultimately forming the tapestry of a vast and encompassing Judaism, the one that would fill the frame of life of Israel, the Jewish people, for 2,000 years.

I address students in courses on Old and New Testament, on early Christianity, and above all, on Western civilization and general education. In particular I introduce those aspects of Judaism that are important in Western civilization. In the case of Judaism, where did it begin? Why did it work when it worked? What questions did it answer for the Jews, and why did those questions strike them as urgent, the answers as self-evidently true? When we can take up the sources of Judaism to answer these particular inquiries, we can make sense of not only the place of Judaism in Western civilization, but also the way in which other important components of the life of the West took shape . The book is meant to do two things. First, it proposes to tell the story of how Judaism began. Second, it means to provide an example of how to tell the stories of other definitive parts of Western civilization as well—Christianity, philosophy, and law, for instance.

Now everyone knows two things about Judaism. The first thing people know about Judaism is simple: it is not Christianity, and Jews are not Christians. The second is that Judaism is the religion of the Old Testament, and that Jews are the people of the Old Testament. That is where everyone starts, it is what everyone knows. One important thesis of this book is that Judaism attained its final definition in its formative age in response to the challenge of Christianity. Judaism is not Christianity because it is Judaism. The second important thesis is that Judaism developed out of the Hebrew Scriptures, the Old Testament, choosing out of that rich heritage its particular points of departure and emphasis, just as Christianity did. We begin with the formation of the Old Testament, because that marks the first stage in the three-stage process by which Judaism developed in its formative period. But we must remember that Christianity too is the religion of the Old Testament; that is why the Hebrew Scriptures are called the Old Testament. So the really central questions are, how did the Judaism we now know emerge from the Old Testament, and what are the writings of the Jews, beyond the Old Testament, that formed and defined Judaism.

What you must keep in mind, therefore, is that when we speak of Judaism in these pages, we do not mean everything every Jew everywhere believed about everything. We mean something much more precise and specific. We have to start back with the notion of a religious system, which will occupy us in later pages of this book, and then apply that notion to Judaism(s). A religious system comprises a world view, a way of life, and a particular social group. A Judaic religious system, or a Judaism, is a particular world view adopted by a group of Jews, a distinct and characteristic way of life of that group, joined to the actual existence of that social group that finds its meaning and purpose in the world view and its proper conduct in the way of life.

Just as today there are diverse world views and ways of life that characterize different groups presenting us with contemporary Judaisms, so it was in ancient times as well. In the aftermath of the destruction of the First Temple in 586 B.C., and the destruction of the Second Temple in A.D. 70, many Judaisms flourished. Biblical literature, which took shape at that time, testifies to the varieties of Judaisms that developed in response to the destruction of the Temple in 586. But we shall not explore all of them. We deal with only one of them—the one that came to its first statement in the Pentateuch, the Five Books of Moses, and that expressed the emphases of the priesthood in charge of the Temple of Jerusalem. The reason is not that that is the only Judaism that mattered in its day. It is that that is the Judaism which would later form the center of the Judaism of the dual Torah, which, from late antiquity to our own day, has predominated. And, it goes without saying, the Judaism expressed in the Pentateuch did not persist unchanged until it emerged in the larger system that came to final expression at the end of this formative age. Quite to the contrary, as we shall see, that Judaic system would undergo vast changes and great expansion over the course of time.

The formation of Judaism can be viewed as having three aspects:

1. The context of the social group that constituted Judaism,
2. The components of the canon of that group—that is, of the literary analysis of Judaism as displayed in its sacred writings, the writings as they emerge at a particular time and place, and
3. Of the system of questions and answers that served that group of Jews.

We ask: What was the human situation confronting the writers of these texts, and why did their message—their particular statement of

God's revelation or, in Hebrew, Torah—prove self-evidently persuasive for as long as it did, and still does?

My thesis is simple: *The Judaism that emerged as the normative religious system answered a particular problem. The problem persisted, and because of that persistent and chronic problem, which was adequately answered by Judaism, the Judaism that solved that problem endured and enjoyed success among the Jewish people.*

This book, therefore, introduces Judaism at its beginnings. Specifically, we take up three moments of radical change in the history of Judaism. The first is marked by the destruction of the Temple of Jerusalem in 586 B.C. (Chapter 1), the second, by the destruction of the Temple of Jerusalem in A.D. 70 (Chapters 2 and 3), and the third, by the Christianization of the Roman Empire beginning with the toleration of Christianity accorded by Constantine in A.D. 312 (Chapters 4, 5, and 6). The impact of the successive destructions of the Temple on the life of the Jews and on Judaism presents few surprises. But the importance of the conversion of Constantine to Christianity in 312 and the later recognition of Christianity as the religion of the Roman Empire is less widely understood. And yet, as I have shown,[1] that moment defined the civilization of the West, which, from the fourth century to nearly our own time has been Christian in its politics and in its deepest layers of consciousness and culture. It has also determined the system and structure of Judaism in the West. So let us dwell for a moment on the impact on Judaism of the Christianization of the Roman Empire.

That crisis presented Jews and Judaism with a challenge more difficult to accommodate than the destruction of the two Temples, difficult and disheartening though the events of 586 B.C. and A.D. 70 proved to be. The reason that the fourth century presented the most severe crisis Judaism ever had to face is simple. Christianity claimed to be Judaism, Christians to be Israel. So more subtle and more insidious, the challenge of Christianity addressed not the frontiers of the people from without, but the soul and heart of the people from within.

As I shall explain, that third critical moment would impart to Judaism the definition it would retain from then to now. I further argue that so long as the challenge of Christianity defined the social world of Israel, the Jewish people, the Judaism that came to definition originally in response to that challenge would enjoy the status of self-evident truth for Israel, the Jewish people. For the shift in the condition of Israel marked by Christ's rise to political power and the Torah's loss of a place in political institutions defined the context and setting of Judaism from then to nearly the present day. And, it must be said, the response of the

---

[1]Neusner, *Judaism in the Matrix of Christianity* (Philadelphia: Fortress Press, 1986) and *Judaism and Christianity in the Age of Constantine* (Chicago: University of Chicago Press, 1987).

day—represented by the Judaism defined in the documents of the late fourth and fifth centuries—proved remarkably successful. Judaism did endure, and the Jews did persist, from then to now. Thus, in the shifts in the symbolic system represented by the redefinitions of canon, teleology, and encompassing symbol, the Judaism which emerged from the fourth century, principally in the pages of the Talmud of the land of Israel, and which 200 years later reached fruition and full statement in the Talmud of Babylonia, enjoyed stunning success. We want to know whether and how the Judaism for which we have data changed in the context of the creation of the Christian polity and the Christian culture. We shall find out that that Judaism did change, and that Christianity had a considerable effect on the change.

We realize, therefore, that there is another long chapter in the history of Judaism, one that is not contained in this book. It concerns the period in which the Judaism that reached its final definition in response to the Christianization of the Roman Empire predominated. So long as Christianity remained self-evident in the West, Judaism retained the quality of self-evidence among Jews. The political and cultural questions Judaism answered, the institutions, the mythic structure, the way of life—all these remained stable in the West, so long as the West remained Christian. When Christianity lost its standing as self-evident truth to a fair sector of Western life, then Judaism too ceased to persuade large numbers of Jews that its picture of the world made sense. But that tale of change in modern times is another story, and I tell it in a different book.[2] This book stands on its own and tells its story entirely within its own covers.

It should be clear that when I approach the study of a religious system—in this case, Judaic systems, described, analyzed, interpreted—I ask a set of social questions. My particular interest in religion is in the relationship between the ideas people hold and the world in which they live—and with which they have to cope. This concern for the interplay of setting and substance, of the circumstance and contents of a religious system, falls in a broad sense into the category of the study of the ecology of religion as an approach to the comparison of religious systems. Let me explain.

When we study the ecology of religion, we study about how humanity in society responded to challenge and change, mediated between the received tradition of politics and social life and the crisis of the age and circumstance. In this book we treat the social side of religion—something people do together. Here religion is not trivial, not private, not individual, not mainly a matter of the heart. Religion is

---

[2]Neusner, *The Death and Birth of Judaism: From Self-Evidence to Self-Consciousness in Modern Times* (New York: Basic Books, 1987). My general theory of the whole of the history of Judaism is in *Judaism: Past, Present, Future* (Boston: Beacon Press, 1987).

public, political, social, economic. My premise about the nature of religion is simple. No single object of study forms so public and social—indeed, so measurable—a presence as religion. Nothing humanity has made constitutes a less personal, a less private, a less trivial fact of human life than religion.

Some people tend to identify religion with belief, to the near exclusion of behavior; by this definition, religion is understood as a personal state of mind, a private attitude. An introduction to Judaism would thus provide an account of things Jews believe. But religion not only transcends matters of belief; it constitutes a social system to which belief is only one contributing factor. The contrary view should be clear: When we study religion, we ask not about society but about self, not about culture and community but about conscience and character. So when people study religion, they tend, in the aggregate, to speak of individuals and not groups: faith and its substance, and, beyond faith, the things that faith represents—faith reified, hence, religion. In my view the power of religion in the world today, as through all of human history, testifies against that narrow view of the content of the study of religion and in favor of the approach of this book.

1

the first crisis: 586 and the judaism of the written torah

1. URGENT QUESTION, OBVIOUS ANSWER: ONE JUDAIC SYSTEM IN ITS SOCIAL AND POLITICAL SETTING

In 586 B.C., the Temple of Jerusalem was destroyed, the Jews were sent into exile in Babylonia, their king was deposed, and they witnessed the end of their state and settlement in their land, the land of Israel. It was at this moment that Judaism made its first statement. That is, over the next century a Judaism reached to full expression in response to that crisis. Looking backward from the end of the period of formation, we realize that it marked the first in the three-stage unfolding of the Judaism that, by the end of the ancient world, came to predominate and define Judaism from that time to this. For a Judaism responds with self-evidently valid answers, composed into a complete and systematic statement of reality, to a critical question, one raised by a crisis.

The three successive and connected Judaisms on which we focus came into being in response to critical turnings in the history of the Jewish people in the land of Israel; the first in 586 B.C., the second in A.D. 70, and the third in A.D. 312, as we shall see. The first of the three Judaisms before us made its principal statement in the pages of the Hebrew Scriptures and took up the question of exile and homecoming, alienation and conciliation. We realize of course, that other Judaisms began at the same time and within the same Scriptures. When we identify the first stage in the formation of the Judaism that became normative with the beginnings of the Pentateuch after 586, therefore, we do not exclude from consideration other Judaisms and their beginnings at the same time and place. But our problem is to describe the formation of a particular Judaism, and that defines the perspective we bring to the Scriptures at hand. If we wanted to describe all of the religious developments after 586 and before A.D. 70, we should consider many more aspects of the matter than we do now.

The Hebrew Scriptures—the Old Testament—came into existence in the aftermath of the exile, in 586, of the Jews from their homeland to Babylonia, and their return approximately 70 years later. In 539 Babylonia fell, and in 538 the new ruler of the Middle East, the Iranian emperor Cyrus, decreed that exiles might return to their homelands, including the Jews to the land of Israel. Some years later, a few did. The destruction of the Temple in 586 was followed by its reconstruction, reaching a conclusion in the time of Ezra and Nehemiah in ca. 450 B.C. The question was obvious: Who are we and why have these things happened to us? The answer provided by the Pentateuch—the Five Books of Moses: Genesis, Exodus, Leviticus, Numbers, and Deuter-onomy—appeared equally self-evident.

The specific ecology of Judaism in this original statement of a Judaic system therefore took up the issue of defining a people that, through exile to a foreign country, had attained an acute sense of self-consciousness, of being special. That definition of Israel in light of exile and return involved such diverse elements as the land and the relationship to the land, the identification of the group and its members' bond to one another, and the meaning of the events that overtook the group, which, in our language, we should call the history of the people. All of these elements—the definition of the social group, the explanation of the world view, the spelling out of the way of life—together comprised the first Judaism—the Judaism that accounted for events of a world-shaking, and therefore (in our terms) also a world-creating, order. We once more remind ourselves that there were other Judaisms that presented answers to the same urgent questions, so the one ecological setting generated more than a single system.

But all Judaisms after 70 began because of two events seen by the framers of Scripture as a single statement: (1) the destruction of the First Temple in 586, and (2) the building of the second about three generations later. The ecological facts worked out by the original Judaisms, including the one on which we focus, required an explanation of both loss and recovery—in theological terms, sin and punishment, atonement and reconciliation. Any Judaic system had to address the stunning fact that the nation had lost its land but had then gotten it back. The facts of the ecology of Judaism are simple. In 586 B.C., the Babylonian empire took and destroyed Jerusalem, taking into exile the bulk of the population of the small Jewish state centered on that city. Three generations later, the Iranian empire, under a Persian king, having conquered much of the Near East, restored to their homelands various peoples, including the Jews to Jerusalem, exiled by the preceding government. In ca. 500–450 B.C., the Temple of Jerusalem was rebuilt under a Jewish regime sponsored by the Iranian government. Everything that would happen for centuries to come, from the rebuilding of the Jerusalem Temple to its destruction in A.D. 70 by the Romans, and long afterward as well, found meaning in the stunning sequence of defeat and exile, followed by return and restoration.

The ecological setting for all Judaic systems took shape in the experience of defeat followed by restoration, loss of political standing and exile from the land, then recovery of standing and renewed possession of the land. What people had lost and then regained they saw in a quite fresh light. Their group life and its location on the land could no longer be taken for granted as a permanent fact of life. What an earlier generation had treated as a birthright, a new generation now found surprising. An intense sense of the land as something lost and then regained, a deep self-consciousness about the people as a special group because it had lost, then regained, its original situation—these demanded a cogent explanation. The original Judaism, expressed in the Five Books of Moses when assembled as a complete and cogent statement, supplied it. Judaism was born in that setting and it answered the question of the meaning of what had happened. That Judaic system comprised of Scripture explained the relationship of the people to the land, and of each person to the other, and of all, land and people alike, to God—a considerable story indeed. The setting is clear. As to the Scriptures, they reached their initial definition—that is, the selection that formed the first Judaic canon—on account of that sequence of calamitous events.

To summarize:

1. Setting: The system in its fundamental structure reached its definition in response to what happened between 586 and 450 B.C.: destruction and political dissolution, followed by reconstruction and political restoration—above all, loss of the land and return to the land.

2. Scripture: The canon comprised the books of Genesis, Exodus, Leviticus, Numbers, and Deuteronomy—that is, the Pentateuch, or Five Books of Moses—and most of the prophetic writings—that is, Joshua, Judges, Samuel, and Kings, as well as important parts of the books of Isaiah, Jeremiah, Ezekiel, and some of the minor prophets.

3. System: The original Judaism is the religion of a people that had suffered defeat and overcome that defeat; from that point onward, the Jews would constitute a people with a strong sense of a special destiny, having lost and regained the land.

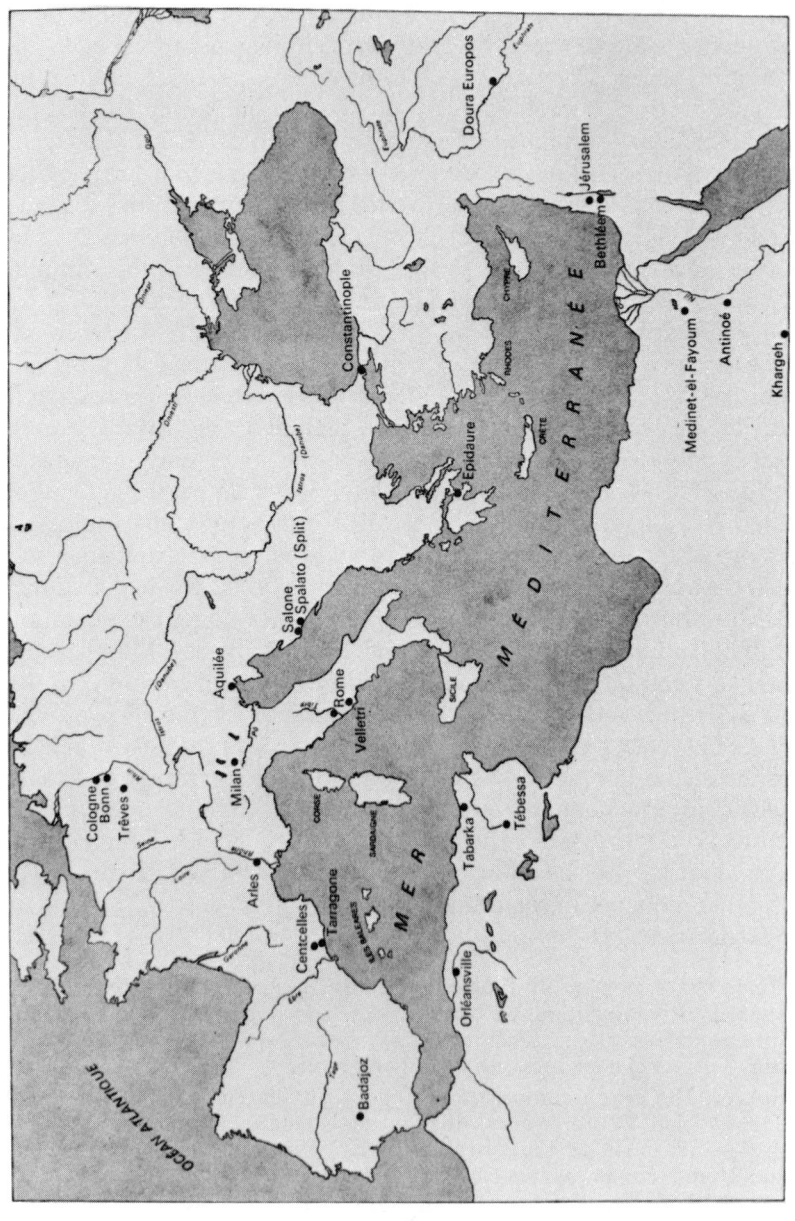

The Ancient World. (From P. Du Bourguet, *Early Christian Art*, trans. by T. Burton (New York: Reynal & Co., Inc., 1971), p. 219. Used with permission of William Morrow & Co., Inc.)

2. *THE PRIESTS' JUDAISM OF THE FIVE BOOKS OF MOSES: SCRIPTURE, SETTING, SYSTEM*

The Scripture of the first Judaism was the Five Books of Moses; the setting, Israel after the exile and return to Zion; and the system centered on the explanation of those rules that would keep Israel holy, separate for God alone. The Scriptures refer to events of a long-ago past, beginning with the creation of the world; the making of man and woman; the fall of humanity through disobedience; the flood that wiped out nearly all of humanity except for Noah, progenitor of all humanity; the decline of humanity from Noah to Abraham; then the rise of humanity through Abraham, Isaac, Jacob (also called Israel), and the twelve sons of Jacob; to exile in Egypt and, ultimately, Sinai. There, the Scriptural narrative continues, God revealed the Torah, revelation to Moses, and that revelation contained the terms of the covenant that God then made with Israel, the family of Abraham, Isaac, and Jacob. The book of Genesis narrates the story of creation and then the beginnings of the family that Israel would always constitute, the children of Abraham, Isaac, and Jacob. The book of Exodus presents the story of the slavery of the children of Israel in Egypt and of how God redeemed them from Egyptian bondage and brought them to Sinai, there to make a covenant, or contract, with them by which they would accept the Torah and carry out its rules. The book of Leviticus portrays the founding of the priests' service of God through the sacrifice of the produce of the holy land to which God would bring Israel, specifying the rules and regulations to govern the kingdom of priests and the holy people. The book of Numbers provides an account of the wandering in the wilderness. The book of Deuteronomy then presents a reprise of the story, a long sermon by Moses looking back on the history of Israel from the beginnings through the point of entry into the promised land, followed by a restatement of the rules of the covenant, or contract, between Israel and God.

Not all of the materials now joined in the Five Books of Moses derived from priestly authors, and a sizable proportion represented views held long before 586. But the priests put it all together, and their perspective comes to expression throughout. For what is important about the Pentateuch, from the perspective of its version of Judaism, is when the work reached the full and complete statement that we now have. The answer is simple. While making ample use of ancient tales, the framers of the Pentateuch as we now have it flourished in Babylonia after 586. There they drew together the elements of the received picture and reshaped them into the fairly coherent set of rules and narratives we now know as the Pentateuch. So the setting of the Judaism of the priests imparts to the scripture of that first setting its ultimate meaning: response to historical disaster followed by (to the Jews' mind) unprecedented triumph.

The Five Books of Moses encompass four sources, originally distinct, three deriving from the period before 586, and one from the period afterward. From our perspective, however, the Judaic system represented by the Pentateuch came into being when the several sources became one—that is, the Five Books of Moses as we now know them. That work was accomplished by priests in the time of Ezra, around 450 B.C. Their vision is characterized as follows:

> In the priests' narrative the chosen people are last seen as pilgrims moving through alien land toward a goal to be fulfilled in another time and place, and this is the vision, drawn from the ancient story of their past, that the priests now hold out to the scattered sons and daughters of old Israel. They too are exiles encamped for a time in an alien land, and they too must focus their hopes on the promise ahead. Like the Israelites in the Sinai wilderness, they must avoid setting roots in the land through which they pass, for diaspora is not to become their permanent condition, and regulations must be adopted to facilitate this. They must resist assimilation into the world into which they are now dispersed, because hope and heart and fundamental identity lay in the future. Thus, the priestly document not only affirms Yahweh's continuing authority and action in the lives of his people but offers them a pattern for life that will ensure them a distinct identity.[1]

The several segments of the earlier traditions of Israel were drawn together so as to make the point peculiarly pertinent to Israel in exile. So the original Judaic system, the one set forth by the Pentateuch, answered the urgent issue of exile with the self-evident response of return. The question was not to be avoided; the answer, not to be doubted. The center of the system, then, lay in the covenant, the contract that set forth the governing rules of Israel. And at the heart of the covenant was the call for Israel to form a kingdom of priests and a holy people.

If we ask ourselves for a single passage to express the priests' Judaism, we look to the book of Leviticus, which concerns the priesthood above all, and its version of the covenant, which is at Lev. 19:1–18 (given in the Revised Standard Version):

> And the Lord said to Moses, "Say to all the congregation of the people of Israel, You shall be holy, for I the Lord your God am holy.
>
> "Every one of you shall revere his mother and his father and you shall keep my sabbaths, I am the Lord your God.
>
> "Do not turn to idols or make for yourselves molten gods; I am the Lord your God.
>
> "When you offer a sacrifice of peace offerings to the Lord, you shall offer it so that you may be accepted. It shall be eaten the same day you offer it or

---

[1]W. Lee Humphreys, *Crisis and Story: Introduction to the Old Testament* (Palo Alto, Calif.: Mayfield Publishing Co, 1979), p. 217.

on the morrow, and anything left over until the third day shall be burned with fire. If it is eaten at all on the third day, it is an abomination, it will not be accepted, and every one who eats it shall bear his iniquity, because he has profaned a holy thing of the Lord; and that person shall be cut off from his people.

"When you reap the harvest of your land, you shall not reap your field to its very border, neither shall you gather the gleanings after your harvest. And you shall not strip your vineyard bare, neither shall you gather the fallen grapes of your vineyard; you shall leave them for the poor and for the sojourner. I am the Lord your God.

"You shall not steal, nor deal falsely, nor lie to one another. And you shall not swear by my name falsely and so profane the name of your God; I am the Lord. You shall not oppress your neighbor or rob him. The wages of a hired servant shall not remain with you all night until the morning. You shall not curse the deaf or put a stumbling block before the blind, but you shall fear your God; I am the Lord.

"You shall do no injustice in judgment; you shall not be partial to the poor or defer to the great, but in righteousness shall you judge your neighbor. You shall not go up and down as a slanderer among your people, and you shall not stand forth against the life of your neighbor; I am the Lord.

"You shall not hate your brother in your heart, but you shall reason with your neighbor, lest you bear sin because of him. You shall not take vengeance or bear any grudge against the sons of your own people, but you shall love your neighbor as yourself; I am the Lord."

The children of Abraham, Isaac, and Jacob are to form a people of God, keeping the rules—the covenant—God sets forth. This mixture of rules we should regard as cultic (as to sacrifice), moral (as to support of the poor), ethical (as to right-dealing), and above all religious (as to "being holy for I the Lord your God am holy") all together portrays a complete and whole society. Elsewhere, the book of Leviticus contains a clear statement of the consequence, and that is geared to the events of the recent past: "If you walk in my statutes and observe my commandments and do them, then I will give you your rains in their season" (Lev. 26:3), "But if you will not hearken to me and will not do all these commandments, . . . I will do this to you: I will appoint over you sudden terror . . . and you shall sow your seed in vain for your enemies shall eat it . . . Then the land shall enjoy its sabbaths as long as it lies desolate while you are in your enemies' land. . . ." (Lev. 26:34). The Judaism of the priests therefore responded to the loss of the land and its restoration to the Jews' possession. It confronted the overwhelming question of the meaning of what had happened and supplied what to the priests was a self-evidently valid answer: Israel must obey the rules of holiness, and, if it does, then by keeping its half of the agreement, or covenant, it could make certain that God would find valid the other half: "And I will give peace in the land, and you shall lie down and none shall make you afraid" (Lev. 26:6).

PALESTINE IN 30 A.D.

TETRARCHY OF HEROD ANTIPAS
TETRARCHY OF PHILIP
UNDER PONTIUS PILATE
CITIES OF THE DECAPOLIS
CITIES AND TOWNS

Palestine in the Ancient World. (Adapted from *Westminster Historical Atlas to the Bible* (rev. ed.), edited by George Ernest Wright and Floyd Vivian Wilson. Copyright 1956 by W.L. Jenkins. Adapted and used by permission of the Westminster Press, Philadelphia, PA.)

3. THE "NORMATIVE JUDAISM" OF THE SECOND TEMPLE PERIOD

As we shall see in Chapter 2, in the period from 586 B.C. to A.D. 70, one basic Judaic system characterized pretty much everybody in the land of Israel ("Palestine"); in addition, some small groups developed Judaic systems of a distinct character. Here we describe the system that was normal and normative, in the descriptive sense that most people, whatever else they believed and cherished and did, found definition here. In Chapter 2 we then consider the broader social context created by this Judaism—and also the special Judaic systems that were generated within, and by, this same general system, this one normal and "normative" Judaism.

While Scripture—the Old Testament—contained many more writings than those of the priests, and the work of drawing together the entire heritage of Israel before 586 encompassed many more authorships than the priestly one, one strand in the larger thread imparts its texture to the whole. The principal Judaism of the period from 586 B.C. to A.D. 70, the one that enjoyed the broadest recognition among the Jews and set the norm for them all, focused upon the Five Books of Moses, with their emphasis upon the Temple and its orderly and meticulous service of God through sacrifice. The principal institutions of that normative Judaism derived from Scripture. The way of life overall expressed the requirements of the covenant of God with Moses and has been rightly called *covenantal nomism*,[2] and the world view explained in terms of the Five Books of Moses the meaning of the everyday life of the people and the historical existence of the nation. And that was the particular Judaism that would impart its shape and structure to the Judaism that would predominate, in vastly different form to be sure, after 70. There are two reasons for the fact that the normative Judaism of the land of Israel from the return to Zion after 586 to the destruction of the Temple should find definition in the priests' conception.

First, the priests are the ones who organized and set forth the Torah revealed by God to Moses at Sinai as the Jews would receive and revere it. Consequently, their perspective, with its emphasis on the Temple and its holiness, the cult and its critical role in sustaining the life of the land and the nation, would predominate. Since the Torah of Moses at Sinai defined the faith, explained what had happened and set forth the rules for God's continuing favor to Israel, the final shape and system of the Torah would have a profound impact. And, as we realize, the structure of the whole—as distinct from its parts—derived from the perspective and paramount influence of the priesthood of the Jerusalem Temple.

---

[2]E. P. Sanders, *Paul and Palestinian Judaism* (Philadelphia: Fortress Press, 1979).

Second, the issue that formed the critical center of the Torah of Moses persisted, with the result that the urgent question answered by the Torah retained its original character and definition—and the self-evidently valid answer—read in the synagogue every Sabbath morning, as well as on Monday and on Thursday—retained its relevance. With the persistent problem renewing, generation after generation, that same resentment, the product of a memory of loss and restoration, of a recognition, in the here and now, of the danger of a further loss, the priests' authoritative answer would not lose its power to persist and to persuade. So the second of the two reasons is the more important: The question answered by the Five Books of Moses persisted at the center of the national life and remained, if chronic, also urgent. The answer provided by the Pentateuch therefore retained its self-evident importance. To those troubled by the question, the answer enjoyed the status of (mere) fact. So let me spell out this question, this answer, that would so shape the Judaism that, at the end of the ancient world, would persist and flourish in the West.

From the formation of the Five Books of Moses, with the Priestly Code at the center and the priests' vision infusing the whole, the priests' conception of the Temple and its world view and way of life provided the structural model for a number of groups within Israel. We may point to three such groups, all of them turning for definitive structure—points of emphasis and continual concern—back to the Priestly Code and its generative symbols and myths: the Essenes of Qumran and the Pharisees, whom we shall meet in the next chapter, and the framers of the earlier strata of the Mishnaic system (who may or may not also have been Pharisees), whose work we shall consider at length in Chapter 3. The literary statements of all three groups make frequent reference to issues of the Priestly Code. One encompassing example of that fact is the stress placed by all three groups upon cultic cleanness and uncleanness, preservation of food and of meals in conditions required, in the Priestly Code of Leviticus and Numbers, only for the Temple and the priests.

Each of these groups—sects expressing in an extreme and pure way the values of the society as a whole—emphasized the holy Temple. In each case, the members of the sect wanted to obey the rules of holiness, as they applied to the Temple, even when they were in their homes. As we realize, those rules involved aspects of everyday life. But one point of emphasis was on the conduct of the priests in their eating of their share of the holy offerings to God. Specifically, the priests had to keep a set of rules of consecration when they ate their meals, which were made up of the priests' portion of the sacrifice. The Essenes of Qumran observed a set of rules of cultic cleanness when eating their meals. The Pharisees, a group of people bound by common rules of observance governing the preparation and eating of meals, also had special dietary laws. Both groups imitated the priests (in one way or another) and so entered into that state of holiness achieved by the priests in the temple. Each of these social groups defined itself around the eating of cultic meals in the state of cleanness prescribed by Leviticus for Temple priests in the eating of their share of the Temple sacrifices.

This brings us back to our original question: Why should the Temple and the ideas of its priests have played so important a role in the mind of the people later on? Given the range and variety of teachings in the Five Books of Moses, we wonder why these sectarian groups found so authoritative a model in the rules of sanctification. Of still greater interest, we know that the Temple and its rites formed the centerpiece of the national life of Israel. Large numbers of people came to Jerusalem on the pilgrim festivals—Tabernacles in the autumn, Passover and Pentecost in the spring. So it was not only the minor sects who testify to the centrality of the priests' vision in the life of Israel, the Jewish people. The very critical role played by Jerusalem, with stress on the holiness of the Temple and the supernatural importance of its cult, makes us realize the importance of that original Judaism, the Judaism of the Five Books of Moses, that took shape after 586. Accordingly, we have to wonder why the priestly themes and repertoire of concerns should have so occupied the imagination and fantasy of the people as a whole, not only of those who formed the group (or groups) represented by the holiness sects. It is the continuity from the priestly code of the seventh through the fifth century B.C., to the beginnings of the Mishnaic code of the first and second centuries A.D. which requires explanation. For, as we shall see, the Mishnah, and therefore the Judaism, that flowed from that central document presents the priestly perspective on the condition of Israel.

The deep syntax of the sacred belonged to the priesthood from olden times. That is why it becomes urgent to speculate on why the priestly code should have exercised so profound and formative an influence upon the life of the Second Temple. The priestly code of the Five Books of Moses that expressed the priestly emphasis on sanctification exercised formative power. The reason is that the problems addressed and solved by the Judaism of the Five Books of Moses remained chronic long after the period of its formation, from the seventh century onward, until its closure in the time of Ezra and Nehemiah. The Priestly Code states a powerful answer to a pressing and urgent question. The question continued to trouble people. Since, as I shall now suggest, that question would remain a perplexity continuing to trouble Israelites for a long time, it is not surprising that the priestly answer to it, so profound and fundamental in its character, should for its part have continued to attract and impress people too.

We have once more to locate ourselves in the time of closure of the Mosaic Scriptures—that is, in the late sixth and fifth centuries B.C.—and to specify the critical tensions of that period. Once we have seen the character of these tensions, we shall realize without needing much exposition that the same tensions persisted and confronted the thinkers whose reflection led to the conclusions, in resolution of those ongoing points of dissonance, that the Temple's holiness enveloped and surrounded Israel's Land and demarcated its people. What distinguishes ancient Israel is its preoccupation with defining itself. And the reason for that obsession was the loss and recovery of the land and of political sovereignty. Israel, because of its (in its mind) amazing experience had attained a self-consciousness that continuous existence in a single place under a single government denied others. There was nothing given, nothing to be taken for granted, in the life of a nation that had ceased to be a nation on its own land and then once more regained that (once normal, now abnormal) condition.

So the issue was, and would remain, Who is Israel? And what are the rules that define Israel as a social, and therefore also a political, entity? In one way or another, Israel, the Jewish people wherever they lived, sought means of declaring itself distinct from its neighbors. The stress on exclusion of the neighbors from the group, and of the group from the neighbors, in fact runs contrary to the situation of ancient Israel, with unmarked frontiers of culture, the constant giving and receiving among diverse groups, generally characteristic of ancient times. The persistent stress on differentiation, yielding a preoccupation with self-definition, also contradicts the facts of the matter. In the time of the formation of the Pentateuch, Israel was deeply affected by the shifts and changes in social, cultural, and political life and institutions. A century and a half after the formation of the Pentateuch under Ezra and Nehemiah, when the Greeks under Alexander the Great conquered the entire Middle East (ca. 320 B.C.) and incorporated the land of Israel into the international Hellenistic culture, the problem of self-definition came to renewed expression. And when the war of independence fought by the Jews under the leadership of the Maccabees (ca. 160 B.C.) produced an independent state for a brief period, that state found itself under the goverment of a court that accommodated itself to the international style of politics and culture. What was different, and what made Israel separate and secure on its land and in its national identity? In that protracted moment of confusion and change, the heritage of the Five Books of Moses came to closure. And that same situation persisted that had marked the age in which the Pentateuch had delivered its message, answering with self-evidently valid responses the urgent question of the nation's existence.

The codification and closure of the law under Ezra and Nehemiah produced a law code which heavily emphasized the sanctification of Israel, in secular terms, on the exclusivist character of the Israelite God and cult. "Judaism" gained the character of a cultically centered way of life and world view. Both rite and myth aimed at the continuing self-definition of Israel by separation from, and exclusion of, the rest of the world. Order against chaos meant holiness over uncleanness, life over death. The purpose was to define Israel against the background of the other peoples of the Near and Middle East, with whom Israel had much in common, and, especially, to differentiate Israel from its neighbors (for example, Samaritans) in the same country. Acute differentiation was required because the social and cultural facts were precisely to the contrary—common traits hardly bespeaking clear-cut points of difference, except of idiom. The mode of differentiation taken by the Torah literature in general, and the priestly sector of that literature in particular, was cultic. The meaning, however, was also social. The power of the Torah composed in this time lay in its control of the Temple. The Torah made that Temple the pivot and focus. The Torah literature, with its concerned God, who cares what people do about rather curious matters, and the Temple cult, with its total exclusion of the non-Israelite from participation, and (all the more so) from cultic commensality, raised high those walls of separation and underscored the distinctiveness that already existed. The life of Israel flowed from the altar; what made Israel Israel was the center, the altar.

Note the contrast to the life of Israel, the Jewish people, before 586. So long as Israel remained essentially within its own Land and frame of social reference—that is, before the conflagration of the sixth century B.C.—the issue of separation from neighbors could be treated casually. When the very core and heart of what made Israel into Israel were penetrated by the doubly desolating and disorienting experiences of both losing the Land and then coming back, the issue of who is Israel came to the fore. Exercises in confusion in economic and social relationships, and the fact that the Land to which Israelites returned in no way permitted contiguous and isolated Israelite settlement, made it certain that the issue of self-definition clearly would emerge. It would remain chronically on the surface. And it would persist for the rest of Israelite history, from the return to Zion and the formation of the Torah literature even down to our own day. The reason for this persistence? It is that the social forces that lent urgency to the issue of who is Israel (later, who is a Jew) would remain. It is hardly an exaggeration to say that this confusion about the distinctive and ongoing identification to be assigned to Israel would define the very framework of the social and imaginative ecology of the Jewish people. So long as memory remained, the conflicting claims of exclusivist Torah literature and universalist prophecy, of a people living in utopia, in no particular place, while framing its vision of itself in the deeply locative symbols of cult and center—these conflicting claims would make vivid the abiding issue of self-definition.

When we ask why the Temple with its cult enduringly proved central in the imagination of the Israelites in the country, as indeed it did, we have only to repeat the statements which the priests of the Temple and their imitators in the sects were prepared to make. These explain the critical nature of cult and rite. If we reread the priestly viewpoint as it is contained in the books of Leviticus and Numbers, as well as in priestly passages of Genesis and Exodus, this is the picture we derive. The altar was the center of life, the conduit of life from heaven to earth and from earth to heaven. All things are to be arrayed in relationship to the altar. The movement of the heavens demarcated and celebrated at the cult marked out the divisions of time in relationship to the altar. The spatial dimension of the Land was likewise demarcated and celebrated in relationship to the altar. The natural life of Israel's fields and corrals, the social life of its hierarchical caste system, the political life (by no means only in theory) centered on the Temple as the locus of ongoing government—all things in order and in place expressed the single message. The natural order of the world corresponded to, reinforced, and was reinforced by, the social order of Israel. Both were fully realized in the cult, the nexus between those opposite and corresponding forces, the heavens and the earth.

The lines of structure emanated from the altar. And these lines of structure constituted high and impenetrable frontiers to separate Israel from the gentile's Israel, which was holy, ate holy food, reproduced itself in accord with the laws of holiness, and conducted all of its affairs, both affairs of state and the business of the table and the bed, in accord with the demands of holiness. So the cult defined holiness. Holiness meant separateness. Separateness meant life. Why? Because outside the Land, the realm of the holy, lay the domain of death. The lands are unclean. The Land is holy. For the Scriptural vocabulary, one antonym for *holy* is *unclean*, and one opposite of *unclean* is *holy*. The synonym of *holy* is *life*. The principal force and symbol of uncleanness and its highest expression are death. So the Torah stood for life, the covenant with the Lord would guarantee life, and the way of life required sanctification in the here and now of the natural world.

It is one thing to consider these questions in theory. It is another to peer into the actual life of the country and its people. For that purpose, Chapter 2 presents a tableau of Jerusalem in the first century, an account of that setting that marked the full expression of the Judaism that had begun its life with the destruction of the First Temple and the building of the Second in the sixth century B.C.

2

church and sect: a tableau of israel, the nation, and its judaism(s) in first-century jerusalem

The two great religious traditions of the West that emerged from the Judaism of the Land of Israel/Palestine in the first century A.D. originated among small groups of people who, in one way or another, brought to an extreme expression common beliefs of the nation at large. If we distinguish between a church as the social category of a religion that aspires to address everybody and to include the entire society, and a sect as the category that speaks to the few, the saved, then the nation, Israel, produced a church and sects. The "church" was the normative religion of the nation as a whole (with some isolated groups that segregated themselves from it for their special reasons). That religion appealed, for its world view, to the Hebrew Scriptures (later called by Christianity "the Old Testament") which people believed God had revealed to Moses and the prophets. Its way of life could be described, more or less completely and accurately, by reference to the principal points of observance—festivals, Sabbaths, holy way of life—called for in those Scriptures (or in some passages). Its definition of Israel encompassed all Jews. The pillars of this nation-church-religion, its principal institutions, consisted in the Temple and its cult, the calendar marking

15

Two of the pottery jugs in which
the Dead Sea Scrolls were found
at Qumran. (Courtesy of the Consulate
General of Israel, New York.)

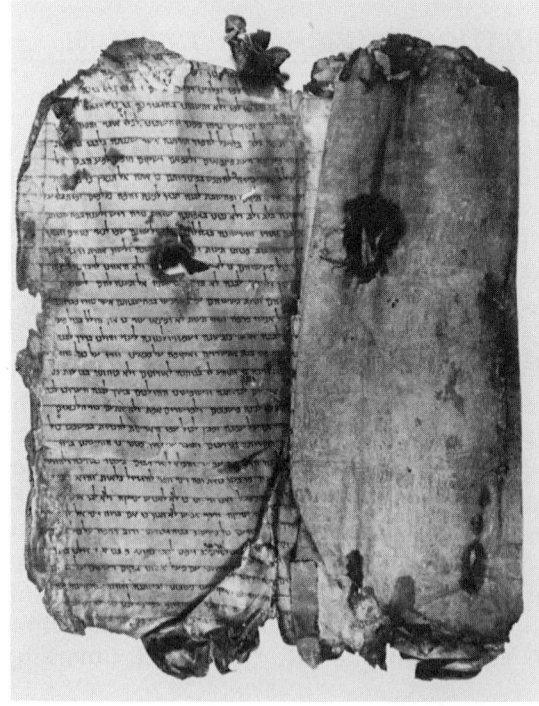

Partially rolled "Thanksgiving
Scroll"—one of the original Dead
Sea Scrolls—containing Psalm
40, which like all hymns begins, "I
thank Thee, O Lord." (Courtesy of
the Consulate General of Israel, New
York.)

the passage of time in the heavens and the seasons down below, the Scriptures. Wise teachers, priests, prophets, figures of politics—all appealed to this same heritage of the kingdom of priests and holy people, once exiled for sin from its holy land, then forgiven, brought back, and blessed.

Within the nation-religion we discern two small groups from whom the world was to hear much. One was nascent Christianity, which carried forward the scriptural heritage of prophecy and apocalyptic, with keen interest in questions of salvation; the other was nascent Judaism, represented in the first century by the Pharisees (of whom we shall hear more in a moment). They carried forward the scriptural heritage of the Five Books of Moses, with the pentateuchal stress upon the questions of the sanctification of Israel. Now the nation-church of Israel encompassed both of these poles of life, salvation out of history at the end of time, with concern for sin, punishment, forgiveness, and atonement, and sanctification of everyday life in the here and now, with concern for living in the workaday world the life that God in heaven commanded. But the one group laid emphasis on the one, the other on the other, each giving powerful and effective statement to a fundamental religious conviction cherished by all in common.

Western civilization over the next four centuries is the tale of how two small sects within the nation-church of Israel turned themselves into churches, encompassing each in its own way the concerns of the other; thus, in its diverse forms, Christianity, with its initial stress on salvation, would address the issues of sanctification, while the Judaism emerging, in part, from Pharisaism would take account not only of the sanctification of the everyday world of nature and supernature, but also of the salvation of the historical life of Israel at the end of time. The sects both became Churches: the one, the Christian Church in all its glory; the other, the faith of Israel, God's people, in all its pilgrim majesty.

2. JERUSALEM AND THE TEMPLE

Let us begin our journey through the Judaism of all Israel, that "church" of which we spoke, with a picture of how a religion looks when it encompasses a nation. The Judaism of Israel, the Jewish people, centered upon the Temple; and at three holy seasons a year, pilgrims came to witness and share in the rites, to celebrate God in the holy communion of the altar of Jerusalem. From near and far pilgrims climbed the paths to Jerusalem. Distant lands sent their annual tribute, taxes imposed by a spiritual, rather than a worldly, sovereignty. Everywhere Jews turned to the Temple mountain when they prayed. Although Jews differed about matters of law and theology, the meaning of history, and the timing of the Messiah's arrival, most affirmed the holiness of the city Isaiah

"The War of the Sons of Light Against the Sons of Darkness," one of the Dead Sea Scrolls. (Courtesy of the Consulate General of Israel, New York.)

called Ariel—Jerusalem, the faithful city. It was here that the sacred drama of the day must be enacted. And looking backward, we know they were right. It was indeed the fate of Jerusalem which in the end shaped the faith of Judaism for endless generations to come—but not quite in the ways that most people expected before 70 A.D.

How had Jerusalem cast its spell upon the Jews of far-off lands, to bring them together in their hearts' yearning? For centuries Israel had sung with the psalmist, "Our feet were standing within thy courts, O Jerusalem." They had exulted, "Pray for the peace of Jerusalem! May all prosper who seek your welfare!" Jews long contemplated the lessons of the old destruction. They were sure that by learning what Jeremiah, Ezekiel, and (Second) Isaiah taught about the meaning of the catastrophe of 586 B.C., by keeping the faith that prophecy demanded, they had ensured the city's eternity. Even then the Jews were a very old people. Their own records, translated into the language of all civilized people, testified to their antiquity. They could look back upon ancient enemies

Mosaic floor showing the 7-branched candelabrum, palm branch, incense shovel, and ram's horn at the Hamat–Tiberias Synagogue, 3rd to 4th century. (Courtesy of the Consulate General of Israel, New York.)

Greek inscription flanked by lions on the mosaic floor of the Hamat–Tiberias Synagogue, 3rd to 4th century. (Courtesy of the Consulate General of Israel, New York.)

now forgotten by history, and ancient disasters, the spiritual lessons of which illuminated current times. People thought that they kept the faith by devotion to the holy city, to the sacred Temple, to divinely ordained rites of service, to the priesthood, to the altar. Many a Jew yearned to see the priests upon their platform, to hear the Levites in their great choir singing the songs of David, to receive the blessing of the Lord in the Temple in Jerusalem.

If people thought they kept the faith, they had good reason. What had the Lord commanded of old, which now they did not do? For three sins the ancient Temple had fallen in 586 B.C.—murder, adultery, and idolatry. Now, five centuries later, idolatry was a grotesque memory. Murder and adultery were surely not so common among those whom God had instructed as elsewhere, they supposed. As to ancient Scriptures, were these not studied in the synagogues Sabbath upon Sabbath? But the most certain testimony of all to the enduring covenant was the Temple, which stood as the nexus between Jew and God. Its services bore witness to Israel's enduring loyalty to the covenant and the commandments of Sinai. They saw Jerusalem with the eye of faith, and that vision transformed the city.

The activity was endless. Priests hurried to and fro—important because of their tribe, sacred because of their task, officiating at the sacrifices morning and eventide, busying themselves throughout the day with the Temple's needs. They were always careful to keep the levitical rules of purity which God decreed, they thought, for just this place and hour. Levites assisting them and responsible for the public liturgies could be seen everywhere. In the outer courts, Jews from all parts of the world, speaking many languages, changed their foreign money for the Temple coin. They brought up their shekel, together with the free will, or peace, or sin, or other offerings they were liable to give. Outside, in the city beyond, artisans created the necessary vessels or repaired broken ones. Incense makers mixed spices. Animal dealers selected the most perfect beasts. In the schools, young priests were taught the ancient law to which they would, in time, conform, as had their ancestors before them, exactly as did their fathers that very day. The entire population was either directly or indirectly engaged in the work of the Temple. The city lived for it, by it, and on its revenues. In modern terms, Jerusalem was a center of pilgrimage, and its economy was based upon tourism.

But no one saw things in such a light. Jerusalem had an industry, to be sure, but a Jew asked "What is the business of this city?" would have replied without guile, "It is a holy city, and its work is the service of God on high." Only a few doubted it. For reasons of their own, the Essenes, who formed the commune at the Dead Sea, abandoned the Temple, regarding it as hopelessly impure, its calendar as erroneous. Others, the Pharisees, thought that the priests should conduct themselves in accordance with the oral tradition they believed God had revealed to

Moses at Sinai, that Moses had transmitted to the prophets, and the prophets to sages, down to that very day and to their own group. But even they were among the Temple's loyal servants. The Temple was the center of the world. They said that the mount was the highest hill in the world. To it, in time, would come the anointed of God. In the meantime, they taught, the Temple sacrifice was the way to serve God, a way he himself in remotest times had decreed. True, there were other ways believed to be more important, for the prophets had emphasized that sacrifice alone was not enough to reconcile the sinner to a God made angry by unethical or immoral behavior. Morality, ethics, humility, good faith—these, too, he required. But good faith meant loyalty to the covenant, which had specified, among other things, that the priests do just what they were doing. The animal sacrifices, the incense, the oil, wine, and bread were to be arrayed in the service of the Most High.

3. "BECAUSE OF THEIR SINS"

So much for the tableau. How did the sects see the church? Both sides found fault—later. The Judaism that would emerge from Pharisaism condemned the generations before 70 because of the historical outcome: the destruction of the Temple. So the sect that stressed sanctification of the here and now saw in a historical and one-time event—one that marked the opposite of salvation—the epitaph. The Christian church condemned the same generations of Israel because so few had accepted Jesus as the promised Messiah, the Christ. The sanctification associated with the Temple was broken on that account, they held, and so no stone would be left on stone. The destruction of Jerusalem marked the end of both Israel's sanctification and the power of its rites based on sanctification, so later Christian thinkers maintained. So the sect that stressed salvation at the end of time interpreted in the historical event a supernatural break in the on-going processes of holiness. In this way each of the sects marked its movement beyond its original limitations—the one toward an interest in salvation, in history and events, the other toward a concern for sanctification, with an account of how life in the here and now would be lived within the rites of God's holiness.

For their own reasons, as stages in their unfolding history, therefore, the emerging Christianity and Judaism would condemn this generation of the first Christian century. Christians and Jews alike reflected upon the destruction of the great sanctuary. They looked to the alleged misdeeds of those who lived at the time for reasons to account for the destruction. No generation in the history of Jewry had been so roundly, universally condemned by posterity as that of Yohanan ben Zakkai. Christians remembered, in the tradition of the church, that Jesus wept over the city and spoke bitterly, and with sorrow:

> O Jerusalem, Jerusalem, killing the prophets and stoning those who are sent
> to you! How often would I have gathered your children together as a hen
> gathers her brood under her wings, and you would not! Behold, your house
> is forsaken and desolate. For I tell you, you will not see me again, until you
> say, "Blessed is he who comes in the name of the Lord."
>
> (Matt. 23:37–39)

> And when the disciples pointed out the Temple buildings from a distance,
> he said to them, "You see all these, do you not? Truly, I say to you, there will
> not be left here one stone upon another, that will not be thrown down."
>
> (Matt. 24:2; cf. Luke 21:6)

So for twenty centuries, Jerusalem was seen through the eye of Christian
faith as a faithless city, killing prophets, and therefore desolated by the
righteous act of a wrathful God.

But Jews said no less. From the time of the destruction, they prayed:

> On account of our sins we have been exiled from our land, and we have
> been removed far from our country. We cannot go up to appear and bow
> down before you, to carry out our duties in your chosen Sanctuary, in the
> great and holy house upon which your name was called.
>
> *Siddur* (the Jewish prayerbook)

It is not a great step from "our sins" to "the sins of the generation in whose
time the Temple was destroyed." It is not a difficult conclusion, and not a
few have reached it. The Temple was destroyed mainly because of the
sins of the Jews of that time, particularly "causeless hatred." Whether
the sins were those specified by Christians or by talmudic rabbis hardly
matters. This was supposed to be a sinning generation.

It was not a sinning generation, but one deeply faithful to the
covenant and to the Scripture that set forth its terms, perhaps more so
than many who have since condemned it. First-century Israelites sinned
only by their failure. Had they overcome Rome, even in the circles of the
rabbis they would have found high praise, for success indicates the will
of Providence. But on what grounds are they to be judged sinners? The
Temple was destroyed, but it was destroyed because of a brave and
courageous, if hopeless, war. That war was waged, not for the glory of a
king or for the aggrandizement of a people, but in the hope that at its
successful conclusion, pagan rule would be extirpated from the holy land.
This was the articulated motive. It was a war fought explicitly for the
sake, and in the name of, God. The struggle called forth prophets and
holy men, leaders whom the people did not kill or stone, but courageously
followed past all hope of success. Jews were not demoralized or cowardly,
afraid to die because they had no faith in what they were doing, fearful
to dare because they did not want to take risks. The Jerusalemites fought
with amazing courage, against unbelievable odds. Since they lost, later

The Zodiac from the mosaic floor of the Beth Alpha Synagogue. (Courtesy of the Consulate General of Israel, New York.)

The Sacrifice of Isaac, from the mosaic floor of the Beth Alpha Synagogue. (The Institute of Archaeology, The Hebrew University of Jerusalem.)

generations looked for their sin, for none could believe that the omnipotent God would permit his Temple to be destroyed for no reason. As after 586 B.C., so after A.D. 70, the alternative was this: "Either our fathers greatly sinned, or God is not just." The choice represented no choice at all. "God is just, but we have sinned—we, but mostly our fathers before us. Therefore, all that has come upon us—the famine, the exile, the slavery to pagans—these are just recompense for our own deeds."

4. HEROD AND ROMAN RULE

Just before the turn of the first century, the Jews were ruled by King Herod, a Roman ally and a strong and able monarch. Herod's sons took over after his death, just before the turn of the century. What was Herod's position within the larger Roman context, and why did he, as a native Jew, enjoy Roman support and allegiance? It was imperial policy in Herod's time to exert authority through territorial monarchs, petty kings who ruled frontier territories still too unruly to receive a Roman viceroy. Rome later came to govern the protectorates through its own agents. It finally incorporated the subjugated lands into the normal provincial structure. Thus in Armenia, Cilicia, and other territories on the Parthian frontier, Rome established or supported friendly kings, ethnarchs, and tetrarchs, thereby governing through subservient agents in lands where Rome itself did not choose to rule. Honored by Rome with the titles *Socius et Amicus Populi Romani*, "associate and friend of Roman people," and, in the East, *Philo-Romaios* and *Philo-Kaiser*, "friend of Rome," "friend of Caesar," Herod governed efficiently. He collected revenues, contrived public works to develop vast tracts of land and eliminate unemployment, and, as we have seen, constructed a magnificent temple in Jerusalem. He also built several large cities, fortresses, and palaces, including Herodion in the south, Sebaste in Samaria, and Caesarea, a seaport in the Sharon. Herod stabilized political life, which had been in turmoil during the reign of the last Hasmonean monarchs. Indeed, under him there were no politics at all, only palace intrigue and slaughter of potentially dangerous wives, sons, and servants. Most Jews simply could not participate in public affairs. Many retired from the stage of political history. Earlier institutions of political life were either transformed into instruments of state, like the high priesthood, or apparently ignored, like the Sanhedrin. Under Herod, official culture increasingly came under Hellenistic domination. Court history was written in Greek by able Syrians, such as Nicholaus of Damascus. The Temple cult was managed by agents of the monarchy, men who purchased the high priesthood at a price, held it at the king's pleasure, and, enriched by the priestly dues, handed it in the accepted Greek manner to the next appointee. It was a brilliant reign, but in the wrong time and over the wrong people.

After Herod's death in 6 B.C., the people begged for direct Roman government. They asked the Romans to unite their country to Syria and to entrust its administration to Roman governors. They would then show that though people said they were contentious and unruly, they knew how to obey a fair government. The Romans tried to keep Herod's sons in power, but when this led to further difficulties, they acquiesced and appointed the first in a line of procurators. The procurators did not share Herod's interest in developing the economy by building port cities and roads, they were mainly concerned with the imperial welfare, if not, first of all, with their own. They lived in Hellenistic Caesarea, went up to Jerusalem when masses of pilgrims came up to celebrate the festivals, and were glad to return to the cosmopolitan capital as soon as possible. When in the spring of 66 A.D., one of them, Cestius, did not survive a bloody ambush on the road back, the revolution began. The procuratorial government ended as abruptly as it had begun.

5. ECONOMIC LIFE

The first act of the procuratorial government was normally to divide the conquered territory into municipal districts; the second was to take a census, determining the rate at which cities could be expected to contribute to the treasury. Taxes were applied to individual persons, houses, animals, sales, imports, and exports (at a moderate rate) and were collected by an efficient bureaucracy. Besides these taxes, Jews paid dues to another sovereignty as well—that imposed by the ancestral faith. The Bible had detailed many kinds of priestly and levitical offerings and animal sacrifices to support the expensive Temple cult. Under a priestly government, these taxes would certainly have supported a large administration. This doubtless was the economic rationale for the multitudinous tithes and offerings. Although the priests had ceased to rule, they still claimed their dues. With Roman help they obtained some of them from the majority of Jews and all from the very pious. Throughout these years, then, Jews were paying a twofold tax. The extent of civil and religious taxation has been estimated at from thirty to forty percent of the gross national income, but it was probably considerably lower since the majority of the Jews paid only a small part of the religious imposts.

In any event, the Jews never regarded Roman rule as legitimate. Taxes were therefore seen to be robbery. The Pharisaic sages made no distinction between a tax collector and a thief or an extortioner. Sages regarded gentile rulers in Palestine as robbers, without any rights whatsoever either in the land or over its inhabitants. No pagan power whatever had any right in the land. No land acquisition could free a field user from the obligation to pay the tithes. Even if a Gentile bought land from a Jew, he was held to be a sharecropper. No Gentile could ever

Full cycle of paintings from the West
Wall, Dura–Europos Synagogue. (The
Dura–Europos Collection, Yale University Art
Gallery.)

Torah Shrine, Dura– Europos Synagogue. (The Dura–Europos
Collection, Yale University Art Gallery.)

take valid, legal possession of any part of the land. This attitude to the rightful ownership of the land affected collection of taxes and much else, as we shall see. But religious imposts were something else again. The Pharisees believed they must be paid. Pharisees therefore separated themselves from Jews who neglected the tithes and heave-offerings or paid only part of them. It was one of the main distinctions between the Pharisaic masters and disciples, on the one hand, and the common people on the other. The former were meticulous in paying the priestly and levitical dues, and the latter were not.

Roman rule was advantageous for some. It opened the way for the adventurous to undertake vast enterprises in commerce and travel. Many took advantage of the opportunities of the Roman Empire to move to more prosperous lands. Throughout this period, one discovers Jews settling in the most remote corners of the empire and beyond. Those who stayed at home benefited from economic stability.

Situated on the trade routes to the east and south, the coastal cities, which contained large Jewish minority populations, imported new wares for sale in the bazaars and markets of back country towns like Jerusalem. The Jewish economy in the land flourished. Roman peace, Herodian enterprise, the natural endowments of the land, and broad economic opportunities combined to yield an adequate subsistence in a relatively stable economy for a very large population.

Nonetheless, living standards were modest. Archaeologists have not turned up pretentious synagogues, treasures of gems, rich pottery, furnishings, or costly sarcophagi dating from the first century. Life was simple. People ate inexpensive foods, such as salted fish, bread made from low grades of local wheat, low-quality grain imported from Egypt, or barley. They drank beer or wine diluted with water and sweetened their food with honey. Meat was eaten mostly on festival occasions, fish on the Sabbath. Judea was famed for its date palms, and the palm tree was sometimes engraved on coins as the emblem of the land. Most lived by farming or handicrafts. Contemporary parables borrow the imagery of fishing, agriculture, and petty trade. Few related to large-scale commerce, since Jews were mainly farmers and craftsmen. Riches meant a long-term food supply or a good wife. No parables refer to sophisticated problems of government, but many allude to a majestic, exalted monarch much magnified from the viewpoint of the mute populace.

6. EDUCATION

Many of the people, rich and poor alike, received an education in the main disciplines of Jewish tradition—that is to say, in the Torah, consisting of the Five Books of Moses, the prophetic writings, the wisdom books, as well as other traditions that spelled out and amplified these

scriptures.   This education, centering on religious learning, was
sufficiently broad to impart civilizing and humanizing lessons. What did
ordinary people study?   They learned the Torah.   They, therefore,
considered the history of the world from creation onward.   They were
taught, in lessons about their forefathers Abraham, Isaac, and Jacob, to
emulate patriarchal hospitality to others and faithfulness to God.   They
studied about the life and laws of Moses.   From those laws they gained an
idea of how a covenanted community should conduct its affairs.   They
were instructed about their obligations to the poor, weak, orphaned,
homeless, the stranger, and the outsider.   They were educated to say that
God is one, and that there are no other gods.   They were told about the
prophets whom God had sent to warn before ancient disasters and to
exhort afterward.   Those prophets had said that what God wanted of
people was that they do justice, show mercy, and walk humbly before
God.   The people learned that Providence guided their fate and that
nothing happened but that God decreed it.   So they were taught to look
for the meaning of daily and cosmic events alike.   A comet, drought,
broken leg, or earthquake—all could equally convey a truth.   In the
biblical writings they studied the wisdom of ancient sages, learning
prudence, piety, and understanding.

In modern terms their curriculum included much attention to matters
of metaphysics, law and morality, ethics and history.   Such lessons were
intended to create a decent human being.   Perhaps everyday conduct
revealed something of their impact, but it was the historical lesson that
seems to have had the greatest effect.   God had given the land to Israel.
Pagans had held it for a time, because in ancient days the people had
sinned.   But Israel had gotten it back after God had purified the people
through suffering.   In time, God again would set things straight and send a
king like David of old, anointed in the manner of the ancient monarchy, to
sit upon Mount Zion and dispense justice and revelation to all nations.   So
the Judaism that shaped the life and culture of the country saw in the
Temple and cult and priesthood marks of God's favor.   At the same time,
that Judaism took to heart the prophets' warnings that God's favor
depended on Israel's loyalty to the covenant that was represented by the
Torah.   The people further understood that what happened to their
country—their history as a people and a state—expressed God's rule and
judgment.   So the continuing conduct of the rite of the cult joined to the
practice of right and just government and public policy would sustain the
nation.   The earlier disaster had proven that law was immutable.   Just as
sin had led to disaster, so regeneration and atonement produced
restoration.   The result, then, was there for all to see: holy life of the
kingdom of priests and the holy people, centered on the Torah and the
Temple, the sages and the priests and the prophets and the king, all as
God had ordered things from the very beginning.

Exodus sequence from the West Wall, Dura–Europos Synagogue. (The Dura–Europos Collection, Yale University Art Gallery.)

Wall painting of Nike, Greek goddess of Victory, Dura–Europos Synagogue. (Photo by Eric F. Long, Smithsonian Photographic Services. Courtesy of SITES, Washington, D.C. from their exhibition, *Ebla to Damascus: Art and Archaeology of Ancient Syria.*)

7. SOCIAL CLASSES

Class divisions were complicated by the regional variations of the land. Jerusalem was the metropolis of the Jews. Its populace included a significant number of wealthy people, both absentee landlords and great merchants, as well as many priests who lived on the priestly dues and Temple endowments. The city also contained a smaller class of Levites, who performed certain nonsacrificial tasks in the sanctuary and managed the buildings. Artisans, whose skills were indispensable in the building and maintenance of the Temple, petty traders, a large urban proletariat, and unskilled laborers filled the crowded streets. Jerusalemites tended to separate themselves from the Judean provincials for both social and ritual reasons. Living in close proximity to the sanctuary, the inhabitants of the city were more concerned about observing the requirements of ritual cleanness, imposed by residence in the holy place, than were the provincials who purified themselves mainly for the festal pilgrimages. The provincials often did not have the benefit of much advanced education. Animosities between urban and rural residents were bitter. The provincials themselves were by no means united. The country gentry, landowners holding considerable property in the fertile lowland plains, had less in common with their highland neighbors than with the urban upper bourgeoisie.

On the other hand, the rural farmers and proletarian submerged classes were divorced from the central issues of national life. They welcomed the ministry of powerful personalities, sometimes sages empowered by learning, but more often wonderworkers able to heal mind and body. Jericho and the southern plain were the main centers of the rural gentry. On the rocky Judean hills lived the rural yeomanry and proletariat. In Galilee, class divisions between wealthier and poor peasants likewise were manifest. Hundreds of rural villages, large and small, clustered in the fertile hills and valleys of the north. Only Sepphoris and Tiberias were large urban centers, and they did not dominate the province as Jerusalem did Judea.

8. THE SECTS: ESSENES, SADDUCEES, AND PHARISEES

This brings us back to those sects, segregated representatives of the values of the "church," with which we began. Minor and unimportant groups, the several sects later assumed an importance that they did not enjoy in their own time. That was because, in the Gospel narratives of the life and teachings of Jesus, these small groups, Pharisees and Sadducees in particular, played a role as part of the opposition (for Matthew and Mark) or part of the sympathetic bystanders (Luke). The Essenes are described by Josephus, and in 1947 their library by the Dead Sea, in their monastic community at Qumran, was discovered. Our knowledge of these groups is diverse. We have detailed facts deriving from the Essenes' own library. About the Sadducees we have only references in the writings of Josephus and in the Gospels. The Pharisees occur in those same documents. Further, there are allusions to Pharisees in the later rabbinic writings, and some ideas originating among the Pharisees find a place in the earliest strata of the Mishnah, as we shall see in a later chapter.

Our interest in these small, if suggestive and later influential, groups exceeds that of their contemporaries. But what to us were the main social and religious events of this period held little interest for contemporary historians. Josephus, for one, paid little attention to the inner life of Israel in his rich narrative of politics and war. His histories provide evidence that the masses had turned away from public affairs. They may have responded to changes in their political situation; they may have felt growing impatience with social inequity or with the alien government whose benefits were not obvious to them. Only in the riots and continuous unrest toward the end of this period, however, does their response become entirely evident. A few indicated their disapproval of the course of events by withdrawing from the common society. Some became hermits; some fled to other lands or entered monastic communities in which contact with the outside world was minimal.

The Essenes. The monastic commune near the shores of the Dead Sea was one such group. To the barren heights came people seeking purity and hoping for eternity. The purity they sought was not from common dirt, but from the uncleanness of this world, symbolized by contact with the impure insects or objects Scripture had declared unclean. In their minds, that uncleanness carried a far deeper meaning. This age was impure and therefore would soon be coming to an end. Those who wanted to do the Lord's service should prepare themselves for a holy war at the end of time. The commune at the Dead Sea, therefore, divided by ranks under captains, lived under military discipline and studied the well-known holy books as well as books others did not know about. These books specified when and how the holy war would be fought and the manner of life of those worthy to fight it.

Men and women came to Qumran with their property, which they contributed to the common fund. There they prepared for a fateful day, not too long to be postponed, scarcely looking backward at those remaining in the corruption of this world. These Jews would be the last, smallest "saving remnant" of all. Yet through them all humankind would come to know the truth. They prepared for Armageddon, and their battle against forces of ritual impurity, evil, and sin alike was for the Lord. The Qumran commune ordained: "This is the regulation for the men of the commune, who devote themselves to turn away from all evil, and to hold fast to all that he has commanded as his will, to separate themselves from the congregation of men of iniquity to be a commune in Torah and property." Likewise the psalmist of Qumran prayed:

> Only as you draw a man near will I love him.
> And as you keep him far away, so will I abominate him.

The members of wilderness communes described by Philo as Essenes avoided the settled society of town and city "because of the inequities which have become inveterate among city dwellers, for they know that their company would have a deadly effect upon their own souls." The communards sanctified themselves by meticulous observance of the rules of ritual purity and tried to found such a society as they thought worthy of receiving God's approval. Strikingly, they held that God himself had revealed to Moses the very laws they now obeyed.

What makes the Essenes of Qumran especially interesting is that they joined together in exquisite balance the two points of stress, sanctification and salvation, interest in the holy way of life in the here and now, concern for the meaning of history and the end of time, that marked the nation-church as a whole. On the one side, as we see, they built a holy community, with its rites of sanctification centered on a sacred meal. So life was sustained and nourished in a state of sanctification, as though lived in the holy Temple. On the other side, the same group prepared for the end of time and anticipated a role in the apocalyptic drama of salvation that was about to begin. So life was moving somewhere, and the Essene community knew where. What marked the Essene community of Qumran as a sect—when, as we see, in distinctive form that community held together the two extremes—was the doctrine of Israel. The Essene community saw itself as the entirety of Israel, the saving remnant that would be saved, ruling out that other, that massive Israel round about. The Essene community made itself a sect even while realizing in its microcosm the beliefs of the great world beyond. This gives us an insight into the importance of that third component in a religious system, in a Judaism: the social element. A Judaism consists of more than a world view—in the case of the Essenes, an apocalyptic one concerning salvation; it involves more than a way of life—in the case at hand, a holy one concerning sanctification. A Judaism also addresses itself to an "Israel," defining whom it includes and excludes within Israel. The Essenes' "Israel" excluded many more than it included, and that is what made that Judaism sectarian.

The Pharisees. Pharisees—probably meaning Separatists—also believed that all was not in order with the world. But they chose another way, likewise attributed to mosaic legislation. They remained within the common society in accordance with the teaching of Hillel, "Do not separate yourself from the community." The Pharisaic community therefore sought to rebuild society on its own ruins with its own mortar

General view of the Christian Baptistery, Dura–Europos Synagogue. (The Dura–Europos Collection, Yale University Art Gallery.)

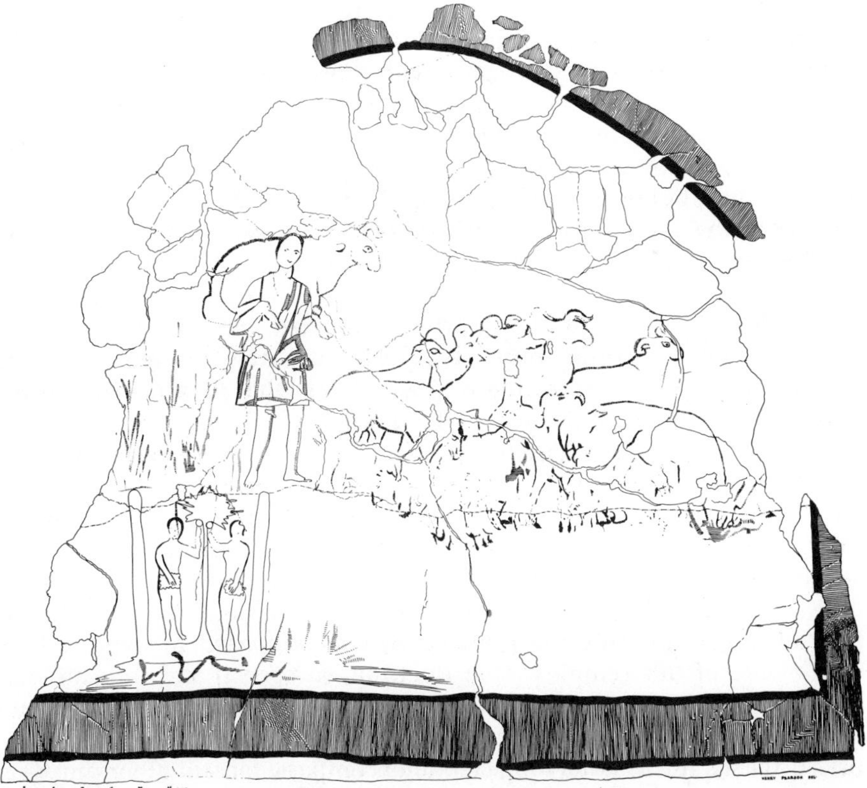

The Good Shepherd, and Adam and Eve, from the Christian Baptistery, Dura–Europos Synagogue. (The Dura-Europos Collection, Yale University Art Gallery.)

33

and brick. The Pharisees actively fostered their opinions on tradition and religion among the whole people. According to Josephus, "They are able greatly to influence the masses of people. Whatever the people do about divine worship, prayers, and sacrifices, they perform according to their direction. The cities give great praise to them on account of their virtuous conduct, both in the actions of their lives and their teachings also." Though Josephus exaggerated the extent of their power, the Pharisees certainly exerted some influence in the religious life of Israel before they finally came to power in the centuries after A.D. 70.

The Haverim and their Havurah.   Among those sympathetic to the Pharisaic cause were some who entered into an urban religious communion, a mostly unorganized society known as the fellowship (*havurah*). The basis of this society was meticulous observance of laws of tithing and other priestly offerings as well as the rules of ritual purity outside the Temple, where they were not mandatory. The members undertook to eat even profane foods (not sacred tithes or other offerings) in a state of rigorous levitical cleanness. At table, they compared themselves to Temple priests at the altar. These rules tended to segregate the members of the fellowship, for they ate only with those who kept the law as they thought proper. The fellows thus mediated between the obligation to observe religious precepts and the injunction to remain within the common society. By keeping the rules of purity, the fellow separated from the common man, but by remaining within the towns and cities of the land, he preserved the possibility of teaching others by example. The fellows lived among, but not with, the people of the land. With neither formal structure nor officers and bylaws as at Qumran, the fellowship represented the polity of people who recognized one another as part of the same inchoate community. They formed a new, if limited, society within the old. They were the few who kept what they held to be the faith in the company of the many who did not.

In their day the Pharisees formed a sect, with a special interest. Their way of life required them to identify with the Temple and its holy meals and to pretend that they were priests; their homes, the Temple; their hearth, the table of God. They lived out life as a metaphor for sanctification. What made them emerge as the "church" of all Israel when, later, they did, was a detail of their world view early on. It was that all Israel, not only the priesthood, was supposed to live the holy way of life of the Temple. That doctrine, so special and indicative of their group alone, contained within itself the seed that would later germinate. From the notion that all Israel was expected to live like the priestly caste, it was not a long step to encompass, for still other purposes within the disciplines and concerns of the group, the whole of Israel. The sectarian doctrine in its fundamental structure would accommodate the entirety of society, so, in a curious paradox, what made the sect sectarian would ultimately transform the sect into a church: all Israel and its single, uniform, normative, and therefore "orthodox," Judaism.

The Sadducees. Upper-class opinion was expressed in the viewpoint of still another group, the Sadducees. They stood for strict adherence to the written word in religious matters, conservatism in both ritual and belief. Their name probably derived from the priesthood of Zaddoq, established by king David ten centuries earlier. They differed from the Pharisees especially on the doctrine of revelation. They acknowledged Scripture as the only authority, themselves as its sole arbiters. They denied that its meaning might be elucidated by the Pharisees' allegedly ancient traditions attributed to Moses or by the Pharisaic devices of exegesis and scholarship. The Pharisees claimed that Scripture and the traditional oral interpretation were one. To the Sadducees, such a claim of unity was spurious and masked innovation. They differed also on the eternity of the soul. The Pharisees believed in the survival of the soul, the revival of the body, the day of judgment, and life in the world to come. The Sadducees found nothing in Scripture that to their way of thinking supported such doctrines. They ridiculed both these ideas and the exegesis that made them possible. They won over the main body of officiating priests and wealthier men. With the destruction of the Temple, their ranks were decimated. Very little literature later remained to preserve their viewpoint. It is difficult indeed to compare them to the other sects. They may have constituted no social institution like the Pharisaic and Essenic groups. In their day, however, the Sadducees claimed to be the legitimate heirs of Israel's faith. Holding positions of power and authority, they succeeded in leaving so deep an impression on society that even their Pharisaic, Essenic, and Christian opponents did not wholly wipe out their memory.

The Sadducees were most influential among landholders and merchants, the Pharisees among the middle and lower urban classes; the Essenes, among the disenchanted of both these classes. These classes and sectarian divisions manifested a vigorous inner life, with politics revolving around peculiarly Jewish issues such as matters of exegesis, law, doctrine, and the meaning of history. The vitality of Israel would have astonished the Roman administration, and when it burst forth, it did.

9. CONVERSION: "NORMATIVE" OR "ORTHODOX" JUDAISM

The rich variety of Jewish religious expression in this period ought not to obscure the fact that for much of Jewish Palestine, Judaism was a relatively new phenomenon. Herod was the grandson of pagans. Similarly, the entire Galilee had been converted to Judaism only 120 years B.C. In the later expansion of the Hasmonean kingdom, other regions were forcibly brought within the fold. The Hasmoneans used Judaism imperially, as a means of winning the loyalty of the pagan Semites in the regions of Palestine they conquered. But in a brief period of three or four generations, the deeply rooted practices of the Semitic natives of Galilee, Idumea, and other areas could not have been wiped out. Rather, they were covered over with a veneer of monotheism. Hence the newly converted territories, though vigorously loyal to their new faith, were no more Judaized in so short a time than were the later Russians, Poles, Celts, or Saxons Christianized within a century.

It took a great effort to transform an act of circumcision of the flesh, joined with a mere verbal affirmation of one God, done under severe duress, into a deepening commitment to faith. And yet in the war of A.D. 66, the Jews of newly converted regions fought with great loyalty. While the Galileans had proved unable to stand upon the open battlefield, many of them, together with Idumeans, retreated to the holy city. There they gave their lives in the last great cataclysms of the war. The exceptional loyalty of the newly converted regions would lead one to suppose that it was to the Temple cult, to the God whom it served, and to the nation that supported it that the pagan Semites were originally converted. They could have known little of the more difficult service of the heart, through study of Torah and ethical and moral action, which the Pharisees demanded.

While the central teachings of the faith were ancient, the adherence of many who professed it was, therefore, only relatively recent and superficial. The Pharisaic party, dating (in Josephus's account) at least from the second century B.C., never solidly established itself in Galilee before the second century. The religious beliefs of recently converted people could not have encompassed ideas and issues requiring substantial study, elaborate schooling, and a well-established pattern of living. Conversion of one group to another faith never obliterates the former culture, but rather entails the translation of the new into the idiom of the old, so that in the end it results in a modification of both. The newly Judaized regions similarly must have preserved substantial remnants of their former pagan Semitic and Hellenistic cultures. The inhabitants could not have been greatly changed merely by receiving "Judaism," which meant in the beginning little more than submitting to the knife of the circumciser rather than to the sword of the slaughterer. Only after many generations was the full implication of conversion realized in the lives of the people in Galilee, and then mainly because great centers of tannaitic law and teaching were established among them.

For this period, however, no such thing as "normative Judaism" other than the Judaism of the Torah of Moses existed. In the great center of the faith, Jerusalem, we find numerous competing groups, two of which would later become important, as we realize full well, and throughout the country and abroad we may discern a religious tradition in the midst of great flux. It was full of vitality, but in the end it was without a clear

Ceiling tile with fish, Dura–Europos Synagogue. (The
Dura–Europos Collection, Yale University Art Gallery.)

and widely accepted view of what was required of each individual, apart from acceptance of mosaic revelation. And this could mean whatever one took it to mean. People would ask one teacher after another, "What must I do to enter the kingdom of heaven?" precisely because no authoritative answer existed. In the end two groups emerged, the Christians and the rabbis, heirs of the Pharisaic sages. Each offered an all-encompassing interpretation of Scripture, explaining what it did and did not mean. Each promised salvation for individuals and for Israel as a whole.

Of the two, the rabbis and their Judaic system would achieve total success among the Jews. The story of the formation of their Judaic system, the stages of its development, the writings they created to define their world view and spell out their way of life—that story will occupy us for the rest of this book. Wherever the rabbis' views of Scripture were propagated the Christian view of the meaning of biblical, especially prophetic, revelation and its fulfillment made relatively little progress. This was true, specifically, in Jewish Palestine itself, in certain cities in Mesopotamia, and in central Babylonia.

Where the rabbis were not to be found, as in Egyptian Alexandria, Syria, Asia Minor, Greece, and in the West, Christian biblical interpretation and salvation through Christ risen from the dead found a ready audience among the Jews. It was not without good reason that the gospel tradition of Matthew saw in the "scribes and Pharisees" the chief opponents of Jesus' ministry. Whatever the historical facts of that ministry, the rabbis proved afterward to be the greatest stumbling block for the Christian mission to the Jews. But Christianity did bring its message of salvation through Jesus Christ, risen from the dead, to the world at large, and what had been a small sect would become the defining and governing church of the whole of Western civilization from the fourth century, when the Roman government first treated the Christian Church as licit, then declared it the most favored religion, and, finally, established it as the religion of the Church, or, more truly, declared itself to be the state of the Church. Each party to what became an argument of twenty-one centuries would therefore rule precisely that group to which it aspired: Each became the Israel it wanted to be.

10. SELF-GOVERNMENT

It was a peculiar circumstance of Roman imperial policy that facilitated the growth of such a vigorous inner life and permitted the development of nonpolitical institutions to express it. Rome carefully respected Jewish rights to limited self-government. The populace was subject to its own law, and quarrels were adjudicated by its own judges. Rome had specific and clearly defined purposes for the empire. Her policies could be adequately effected without totalitarian interference in the inner affairs of the conquered peoples. The same indifference to local sensitivities that occasionally permitted a procurator to bring his military standards into a city pure of "graven images" likewise encouraged him to ignore territorial affairs of considerable weight.

The national tribunal, called variously the Sanhedrin or High Court, acted with a measure of freedom to determine internal policy in religion, ritual, cult, and local law. The Sanhedrin lost authority to inflict capital punishment, it is generally assumed, shortly after Judea became a part of the Syrian provincial administration. Whether, in fact, it had administered the death penalty in Herod's reign is not entirely clear. The court certainly maintained the right to direct Temple affairs. It decided matters of civil and commercial law and torts and defined personal and family status and marriage procedure. The court also collected the biblical levies and determined the sacred calendar. It thus represented the one abiding institutional expression of Israel's inner autonomy during the procuratorial regime.

Both the Pharisees and Sadducees took an active interest in the religious, social, and economic administration of Israel's life. The Sanhedrin provided a means to formulate and effect these interests. The leaders of both major viewpoints played a considerable part in the nation's autonomous affairs. The exact nature of Jewish self-government and the institutions that embodied it has not yet been finally clarified.

The sources are difficult; no body of sources presents a picture that can be wholly verified in some other independent tradition.

11. THE IRREPRESSIBLE CONFLICT AND THE CRISIS OF 70

Jesus came into a world of irrepressible conflict. That conflict was between two pieties, two universal conceptions of what the world required. The Roman imperialist thought that good government—that is, Roman government—must serve to keep the peace. Rome would bring the blessings of civil order and material progress to many lands. For the Roman, that particular stretch of hills, farmland, and desert that Jews called "the land of Israel" meant little economically, but a great deal strategically. No wealth could be hoped for, but the loss of Palestine would mean the loss of the keystone of empire in the East. We see Palestine from the perspective of the West. It appears as a land bridge between Egypt and Asia Minor, the corner of a major trade route. But to the imperial strategist, Palestine loomed as the bulwark of the eastern frontier against Parthia. The Parthians, holding the Tigris-Euphrates frontier, were a mere few hundred miles from Palestine, separated by a desert no one could control. If the Parthians could take Palestine, Egypt would fall into their hands. Parthian armies, moreover, were pointed like a sword toward Antioch and the seat of empire established there. Less than a century earlier they had actually captured Jerusalem and seated upon its throne a puppet of their own. For a time they thrust Roman rule out of the eastern shores of the Mediterranean.

For Rome, therefore, Palestine was too close to the most dangerous frontier of all to be given up. Indeed, among all the Roman frontiers, only the oriental one was now contested by a civilized and dangerous foe. Palestine lay behind the very lines upon which that enemy had to be met. Rome could ill afford such a loss. Egypt, moreover, was her granary, the foundation of her social welfare and wealth. The grain of Egypt sustained the masses of Rome herself. Economic and military considerations thus absolutely required the retention of Palestine. Had Palestine stood in a less strategic locale, matters might have been different. Rome had a second such frontier territory to consider—Armenia. While she fought vigorously to retain predominance over the northern gateway to the Middle East, she generally remained willing to compromise on joint suzerainty with Parthia in Armenia—but not in Palestine.

For the Jews, the land of Israel meant something of even greater import. They believed that history depended upon what happened in the land of Israel. They thought that from creation until the end of time, the events that took place in Jerusalem would shape the fate of all humankind. Theirs, no less than Rome's, was an imperial view of the world, but with this difference: The empire was God's. If Rome could not lose Palestine, the Jew was unwilling to give up the land of Israel. Rome scrupulously would do everything possible to please Jewry, permitting the Jews to keep their laws in exchange only for peaceful acquiescence to Roman rule. There was, alas, nothing Rome could actually do to please Jewry but evacuate Palestine. No amiable tolerance of local custom could suffice to win the people's submission.

The crisis of 70 came about because of the simple fact of ecology, to which every Judaism would have to attend. The Jews were a small people, living in a strategic land. They imagined that there were rules that would guide their national life, rules they could understand and keep. But others had their own interests, and lived by other rules entirely. Consequently, the Judaic system resting on the Five Books of Moses would eventually have to accommodate itself to facts created by others, not by Jews, and address a history and a destiny by no means subject to the will of Israel. But, that Judaic system knew as fact that Israel's God, the one God who created heaven and earth and governed all humanity, nonetheless ruled. Accordingly, when the Second Temple was destroyed in August 70, a crisis of faith reframed the acute question of 586 and marked the second phase in the formation of Judaism.

3
the second crisis:
70 and the Judaism
of sanctification

1. SETTING: FROM PHARISAISM TO JUDAISM

The second crisis was precipitated by an event of the same character as the first—namely, the destruction of Jerusalem and its Temple, along with the dissolution of the Jewish political institutions that had formerly prevailed. The second crisis, unlike the first, was protracted, running over a period of three generations; for two important events defined the history of the Jews in the land of Israel from the first century to the fourth: the destruction of the Temple of Jerusalem in 70, and the catastrophic failure of the rebellion against Rome led by Bar Kokhba in 132–135. As to the former, the Romans had faced a serious rebellion from 66 onward, and, having systematically reduced resistance through the rest of the country, in 69–70 took Jerusalem and razed it. As to the latter event, three generations later a second major war sealed matters and left the Jews of the land of Israel without serious hope of recovering Jerusalem for some time to come. If this second war was fought with the expectation of rehearsing the events of the sixth century B.C., then the disappointment at the end must have proved extreme. For the original pattern no longer provided guidance on the direction, and therefore also the meaning, of events. And people could refer to no other.

It follows that these two catastrophic defeats formed, in reality, a single historical moment. For, in the minds of many, the defeat in the first war set in motion the expectations that led to the second. When the Temple was destroyed, Jews naturally looked to Scripture to find the meaning of what had happened and, more important, to learn what to expect. There they discovered that when the Temple had been destroyed earlier, a period of three generations—"seventy years"—intervened. Then, in the aftermath of atonement and reconciliation with God, Israel was restored to its Land, the Temple to Jerusalem, the priests to the service of the altar. So, many surmised, in three generations the same pattern would be reenacted, now with the Messiah at the head of the restoration. So people waited patiently and hopefully. But whether or not Bar Kokhba said he was the Messiah, he was to disappoint the hopes placed in him. The Jews, possessed of a mighty military tradition then as now, fought courageously, but lost against overwhelming force. The result left Jerusalem closed to the Jews, except on special occasions.

Much Jewish settlement in the southern part of the country was wiped out, though the Jews in Galilee quickly regained their economic health. The long-term cost of the two defeats exacted a heavy charge against the confidence of the people in the fundamental rules of reality, such as they had long assumed the Torah provided. Deep disappointment settled over the people. The setting for the Judaic system reached full statement in the Mishnah, which came to closure in about A.D. 200—that is, approximately three generations beyond the defeat of Bar Kokhba. That setting found definition in the chaos not of economics or politics—the Romans quickly restored the Jews' self-government under Roman supervision. The real issue was the order and meaning of the national life. For the one thing people had anticipated—that is, that the scriptural patterns would pertain—is what did not happen. And no one knew what would now happen.

In ancient Israelite times, the history of Israel defined the issues of faith, and the prophets, in God's name interpreted events as statements of God's will to Israel. So it was perfectly natural, in the period at hand, that the Judaism that took shape should respond in a direct and immediate way to the momentous events of the day. In man˙ ways Judaism, from age to age, has formed what Judaic sages saw as God's commentary on the text that is formed by the events of the history of the Jewish people, and the holy books of Judaism contain that commentary. The Mishnah forms one such commentary. When we understand its points of stress and heavy emphasis, we may outline the answer it proposes, and, from that answer, we further uncover the urgent and critical question at hand. Since the Mishnah presents an essay in the principles of the sanctification of the life of Israel in the natural and social world, we must postulate that the question troubling the authors had to do with sanctification. With the Temple in ruins and the cult no longer in operation, that question focused on whether Israel remained what it had been: God's kingdom of priests and holy people. With the disasters of 70 and 132–135, it was a perfectly natural question.

From Pharisaism to Judaism (the Judaism of the dual Torah). We recall that, before 70, the Pharisees had formed a sect within the larger "nation-church" of Jerusalem. Afterward the Pharisees formed the single most influential group. They were led by a sage, Yohanan ben Zakkai, and represented by elements of the pre-70 aristocracy such as Gamaliel, grandson of the Gamaliel mentioned in Acts 5:34, as well as by the Jewish general Josephus, who had gone over to the Romans during the war. Once the Romans determined to reestablish their system of governing through native allies, they selected the Pharisees as the party most likely to succeed in keeping the peace. The Jewish government recognized by Roman authority, therefore, came under the influence of the descendants of the Pharisees of the period before 70.

The Pharisees contributed more than political representatives in the renewed Jewish government. They also contributed a method and a viewpoint. The viewpoint, we take for granted, addressed "all Israel," and the method focused upon the sanctification of all Israel. So the Pharisees contributed to the nascent system a fundamental attitude that everyone mattered, and a basic point of stress upon the holiness of everyday life. But the aborning Judaism took within itself a second group: the heirs and continuators of the scribes of the period before 70.

These had been a profession, not a sect, and the mark of their profession was knowledge of the Scriptures and traditions of Israel and capacity to bring those Scriptures to bear on the everyday life of the people. Teachers of Scripture, clerks who prepared the documents required for the conduct of an orderly society, and some of the surviving scribes came to the place in which the Jewish government was reorganizing and joined with the Pharisees' successors and continuators (and some Pharisees were scribes, as some scribes were Pharisees). What the scribes contributed to the nascent system was the stress on the Torah and study of the Torah as critical to the holy way of life. They obviously did not invent the Torah, nor did they uniquely espouse its definitive importance. These were commonplaces in the normative religion of Israel before 70. The scribes in the new Judaism contributed their special learning, their detailed knowledge, and, above all, their traditions of correct procedures and conduct of the common affairs of state.

The Judaism that emerged after 70 thus succeeded the Judaic system of Temple and priesthood. It was a Judaism formed upon essentially political lines, and its task was to govern a Jewish state and people in its land. The sect, the Pharisees, and the profession, the scribes—along with surviving priests who joined them—together framed a Judaism to take the place of the Judaism of Temple and cult. It would emerge as a Judaism in which each of the elements of the Judaism of Temple and cult would find a counterpart. Specifically:

1. *In place of the Temple:* the holy people, in which holiness endured even outside of the cult, as the Pharisees had taught;
2. *In place of the priesthood:* the sage, the holy man qualified by learning, as the scribes had taught;
3. *In place of the sacrifices of the altar:* the holy way of life of the people, expressed through carrying out religious duties (*mitzvot*, translated as commandments) and acts of kindness and grace beyond those commanded (*maasim tovim*, translated as good deeds), and, above all, through studying the Torah.

This third element shows us the union of both the Pharisaic sectarian perspective that all Israel must become holy, the kingdom of priests and holy people, and the scribal professional ideal that study of the Torah was the central task. In joining the social ideal of the Pharisees that everyone, not just the priests, undertake to live the holy life, with the professional goal of the scribes that laid emphasis on the study of the Torah, Judaism presented an amalgam. It involved the obligation of everyone to be holy through studying the Torah. All Israel would study the Torah in the model of the sage, the new priest (given the honorific title "rabbi," meaning simply "my lord," a title formerly assigned to diverse holy men and used in Syriac Christianity, as *rabban*, for many centuries to come).

Precisely what comprised this "Torah" that people were to study? That is the next important question. The answer has two parts. First, the Torah comprised precisely what it had always been: the Hebrew Scriptures ("Old Testament"). But, second, in addition to the Torah—now, the Written Torah—certain writings came into being which, in long centuries to come, attained the status of divine revelation, hence of Torah, and so became part of the Torah. The first of these writings, as I shall explain in a moment, was the Mishnah, which was completed in about 200. A generation later, in about 250, a tractate, Avot, the Fathers, joined the Mishnah and explained the authority of the Mishnah in an interesting way. That document began with a list of authorities of the Torah, beginning with Moses at Sinai *and ending with names of important authorities cited in the Mishnah itself!* The implicit proposition, then, was that what the Mishnah authorities teach forms part of the Torah that Moses received from God at Mount Sinai. In the fifth century, documents such as the Talmud of the land of Israel, ca. A.D. 400 begin to refer to these other writings, including the Mishnah, as "the oral Torah," in the theory that when God revealed the Torah to Moses at Sinai, God gave the Torah in two forms—one in writing, the other orally (that is, in memory)—hence, *Torah shebikhtav*, Torah in writing, and *Torah shebeal peh*, Torah in memory, or oral.

It follows that once the Pharisaic ideal that all Israel become holy had joined the scribal professional doctrine that the Torah must define the holy life of all Israel, the next step lay in the development of a fresh ideal of sanctification, one which would use the Torah to explain how—for the moment without a Temple, without a cult, and without a governing priesthood—Israel might carry out the tasks of living a holy way of life. It was the Mishnah's authors, from after Bar Kokhba's war to the year 200, who framed such a full and encompassing statement of the sanctification of the life of Israel, covering both the Temple, then in ruins, and the enduring life of the people in their villages and homes, fields and families. Drawing upon traditions contributed by both the Pharisees from before 70 and the scribes from earlier times, dealing also with topics important to the priesthood (and perhaps accommodating rules preserved by the surviving priests), the authors of the Mishnah presented a document to the living Israel of the households and the farms and drew together into a single, remarkably cogent statement the traditions of Pharisees, scribes, and priests. The Mishnah represents the movement of the Pharisees from the status of sect to church, and the scribes from the status of profession to state, addressing both the program of the priesthood before 70 and the everyday life of all Israel afterward. It is an amazing document, in full and rich detail specifying what the holy life of Israel in the age without the Temple, as well as in the coming age of the restoration of the Temple, must mean.

The Mishnah outlines the many areas of sanctification that endure: land and priesthood, in Agriculture, time, in appointed times, not to mention the record of the Temple, studied and restudied in the mind's reenactment of the cult. But, as we see, the Mishnah stressed sanctification, to the near omission of the other critical dimension of Israel's existence, salvation. Only later—in the aftermath of the third and final crisis in the formation of Judaism—would Scripture exegetes. complete the structure of Judaism, a system resting on the twin foundations of sanctification in this world and salvation in time to come.

2. THE SAGES AND THEIR SYSTEM: THE MISHNAH'S JUDAISM OF SANCTIFICATION

Judaism is the creation of a group of holy men called "sages"—in Hebrew, *hakhamim*. Let us begin with a definition of the sage, and then examine what sages created, beginning with their first and most important document, the Mishnah.

The sages. As we have seen, the sage in the setting of the Mishnah is a special kind of wise man. The Mishnah represents the sage as a man of learning and also of holiness—learning in this world, holiness in the supernatural world. As a teacher of disciples, the sage turned himself into the students' supernatural father and the disciples into his supernatural sons (much as the Gospel of John represents the supernatural transformation through Jesus of the disciples into his holy family). In later writings, the sage as a holy man could do wonders and work miracles, and it was specifically through his learning that the sage became a supernatural man who could do wonders.

The sage at the end became the model for the Messiah, so that the Messiah at the end of time would be in all respects a master of the Torah and the model sage. Thus King David, prototype and progenitor of the Messiah, was represented in the unfolding writings of Judaism as the ideal rabbi—that is, the sage par excellence. The learning of the sage represented, therefore, knowledge of the rules of creation as God had laid them down in the Torah; the rules of the holy way of life as God had revealed them at Sinai; the rules that, in time to come, would make Israel worthy of salvation through the coming of *Rabbi* David's son, the Messiah. The sage bears much in common with the wise men of ancient times in general, clerks and teachers, but the sage also exhibits traits that mark the Judaic sage as distinctive and particularly representative of the Judaic system that he embodied.

The sages' system. This brings us to the Mishnah, the first and greatest work of the sages and, in time to come, recognized as the original document of the Oral Torah. Our approach to describing the Mishnah requires two steps. First, we have to consider the system of the document, looking for its points of emphasis for the reason that has been explained. Second, we shall want to read a passage, which will give us some clear picture of how the document makes its statement.

To define matters simply, the Mishnah is a kind of law code, covering six principal topics: (1) sanctification of the economy and support of the priesthood, the holy caste; (2) sanctification of time, with reference to special occasions, appointed times, and the Sabbath; (3) sanctification of the family and the individual; (4) the proper conduct of points of social conflict and political life; (5) the sanctification of the Temple and its offerings, with special emphasis on the routine occasions; and, (6) the protection of the Temple from uncleanness and the preservation of cultic cleanness. These six principal subjects form the center of the Mishnah's six divisions and, all together, cover the everyday life of the holy people in the here and now. The rules are phrased in the present tense—people do this, people do not do that—and, overall, they provide an account of an ideal world. For at issue was not merely the routine, but the sacred—and holiness persisted even though the routine did not yield such evidence as it had before. So the message is clear: the established sanctification of Israel endured, events changing nothing.

The Mishnah's Judaism of Sanctification. The topical program of
the document, as distinct from the deep issues worked out through
discussion of the topics, therefore focuses upon the sanctification of the
life of Israel, the Jewish people. The question taken up by the Mishnah,
in the aftermath of the destruction of the Temple, is whether, and how,
Israel is still holy. And the self-evidently valid answer is that Israel
indeed is holy, and so far as the media of sanctification persist beyond
the destruction of the holy place—and they do endure—the task of holy
Israel is to continue to conduct that life of sanctification that had centered
upon the Temple. Where now does holiness reside? It is in the life of the
people, Israel—there above all. So the Mishnah may speak of the
holiness of the Temple, but the premise is that the people—that kingdom
of priests and holy people of Leviticus—constitutes the center and focus of
the sacred. The land retains its holiness too, and in raising the crops, the
farmer is expected to adhere to the rules of order and structure laid down
in Leviticus, keeping each thing in its proper classification—observing
the laws of the sabbatical year, for instance. The priesthood retains its
holiness, even without the task of carrying out the sacrificial cult.
Therefore priests must continue to observe the caste rules governing
marriage, such as are specified in Leviticus.

The relationship of husband and wife forms a focus of sanctification,
and that too retains its validity even today. The passage of time—from
day to day with the climax at the Sabbath; from week to week with the
climax at the sanctification of the new month, from season to season with
the climax at the holy seasons, in particular the first new moon after the
autumnal equinox, marked by Tabernacles, and the first new moon after
the vernal equinox, marked by Passover—these too continue to indicate
the fundamental state and condition of Israel the people. All these modes
of sanctification endure, surviving the destruction of the holy Temple. In
these and other foci of interest, the Mishnah lays forth a Judaic system of
sanctification, joining discourse on the foci of sanctification that no longer
survived with discussion on those that flourished even beyond the
disaster. If, therefore, we had to specify the single urgent and critical
question and the single self-evident answer, it would be this colloquy:

> The compelling question: *Is Israel yet holy?*
> The self-evident answer: *Sanctification inheres in the life of the people.*

That is why four of the six principal parts of the Mishnah deal
with the cult and its officers. These are, first, *Holy Things,* which
addresses the everyday conduct of the sacrificial cult; second, *Purities,*
which takes up the protection of the cult from sources of uncleanness
specified in the book of Leviticus (particularly Leviticus Chapters 12
through 15); third, *Agriculture,* which centers on the designation of
portions of the crop for the use of the priesthood (and others in the same
classification of a holy caste, such as the poor), and so provides for the

support of the Temple staff; and, fourth, *Appointed Times*, the larger part of which concerns the conduct of the cult on such special occasions as the Day of Atonement, Passover, Tabernacles, and the like (and the rest of which concerns the conduct in the village on those same days, with the basic conception that what one does in the cult forms the mirror image of what one does in the village). Two further divisions of the document as a whole deal with everyday affairs: one, *Damages*, concerning civil law and government; the other, *Women*, taking up issues of family, home, and personal status. This, sum and substance, is the program of the Mishnah.

Clearly, much of the Mishnah attends to topics of a utopian character. That is to say, the laws on the Temple and its conduct on an everyday basis, in the fifth division, and on special occasions, in the second division, and on the support of the priesthood, in the first division, and on the matter of cultic cleanness, in the sixth division—all of these rules pertained to an institution that lay in ruins. Clearly, the framers hoped and expected that, at some time in the future, the Temple would be rebuilt and its cult resorted. They prayed for that eventuality. But when they produced the Mishnah, there was no Temple, no offerings went up in smoke to God in heaven, no priests presided at the altar, no Levites sang on the platform, no Israelites brought their offerings of the produce of the holy land to send up to the holy God in heaven.

The Mishnah is not only in the main, though not exclusively, a utopian document; it also deals, through discourse on practical details, with remarkably familiar issues of philosophy. To define the document more clearly, the Mishnah is a work of philosophy expressed through laws. That is, on the surface the Mishnah presents a set of rules, phrased in the present tense: One does this; one does not do that. But when we look closely at the issues worked out by those laws, time and again we find profound essays on such philosophical questions as being and becoming, the acorn and the oak, the potential and the actual. Or, again, we find reflection on the essential as against the actual; for instance, is the water in the stream the same water now that was there a moment ago, or is it different water? These and similar issues will have found a ready audience among the peripatetic philosophers who preached throughout the Mediterranean. But as we have seen, the sages were not merely philosophers, though many of their most profound exercises of thought concerned characteristically philosophical issues. They were holy men, and their philosophy sanctified.

When did the document take shape, why did it endure, and what accounts for its importance? The document was completed, the consensus of scholarship holds, around the year 200. That is, approximately three generations after the defeat of Bar Kokhba's armies, the Mishnah came forth. We do not know why its authorship produced the book that it did. But the Mishnah quickly proved influential because of its reception. Specifically, the document served as the basic law book of the Jewish government of the land of Israel, the authority of the patriarchate recognized by Rome, as well as the Jewish government of the Jewish minority in Babylonia, a western province of the Iranian Empire. That empire allowed its many diverse ethnic groups to run internal affairs on their own, and the Jews' regime, in the hands of a "head of the exile," or exilarchate, employed sages who had mastered the Mishnah and therefore imposed the pertinent laws of the Mishnah within its administration and courts. So the Mishnah rapidly became not a work of speculative philosophy in the form of legal propositions or rules, but a law code for the concrete and practical administration of the Jewish people in its autonomous life. Why was the Mishnah important? It was important because of two considerations: the political and the intellectual.

Before we speak of the Mishnah's future as the foundation for Judaism from then to now, we have to take one last look backward, at the Mishnah's message on the recent past. If we were to ask the framers of the document to tell us where, in their writing, they speak of what has happened in their own century, they will disappoint us. For they do *not* refer to historical events except in passing. True, they will direct our attention to a few episodic allusions to the destruction of the Temple, on the one side, and the repression after the war of 132–135, on the other. But if we were to ask them to give us their comment on the catastrophe—the radical turning—of their day, they will direct us to look, not at bits and pieces, but at the *whole* of their document. The message emerges in every detail and also in the entirety of the writing: Israel beyond the destruction and before the restoration of the Temple, its holy rites and its consecrated priesthood, remains the kingdom of priests and the holy people of God.

3. THE MISHNAH'S CONTRIBUTION TO THE FORMATION OF JUDAISM

We turn now to the future. Why did the Mishnah matter to generations to come? The Mishnah mattered, on the near term, because of its importance to the Jewish state(s) of the day. The Romans reestablished Jewish self-government after the Bar Kokhba war, and by the middle of the second century a Jewish government conducted the politics of the Jewish community of the Land of Israel. When the Mishnah was published in approximately 200, it immediately became the foundation document of that Jewish government. The clerks of the Jewish government mastered the document and applied it, appealing to their knowledge of the Mishnah's laws as validation for their authority. So on the near term, the code exercised immediate and practical authority in those matters to which it was relevant.

But the Mishnah mattered on the long term because of its centrality in the intellectual life of the Jews' sages. These sages, many of them employed by the Jewish governments of the Land of Israel and of Babylonia, believed, and persuaded many, that the Mishnah formed part of the Torah, God's will for Israel revealed to Moses at Sinai. So the Mishnah, originally not a work of religion in a narrow sense, attained the status of revelation. How did this happen? A look at the first great apologetic for the Mishnah, the Sayings of the Founders (Pirqé Avot), issued in around 250, approximately a generation after the Mishnah itself, tells us the answer. As we shall see when we read the text itself, it begins, "Moses received Torah on Sinai and handed it on to Joshua...," and, the chain of tradition goes on, the latest in the list turn out to be authorities of the generations who form the named authorities of the Mishnah itself. So that which these authorities teach they have received in the chain of tradition from Sinai. And what they teach is Torah. Now the Mishnah, which is their teaching, enjoys its standing and authority because it comes from sages—and, it follows—sages' standing and authority comes from God.

Such a claim imparted to the Mishnah and its teachers a position in the heart and mind of Israel, the Jewish people, that would ensure the long-term influence of the document. What happened after 200 and before 400 were two processes, one of which generated the other.

The first of the two was that the Mishnah was extensively studied, line by line, word by word. The modes of study were mainly three. First, the sages asked about the meanings of words and phrases. Then they worked on the comparison of one set of laws with another, finding the underlying principles of each and comparing, and harmonizing, those principles. They thereby formed of the rather episodic rules a tight and large fabric. Third, they moved beyond the narrow limits of the Mishnah into still broader and more speculative areas of thought. So, in all, the sages responsible to administer the law also expounded, and, willy-nilly, expanded the law. Ultimately, in both countries, the work of Mishnah commentary developed into two large-scale documents, each called a Talmud. We have them as the Talmud of the land of Israel, which I have translated into English, completed by about 400, and the Talmud of Babylonia, completed by about 600.

The second process—besides the work of Mishnah commentary—drew attention back to Scripture. Once the work of reading the new code got under way, an important problem demanded attention. What is the relationship between the Mishnah and the established Scripture of Israel, the written Torah? The Mishnah only occasionally adduces texts of the Scriptures in support of its rules. Its framers worked out their own topical program, only part of which intersects with that of the laws of the Pentateuch. They followed their own principles of organization and development. They wrote in their own kind of Hebrew, which is quite different from biblical Hebrew. So the question naturally

Last passages from the Manual of Discipline. (Samuel and Jeane H. Goltesman Center for Biblical Manuscripts, The Shrine of the Book, the Israel Museum, Jerusalem.)

Page from the Kaufmann Manuscript of the *Mishnah,* 12th to 14th centuries. Kaufmann Collection, Ms. A 50. (From *Encyclopedia Judaica,* Volume 12, p. 94.)

arose, Can we, through sheer logic, discover the law? Or must we tease laws out of Scripture through commentary, through legal exegesis? Their Mishnah represented an extreme in this debate, since, as we have noted, so many of its topics do not derive from Scripture, to begin with, and, further, a large part of its laws ignores Scripture's pertinent texts in that these texts are simply not cited. When, moreover, the framers of the Sayings of the Founders placed sages named in the Mishnah on the list of those who stand within the chain of tradition beginning at Sinai, they did not assign to those sages verses of Scripture, the written Torah (except in one or two instances). Rather, the Torah-saying assigned to each of the named sages is not scriptural at all. So the sages enjoy an independent standing and authority on their own, they are not subordinate to Scripture, and their sayings enjoy equal standing with sentences of Scripture.

The work of exegesis of the Mishnah therefore drew attention, also, to the relationship of the Mishnah to Scripture. Consequently, important works of biblical commentary emerged in the third and fourth centuries. In these works, focused on such books as Leviticus (Sifra), Numbers (Sifré to Numbers) and Deuteronomy (Sifré to Deuteronomy), a paramount issue is whether law emerges solely on the basis of processes of reasoning, or whether only through looking at verses of Scripture are we able to uncover solid basis for the rules of the Mishnah. In that discourse we find the citation of a verse of Scripture followed by a verbatim citation of a passage of the Mishnah.

Since this mode of reading Scripture is apt to be unfamiliar to many readers, let me give a concrete example of how the process of Mishnah exegesis in relationship to Scripture exegesis was carried forward in the third and fourth centuries. What follows is from Sifré to Numbers:

PISQA VI:II.1

A.   "...every man's holy thing shall be his; whatever any man gives to the priest shall be his" [Num. 5:10].

B.   On the basis of this statement you draw the following rule:

C.   **If a priest on his own account makes a sacrificial offering, even though it falls into the week [during which] another priestly watch than his own [is in charge of the actual cult, making the offerings and receiving the dues], lo, that priest owns the priestly portions of the offering, and the right of offering it up belongs to him [and not to the priest ordinarily on duty at that time, who otherwise would retain the rights to certain portions of the animal] [T. Men. 13:17].**

What we have is simply a citation of the verse plus a law in a prior writing (in this case not the Mishnah, but the Tosefta, a compilation of supplements to the Mishnah's laws) which the verse is supposed to sustain. The formal traits require (1) citation of a verse, with or without comment, followed by (2) verbatim citation of a passage of the Mishnah or the Tosefta. We thus have a formal construction in which we simply juxtapose a verse, without or with intervening words of explanation, with a passage of the Mishnah or the Tosefta. So we see that, when sages proposed to provide for Scripture a counterpart, a commentary, to what they were even then creating for the Mishnah, they sought to build bridges from the Mishnah to Scripture.

In so doing, they articulated the theme of the Mishnah, the sanctification of Israel. But what of salvation? Where, when, and how did sages then shaping Judaism address that other and complementary category of Israel's existence? And, we further ask, is the work of linking the Mishnah to Scripture the only kind of scriptural commentary sages produced between the first and the fourth century? Not at all. Sages turned to Scripture to seek the laws of Israel's history, to ask the questions of salvation, of Israel's relationship to God, that, in the Mishnah and in the works of amplification of the Mishnah, they tended to neglect. In Chapter 4 we shall see when, where, how, and why they did so. First let us consider the text under discussion and see for ourselves some of its salient traits.

4. A SAMPLE CHAPTER OF THE MISHNAH

The rules before us tell about the rights and prerogatives of the high priest and then the king. Since, as we have seen, the Mishnah rapidly served as the foundation document of the politics of the Jews of the land of Israel and Babylonia, we do well to take up a chapter of the Mishnah that treats a political question. What we see is the utopian character of discourse. That is to say, the Mishnah chapter at hand deals not with the government that did exist—that is, of a Jewish ethnarch (ruler of the ethnic group) and a Jewish bureaucracy made up of sages and clerks—but with the government that did not exist. The rules concern the dual authority of high priest and king, both of them based on the Temple of Jerusalem. At the time of the publication of the Mishnah, there was no Temple, no government in the hands of the Temple authority, no king. Perhaps people hoped that there would be; I have no doubt that they did. But the document before us presents a picture of a world that did not exist, and does not present an account of the world that did exist.

MISHNAH-TRACTATE SANHEDRIN 2:1-2

2:1

A. A high priest judges, and [others] judge him;

B.   gives testimony, and [others] give testimony about him;

C.   performs the rite of removing the shoe [Deut. 25:7–9], and [others] perform the rite of removing the shoe with his wife.

D.   [Others] enter levirate marriage with his wife, but he does not enter into levirate marriage,

E.   because he is prohibited to marry a widow.

F.   [If] he suffers a death [in his family], he does not follow the bier.

G.   "But when [the bearers of the bier] are not visible, he is visible; when they are visible, he is not.

H.   "And he goes with them to the city gate," the words of R. Meir.

I.   R. Judah says, "He never leaves the sanctuary,

J.   "since it says, *'Nor shall he go out of the sanctuary'* (Lev. 21:12)."

K.   And when he gives comfort to others

L.   the accepted practice is for all the people to pass one after another, and the appointed [prefect of the priests] stands between him and the people.

M.   And when he receives consolation from others,

N.   all the people say to him, "Let us be your atonement."

O.   And he says to them, "May you be blessed by Heaven."

P.   And when they provide him with the funeral meal,

Q.   all the people sit on the ground, while he sits on a stool.

2:2

A.   The king does not judge, and [others] do not judge him;

B.   does not give testimony, and [others] do not give testimony about him;

C.   does not perform the rite of removing the shoe, and others do not perform the rite of removing the shoe with his wife;

D.   does not enter into levirate marriage, nor [do his brothers] enter levirate marriage with his wife.

E.   R. Judah says, "If he wanted to perform the rite of removing the shoe or to enter into levirate marriage, his memory is a blessing."

F.   They said to him, "They pay no attention to him [if he expressed the wish to do so]."

G.   [Others] do not marry his widow.

H.   R. Judah says, "A king may marry the widow of a king.

I.   "For so we find in the case of David, that he married the widow of Saul,

J.   "For it is said, *'And I gave you your master's house and your master's wives into your embrace'*" [II Sam. 12:8].

2:3

A.   [If] [the king] suffers a death in his family, he does not leave the gate of his palace.

B.   R. Judah says, "If he wants to go out after the bier, he goes out,

C.   "for thus we find in the case of David, that he went out after the bier of Abner,

D.   "since it is said, *'And King David followed the bier'*" [2 Sam. 3:31].

E.   They said to him, "This action was only to appease the people."

F. And when they provide him with the funeral meal, all the people sit on the ground, while he sits on a couch.

2:4A–D

A. [The king] calls out [the army to wage] a war fought by choice on the instructions of a court of seventy-one.
B. He [may exercise the right to] open a road for himself, and [others] may not stop him.
C. The royal road has no required measure.
D. All the people plunder and lay before him [what they have grabbed], and he takes the first portion.

2:4E–I

E. *"He should not multiply wives to himself"* [Deut. 17:17]—only eighteen.
F. R. Judah says, "He may have as many as he wants, so long as they *do not entice him* [to abandon the Lord]" [Deut. 7:4].
G. R. Simeon says, "Even if there is only one who entices him [to abandon the Lord]—lo, this one should not marry her."
H. If so, why is it said, "He should not multiply wives to himself"?
I. Even though they should be like Abigail [1 Sam. 25:3].

2:4J–N

J. *"He should not multiply horses to himself"* [Deut. 17:16]—only enough for his chariot.
K. *"Neither shall he greatly multiply to himself silver and gold"* [Deut. 17:16]—only enough to pay his army.
L. *"And he writes out a scroll of the Torah for himself"* [Deut. 17:17].
M. When he goes to war, he takes it out with him; when he comes back, he brings it back with him; when he is in session in court, it is with him; when he is reclining, it is before him,
N. as it is said, *"And it shall be with him, and he shall read in it all the days of his life"* [Deut. 17:19].

2:5

A. [Others may] not ride on his horse, sit on his throne, handle his sceptre.
B. And [others may] not watch him while he is getting a haircut, or while he is nude, or in the bathhouse,
C. since it is said, *"You shall surely set him as king over you"* [Deut. 17:15]—that reverence for him will be upon you.

The passage is readily accessible and requires only little comment. We note, first of all, the use of the progressive present tense: This is how things are. There is no appeal to authority; the document speaks as with an authority of its own. In fact, there is no account of the history of the Mishnah to justify the adoption of the laws for the Israelite government. The model of Deuteronomy, with its powerful account of God's redemption of Israel prior to its statement of the laws God wants Israel to observe, finds no counterpart here. At the same time, the facts of Scripture, the Written Torah, are everywhere taken for granted where they are relevant. But the appeal to prooftexts—that is, here is the law, here is the biblical warrant for the law—tends to be sparing. The passage at hand, in fact, presents an uncommonly sizable repertoire of prooftexts. Overall, the Mishnah's authors rarely find it interesting to cite verses of the Hebrew Scriptures to support their rulings. M. 2:4 shows us how the law code could have looked, had people wished to invoke Scripture as support for their rulings. We note, finally, that the document includes minority opinion, in the name of the individual who holds that view, as against the anonymous ruling of the majority. Judah, a second-century figure, enjoys the opportunity to register his own views. If we examine M. Sanhedrin 2:1 and 2:2, we note a further trait—namely, a rather formalized rhetoric. The one passage is matched against the other. Overall, the Mishnah tends to resort to highly patterned language.

5 . A SAMPLE CHAPTER OF THE TOSEFTA

The Mishnah chapter before us obviously requires amplification. For one thing, the relationship of the rules to their corresponding passages in Scripture demands more sustained attention than the authors of the Mishnah generally provide. The existence, in the Mishnah, of dissenting views alerts us to the fact that alternative opinion circulated in the time of the making of the Mishnah. Materials that fall into these categories—amplification of the Mishnah, alternative and omitted statements on topics that appear in the Mishnah—coalesced into the Mishnah's first systematic commentary, called the *Tosefta,* meaning "supplements." The Tosefta's principal characteristic is its close and loyal adherence to the program—ideas, points of stress and concern—of the Mishnah itself. Here is how the Tosefta takes up the Mishnah chapter we have seen. Citations of the Mishnah chapter are in boldface type, and citations of Scripture are in italics.

TOSEFTA TO TRACTATE SANHEDRIN

4:1

A.   A high priest who committed homicide --

B.   [if he did so] deliberately, he is executed; if he did so inadvertently, he goes into exile to the cities of refuge [Num. 35:9ff].

C.   [If] he transgressed a positive or negative commandment or indeed any of the commandments, lo, he is treated like an ordinary person in every respect.

D. He does not perform the rite of removing the shoe [Deut. 25:7–9], and others do not perform the rite of removing the shoe with his wife [*vs.* M. San. 2:1C].

E. He does not enter into levirate marriage, and [others] do not enter into levirate marriage with his wife [cf. M. San. 2:1C–E].

F. [When] he stands in the line [to receive comfort as a mourner], the prefect of the priests is at his right hand, and the head of the father's houses [the priestly courses] at his left hand.

G. **And all the people say to him, "Let us be your atonement."**

H. **And he says to them. "May you be blessed by Heaven" [M. San. 2:1N–O].**

I. [And when] he stands in the line to give comfort to others, the prefect of the priests and the [high] priest who has now passed out of his position of grandeur are at his right hand, and the mourner is at his left.

J. **[People may] not watch him while he is getting a haircut, [or while he is nude] or in the bathhouse [M. San. 2:5B],**

K. since it is said, *And he who is high priest among his brothers* [Lev. 21:10]—that his brethren should treat him with grandeur.

L. But if he wanted to permit others to wash with him, the right is his.

M. R. Judah says, "If he wanted to disgrace himself, they do not pay attention to him,

N. "as it is said, *And you will keep him holy* [Lev. 21:8]—even against his will."

O. They said to R. Judah, "To be sure [Scripture] says, *From the Temple he shall not go forth* [Lev. 21:12], [but this is referring] only to the time of the Temple service" [M. San. 2:1I–J].

P. He goes out to provide a funeral meal for others, and others come to provide a funeral meal for him.

4.2

A. **An Israelite king does not stand in line to receive comfort [in the time of bereavement],**

B. **nor does he stand in line to give comfort to others.**

C. **And he does not go to provide a funeral meal for others.**

D. **But others come to him to give a funeral meal [M. San. 2:3F],**

E. as it is said, *And the people went to provide a funeral meal for David* [II Sam. 3:35].

F. And if he transgressed a positive or a negative commandment or indeed any of the commandments, lo, he is treated like an ordinary person in every respect.

G. **He does not perform the rite of removing the shoe, and others do not perform the rite of removing the shoe with his wife;**

H. **he does not enter into levirate marriage, nor [do his brothers] enter into levirate marriage with his wife [M. San. 2:2C–D].**

I. **R. Judah says, "If he wanted to perform the rite of removing the shoe [M. San. 2:9], he has the right to do so."**

J. They said to him, "You turn out to do damage to the glory owing to a king."

K. *And [others] do not marry his widow* [M. San. 2:3G], as it is said, *So they were shut up to the day of their death, living in widowhood* [II Sam. 20:3].

L. And he has the right to choose wives for himself from any source he wants, whether daughters of priests, Levites, or Israelites.

M. ***And they do not ride on his horse, sit on his throne, handle his* crown or *scepter* or any of his regalia [M. San. 2:5].**

N.   [When] he dies, all of them are burned along with him, as it is said, *You shall die in peace and with the burnings of your fathers, the former kings* [Jer. 34:5].

4.3

A.   Just as they make a burning for kings [who die], so they make a burning for patriarchs [who die].

B.   But they do not do so for ordinary people.

C.   What do they burn on their account?

D.   Their bed and other regalia.

4.4

A.   Everybody stands, while he sits.

B.   And sitting was [permitted] in the Temple courtyard only for kings of the house of David.

C.   All the people keep silent, when he is talking.

D.   He would call them, "My brothers" and "My people," as it is said, *Hear you, my brothers and my people* [I Chron. 28:2].

E.   And they call him, "Our Lord and our master,"

F.   as it is said, *But our Lord David, the King, has made Solomon king* [I Kings 1:43].

4.5

A.   *"He should not multiply wives for himself* [Deut. 17:17]—like Jezebel. But [if the wives are like] Abigail, it is permitted," the words of R. Judah [*vs.* M. San. 2:4H–I].

B.   *He should not multiply horses for himself* [Deut. 17:16]—if the horses are left idle, even one [he may not keep],

C.   as it is said, *Lest he multiply horses.*

D.   R. Judah says, "Lo, it says, *And Solomon had forty thousand stalls of horses* [I Kings 4:26]—yet he did well,

E.   "for it is written, *And Judah and Israel were as many as the sand that is on the seashore for multitude* [I Kings 4:20].

F.   "And since it is written, *Twelve thousand horsemen* [I Kings 4:26], one has to conclude that the rest of the horses were left idle."

G.   But an ordinary person is permitted [to do] all of these things.

H.   R. Yosé says, "Everything that is spelled out in the pericope of the king [Deut. 17:14] is [an ordinary person] permitted to do."

I.   R. Judah says, "That pericope is written only to make the people revere him [cf. M. San 2:5C],

J.   "for it is written, *You will surely set a king over you"* [Deut. 17:14]."

K.   And so did R. Judah say, "Three commandments were imposed upon the Israelites when they came into the land.

L.   "They were commanded to appoint a king, to build the chosen house, and to cut off the descendants of Amalek.

M.   "If so, why were they punished in the days of Samuel [for wanting a king]? Because they acted too soon."

N. R. Nehorai says, "This pericope was written only because of [future] complaints [with the king].

O. "For it is said, *And you will say, I will set a king over me*" [Deut. 17:14].

P. R. Eleazar b. R. Yosé says, "The elders asked in the proper way, as it is said, *Give us a king to judge us* [I Sam. 8:6].

Q. "But the ordinary folk went and spoiled matters, as it is said, *That we also may be like all the nations, and our king will judge us and go before us to fight our battles*" [I Sam. 8:20].

4.6

A. "Those put to death by the court—their property goes to their heirs.

B. "But those put to death by the king—their property goes to the king," [the words of R. Judah].

C. And sages say, "Those put to death by their king—their property goes to their heirs."

D. Said R. Judah to them, "It says, *Behold, he [Ahab] is in the vineyard of Naboth, where he has gone down to take posession*" [I Kings 21:18].

E. They said to him, "It was because he was the son of his father's brother [and] it was appropriate [to come] to him as in inheritance."

F. They said to him, "And did [Naboth] have no children?"

G. They said to him, "And did he not kill both him and his children,

H. "as it is said, *Surely I have seen yesterday the blood of Naboth and the blood of his sons, says the Lord; and I will requite you in this plot, says the Lord* [II Kings 9:26]?"

4.7

A. *And he writes for himself a scroll of the Torah* [Deut. 17:17] —

B. for his own use, that he not have to make use of the one of his fathers, but rather of his own,

C. as it is said, *And he will write for himself* —

D. that the very writing of the scroll should be for him [in particular].

E. And an ordinary person has no right to read in it,

F. as it is said, *And he will read in it* —

G. he, and no one else.

H. And they examine [his scroll] in the court of the priests, in the court of the Levites, and in the court of the Israelites who are of suitable genealogical character to marry into the priesthood.

I. [When] he goes to war, it is with him, when he comes back, it is with him [cf. M. San. 2:4M]; when he goes to court, it is with him; when he goes to the urinal, it waits for him [outside] at the door,

J. and so does David say, *I have set God always before me [and he is on my right hand]* [Ps. 16:8].

K. R. Judah says, "A scroll of the Torah is at his right hand, and tefillin are on his arm."

L. R. Yosé said, "Ezra was worthy for the Torah to have been given by him, had not Moses come before him.

M. "Concerning Moses *going up* is stated, and concerning Ezra *going up* is stated.

N. "Concerning Moses *going up* is stated, as it is said, *And Moses went up to God* [Ex. 19:3].

O. "And concerning Ezra going up is stated, as it is written, And *he, Ezra, when up from Babylonia* [Ezra 7:6].

P. "Just as, in the case of *going up* mentioned in connection with Moses, he taught Torah to Israel, as it is stated, *And the Lord commanded me at that time to teach you statutes and judgments* [Deut. 4:14],

Q. "so, in the case of *going up* mentioned in connection with Ezra, he taught Torah to Israel, as it is said, *For Ezra had prepared his heart to expound the law of the Lord and to do it and to teach in Israel statutes and judgments*" [Ezra 7:0].

R. Also through him were given [both] a form of writing and language, as it is said, *And the writing of the letter was written in the Aramaic character and interpreted in the Aramaic tongue* [Ezra 4:7].

S. Just as its interpretation was in Aramaic, so its writing was in Aramaic.

T. And it says, *"But they could not read the writing, nor make known to the king the interpretation thereof"* [Dan. 5:8]—

U. this teaches that on that very day it was given.

V. And it says, *And he shall write a copy of this law* [Deut. 17:18]—A Torah which is destined to be changed.

We note that the Tosefta contains formulations of rules on the same topic as in the Mishnah—but with different opinions on what those rules should require, as in the contradiction, at the outset, M. 4:1D. We may conclude that opinions circulated on topics treated in the Mishnah, and that the framers of the Tosefta drew upon some of these opinions and preserved them. Called "supplements," the document performed that important task. We note also how, at I, the Tosefta's authorship presents an amplification of the cited passage of the Mishnah. Tosefta 4:3, 4 then goes on to fresh information on the established topic at hand. The overall character of this rich document emerges from the passage before us.

6. THE SAYINGS OF THE FOUNDERS

We recall that in around 250, approximately a generation after the publication of the Mishnah, tractate Avot made its appearance. Providing the first apologetic of the Mishnah, the opening chapter links the names of authorities in the Mishnah itself to God's revelation to Moses at Sinai. The authority of the Mishnah therefore rests on God's revelation of the Torah to Moses, because the authorities of the Mishnah present traditions handed on orally from one sage to the next, backward to Sinai. The fundamental apologetic for the Judaism of the dual Torah begins in the words that follow. Note two things. First of all, beyond number 1, we deal with names of figures who flourished long after most of the books of the Hebrew Scriptures were written, and from number 7 onward, the named sages figure, also, in the pages of the Mishnah. Second, what the authorities who are listed teach is not simply a teaching of Scripture. Quite to the contrary, all of them give teachings not in Scripture, and the wording of these teachings rarely accords with patterns of wording we find in Scripture. So new authorities, in a language of their own, lay down teachings of their own—and the whole goes back to the Torah that Moses received at Sinai and handed on to Joshua. It would not be long before that other corpus of teachings that Moses received and handed on would gain the status that Sinai accorded, also, to the written Torah—that is to say, the status of Torah, but Torah the opposite of the written one—hence the Oral Torah. When the teachings of the sages, their books and traditions, entered the status of Oral Torah, then their system of Judaism became the Judaism of the dual Torah. But we stand at some distance from that important development, and we have no clear notion of what precipitated it. What urgent question found its self-evidently true answer in the doctrine of Torah in two media—and in the particular world view and way of life laid forth in these *particular* statements of that Torah?

TRACTATE AVOT CHAPTER ONE

1. Moses received Torah at Sinai and handed it on to Joshua, Joshua to elders, and elders to prophets. And prophets handed it on to the men of the great assembly. They said three things: Be prudent in judgment. Raise up many disciples. Make a fence for the Torah.

2. Simeon the Righteous was one of the last survivors of the great assembly. He would say: On three things does the world stand: On the Torah, and on the Temple service, and on deeds of loving kindness.

3. Antigonus of Sokho received [the Torah] from Simeon the Righteous. He would say: Do not be like servants who serve the master on condition of receiving a reward, but [be] like servants who serve the master not on condition of receiving a reward. And let the fear of Heaven be upon you.

4. Yosé ben Yoezer of Zeredah and Yosé ben Yohanan of Jerusalem received [the Torah] from them. Yosé ben Yoezer says: Let your house be a gathering place for sages. And wallow in the dust of their feet, and drink in their words with gusto.

5. Yosé ben Yohanan of Jerusalem says: Let your house be open wide. And seat the poor at your table ["make the poor members of your household"]. And don't talk too much with women. (He referred to a man's wife; all the more so is the rule to be applied to the wife of one's fellow. In this regard did sages say: So long as a man talks too much with a woman, he brings trouble on himself, wastes time better spent on studying Torah, and ends up an heir of Gehenna.)

6. Joshua ben Perahyah and Nittai the Arbelite received [the Torah] from them. Joshua ben Perahyah says: Set up a master for yourself. And get yourself a companion-disciple. And give everybody the benefit of the doubt.

7. Nittai the Arbelite says: Keep away from a bad neighbor. And don't get involved with a bad person. And don't give up hope of retribution.

8. Judah ben Tabbai and Simeon ben Shetah received [the Torah] from them. Judah ben Tabbai says: Don't make yourself like one of those who advocate before judges [while you yourself are judging a case]. And when the litigants stand before you, regard

> them as guilty. But when they leave you, regard them as acquitted (when they have accepted your judgment).
>
> 9. Simeon ben Shetah says: Examine the witnesses with great care. And watch what you say, lest they learn from what you say how to lie.
> 10. Shemaiah and Avtalyon received [the Torah] from them. Shemaiah says: Love work. Hate authority. Don't get friendly with the government.
> 11. Avtalyon says: Sages, watch what you say, lest you become liable to the punishment of exile, and go into exile to a place of bad water, and disciples who follow you drink bad water and die, and the name of Heaven be thereby profaned.
> 12. Hillel and Shammai received [the Torah] from them. Hillel says: Be disciples of Aaron, loving peace and pursuing grace, loving people and drawing them near to the Torah.
> 13. He would say [in Aramaic]: A name made great is a name destroyed, and one who does not add, subtracts.
>   And who does not learn is liable to death. And the one who uses the crown, passes away.
> 14. He would say: If I am not for myself, who is for me? And when I am for myself, what am I? And if not now, when?
> 15. Shammai says: Make your learning of Torah a fixed obligation. Say little and do much. Greet everybody cheerfully.
> 16. Rabban Gamaliel says: Set up a master for yourself. Avoid doubt. Don't tithe by too much guesswork.
> 17. Simeon his son says: All my life I grew up among the sages, and I found nothing better for a person [the body] than silence. And not the learning is the thing, but the doing. And whoever talks too much causes sin.
> 18. Rabban Simeon ben Gamaliel says: On three things does the world stand: on justice, on truth, and on peace. As it is said, *Execute the judgment of truth and peace in your gates* [Zech 8:16].

What is important in this chain of tradition, from Sinai forward, is the simple fact that the cited authorities include important first-century figures, whose sayings also occur in the Mishnah. Later passages in tractate Avot place into that same chain of tradition authorities of the second century, including sages separated from the actual publication of the Mishnah by no more than a generation. So the message is clear: The Mishnah takes its place in the line of Sinai.

7. JUDAISM WITHOUT CHRISTIANITY

Christians and Jews in the first century and for the next two hundred years, to the fourth century, did not argue with one another. Each group went its way, emphasizing matters of concern to its own group. Specifically, the one stressed the matter of salvation; the other, of sanctification. When Christianity came into being, in the first century, one important strand of the Christian movement laid stress on issues of salvation, in the Gospels maintaining that Jesus was, and is, Christ, come to save the world and impose a radical change on history. At that same time, as we have seen, the Pharisees emphasized issues of sanctification, maintaining that the task of Israel is to attain that holiness of which the Temple was a singular embodiment. When, in the Gospels, we find the record of the Church placing Jesus into opposition with the Pharisees, we witness the confrontation of different people talking about different things to different people.

The Judaism without Christianity portrayed in the Mishnah did not present a richly developed doctrine of the Messiah. It worked out issues of sanctification, rather than those of salvation. The reason is that the Mishnah laid its emphasis upon issues of the destruction of the Temple and the subsequent defeat in the failed war for the restoration. These issues, the framers of the Mishnah maintained, raised the question of Israel's sanctity: Is Israel still a holy people, even without the holy temple, and if so, what are the enduring instrumentalities of sanctification? When sages worked out a Judaism without a Temple and a cult, they produced in the Mishnah a system of sanctification focused on the holiness of the priesthood, the cultic festivals, and the Temple and its sacrifices, as well as on the rules for protecting that holiness from levitical uncleanness—four of the six divisions of the Mishnah on a single theme. In the aftermath of the conversion of the Roman Empire to Christianity and the triumph of Christianity in the generation beyond Julian "the apostate," sages worked out in the pages of the Talmud of the land of Israel and in the exegetical compilations of the age, a Judaism intersecting with the Mishnah's but essentially asymmetrical with it. That Talmud presented a system of salvation, but one focused on the salvific power of the sanctification of the holy people. The first of the two Talmuds, the one closed at the end of the fourth century, set the compass and locked it into place. The Judaism that was portrayed by the final document of late antiquity, the Talmud of Babylonia, at the end laid equal emphasis on sanctification in the here and now and salvation at the end of time.

If Christianity presented an urgent problem to the sages behind the Mishnah—for example, giving systemic prominence to a given category rather than some other—we cannot point to a single line of the document that says so. The figure of the Messiah in no way provided the sages of the Mishnah with an appropriate way of explaining the purpose and goal of their system, its teleology. That teleology, appealing to the end of history with the coming of the Messiah, came to predominate only in the Talmud of the Land of Israel and in sages' documents beyond. What issues then proved paramount in a Judaism utterly out of relationship to Christianity in any form? We turn back to the Mishnah to find out.

The Mishnah presents a Judaism that answered a single encompassing question concerning the enduring sanctification of Israel, the people, the land, the way of life. What, in the aftermath of the destruction of the holy place and holy cult, remained of the sanctity of the holy caste, the priesthood, the holy land, and, above all, the holy people and its holy way of life? The answer: Sanctity persists, indelibly, in *Israel, the people,* in its way of life, in its land, in its priesthood, in its food, in its mode of sustaining life, in its manner of procreating and so sustaining the nation. That holiness would endure. And the Mishnah then laid out the structures of sanctification: What it means to live a holy life. But that answer found itself absorbed, in time to come, within a successor system, with its own points of stress and emphasis. That successor system, both continuous and asymmetrical with the Mishnah, would take over the Mishnah and turn it into "the one whole Torah of Moses, our rabbi," that became Judaism. The indicative marks are, first, the central symbol of Torah as sages' teaching, second, the figure of Messiah as sage; and third, the doctrine that Israel today is the family of Abraham, Isaac, and Jacob, heirs to the legacy and heritage of merit that, in the beginning, they earned and handed on to their children.

The system portrayed in the Mishnah emerged in a world in which as a political power there was no Christianity. What points do we *not* find? First, we find in the Mishnah no explicit and systematic theory of scriptural authority. We now know how much stress the Judaism in confrontation with Christianity laid on Scripture, with important commentaries produced in the age of Constantine. What the framers of the Mishnah did not find necessary was a doctrine of the authority of Scripture. Nor did they undertake a systematic exegetical effort at the linking of the principal document, the Mishnah, to Scripture. The authors saw no need. Christianity made pressing the question of the standing and status of the Mishnah in relationship to Scripture, claiming that the Mishnah was man-made and a forgery of God's will, which was contained only in Scripture. Then the doctrine of the dual Torah, explaining the origin and authority of the Mishnah, came to full expression.

Sages therefore produced a document, the Mishnah, so independent of Scripture that, when the authors wished to say what Scripture said, they chose to do so in their own words and in their own way. Whatever the intent of the Mishnah's authors, therefore, it clearly did not encompass explaining to a competing Israel, heirs of the same Scriptures of Sinai, just what authority validated the document and how the document related to Scripture.

Second, we look in vain for a teleology focused on the coming of the Messiah as the end and purpose of the system as a whole. The Mishnah's teleology in no way invokes an eschatological dimension. This Judaism, for a world in which Christianity played no considerable role, took slight interest in the Messiah and presented a teleology lacking all eschatological, therefore messianic, focus. Third, the same Judaism laid no considerable stress on the symbol of the Torah, though, of course, the Torah as a scroll, as a matter of status, and as revelation of God's will at Sinai, enjoyed prominence.

It follows that the issues presented to Jews by the triumph of Christianity, which, as we shall see, informed the documents shaped in the land of Israel in the period of that triumph, did not play an important role in prior components of the unfolding canon of Judaism—in particular, the Mishnah and closely allied documents which reached closure before the fourth century. These present a Judaism, not despite Christianity, but a Judaism defined in utter indifference to Christianity. The contrast that we shall shortly draw between the Mishnah and the Judaic system emerging in the fourth-century documents tells the tale.

The Mishnah shows us a Judaic system completely unaffected by the challenge of Christianity. The great motifs important to Christianity, and therefore later critical to Judaism as well, play scarcely any role. To give four important examples:

1. The Mishnah presents no doctrine of the Messiah, when he will come, what Israel must do to warrant his coming.
2. The Mishnah contains no picture of the meaning of history and the place of Israel in the unfolding universal history of humanity.
3. The Mishnah provides no systematic account of the Torah and its contents—what books produced by the sages are part of the Torah of Sinai for example—and its meaning and relationship to the Mishnah's own documents.
4. The Mishnah in no way asks the question of who is Israel, or who is the true Israel, and provides no theory of what it means to be Israel.

But Judaism would later address all these issues, and the doctrines that would define matters for Judaism would emerge, in particular, in the aftermath of the crisis of the fourth century. At that time we find a fully articulated doctrine of the Messiah, a theory of who is Israel, a picture of the entirety of human history, and an account of what is in the Torah. All these matters, so critical as indicators of Judaism from the fourth century to our own day, emerged in response to the challenge of the political triumph of Christianity, as we shall now see.

4

the thirð crisis: the conversion of constantine in 312 anð the judaism of sanctification anð salvation

1. SETTING

The West as we have known it from the fourth century, the age of Constantine, carried forward four principal elements of the heritage of antiquity: (1) Greek philosophy, (2) Roman law and institutions, (3) the religious legacy of ancient Israel contained in the Hebrew Scriptures, and (4) Christianity, religion of the state and formative force in culture. But above all, the West was what it was because of Christianity. It follows that the history of the West began in the fourth century, from the conversion of Constantine, the Roman emperor, when Christianity attained that paramount position in politics and culture that it was to occupy throughout Western history until nearly the present day. And, as we shall see, it was in that same critical century that the Judaism of the dual Torah—with its world view framed by the texts of the Talmuds and Midrash compilations; its way of life defined as sanctification of the here and now pointing toward salvation at the end of time; and its address to genealogical Israel, meaning the family of Abraham, Isaac, and Jacob—reached its full and definitive expression. So the third crisis in the formative history of Judaism is marked by the political triumph that not only legalized Christianity but also accorded to it the status, by the end of the century, of the official and governing religion of the Roman Empire.

During the next century, however, from 312 onward, the Roman Empire, its government and institutions, came under Christian domination. Writing nearly a century later, for example, the great exegete and translator of the Hebrew Scriptures into Latin, Jerome—cited by Kelly—captures the astonishment that Christians felt:

> ...every island, prison, and salt-mine was crowded with Christian captives in chains...with the present era when (such as the seemingly impossible transformations worked by God in his goodness) the selfsame imperial government which used to make a bonfire of Christian sacred books has them adorned sumptuously with gold, purple, and precious stones, and, instead of razing church buildings to the ground, pays for the construction of magnificent basilicas with gilded ceilings and marble-encrusted walls.[1]

Kelly states the simple fact: "At the beginning of the century [the Church] had been reeling under a violent persecution...Now it found itself showered with benefactions and privileges, invited to undertake responsibilities, and progressively given a directive role in society."[2] The age of Constantine thus presented even to contemporaries an era of dramatic change. When under Constantine the religious systems of Christianity became licit, then favored, and finally dominant in the government of the Roman Empire, Christians confronted a world for which nothing had prepared them. But they did not choose to complain. For the political triumph of Christ, now ruler of the world in dimensions wholly unimagined, brought its own lessons. All of human history required fresh consideration, from the first Adam to the last. The writings of churches now asked to be sorted out, so that the canon, Old and New, might correspond to the standing and clarity of the new Christian situation. So, too, one powerful symbol, that selected by Constantine for his army and the one by which he won, the cross, took a position of dominance and declared its distinctive message of a Christianity in charge of things. Symbol, canon, systemic teleology—all three responded to the unprecedented and hitherto not-to-be-predicted circumstance of Christ on the throne of the nations.

At the end of that century of surprises, in the year 429, the Jews of the land of Israel for their part confronted a situation without precedent. That year marked the end of Roman recognition of the political standing of the patriarchal government that had ruled the Jews of the land of Israel for the preceding three centuries. It was the end of their political entity, their instrument of self-administration and government in their own land. Tracing its roots back for centuries and claiming to originate in the family of David, the Jewish government, that of the patriarch, had

---

[1]Kelly, *Jerome* (Oxford: Oxford University Press, 1981), p. 295.
[2]Ibid., pp. 1–2.

succeeded the regime of the priests in the Temple and the kings, first allies, then agents, of Rome on their throne. Israel's political tradition of government, of course, went back (in the mind of the nation) to Sinai. No one had ever imagined that the Jews would define their lives other than together, other than as a people, a political society, with collective authority and shared destiny and a public interest. The revelation of Sinai addressed a nation; the Torah gave laws to be kept and enforced; and, as is clear, Israel found definition in comparison to other nations. It would have rulers, subject to God's authority to be sure, and it would have a king now, and a king-messiah at the end of time. So the fourth century brought a hitherto unimagined circumstance: an Israel lacking the authority to rule itself under its own government, even the ethnic and patriarchal one that had held things together on the other side of the end of long centuries of priestly rule in the Temple and royal rule in Jerusalem.

In effect, the two systems, Christian and Judaic, had prepared for worlds that neither would inhabit: the one for the status of governed, not governor; the other for the condition of a political entity. But Christianity in politics would now define, not the fringes, but the very fabric of society and culture. Judaism, out of politics altogether, would find its power in the voluntarily donated obedience of people in no way to be coerced to conform and obey, except from within or from on high.

Whatever "Christianity" and "Judaism" would choose as their definition beyond this time of turning, therefore, would constitute mediating systems, with the task, for the new systems to emerge, of responding to a new world out of materials deriving from an inappropriate old one. The Judaism that would take shape beyond the fourth century, beginning in writings generally thought to have come to closure at the end of that momentous age, would use writings produced in one religious ecological system to address a quite different one, and so too would the Christianity that would rule, both in its Western and in its Eastern expressions.

The importance of the radical political shift of the fourth century should not be missed. It is what forced Israel's sages to respond to the existence and claims of Christianity, which, as we have seen, they had been able to ignore for 300 years. The position outlined in the fourth-century documents of Judaism represents the first reading of Christianity on the part of Israel's sages. Prior to that time they did not take to heart the existence of the competition. Afterward, of course, they would draw on the position outlined in their fourth-century writings to sort out the issues made urgent by the success of Christianity throughout the Roman world. Prior to the time of Constantine, as we have seen, the documents of Judaism that evidently reached closure before 300—the Mishnah, tractate Avot, and the Tosefta—scarcely took cognizance of Christianity and did not deem the new faith to be much of a challenge. If the unsystematic and scattered allusions do mean to refer to Christianity at all, then sages regarded Christianity as an irritant, an exasperating heresy among Jews who should have known better. But then, neither Jews nor pagans took much interest in Christianity in the new faith's first century and a half. The authors of the Mishnah framed a system to which Christianity bore no relevance whatsoever; theirs were problems presented in an altogether different context. For their part, pagan writers were indifferent to Christianity, not mentioning it until about 160.[3] Only when Christian evangelism enjoyed some solid success, toward the later part of that century, did pagans compose apologetic works attacking Christianity. Celsus stands at the start, followed by Porphyry in the third century. But by the fourth century, pagans and Jews alike knew that they faced a formidable enemy.

In point of fact, the ecology of Judaism in its formative century finds definition in the ecology of Christianity in the fourth century—the century that marks the first in the history of Christianity as the formative power in the history of the West. Judaism and Christianity have related to each other intensely and continuously from that beginning point to the present. Christianity began its life on earth within Israel, the Jewish people, and for a long time remained a kind of Judaism. It never gave up the claim to carry forward the revelation to Israel by God at Sinai. Judaism, for its part, would live out its history within two worlds—first the Christian, later the Muslim. But it was in the Christian setting, defined by the triumph of the fourth century, that Judaism as it would emerge from late antiquity reached the definition that would prove characteristic from then to now.[4] In the definition of each of its systemically definitive characteristics, Judaism found its points of emphasis and stress in the ecology framed by Christianity at its moment of triumph.

When in 312 Constantine declared Christianity a legal religion, then favored the Church, and finally converted, and when his successors, by the end of the fourth century, had made Christianity the religion of the Roman Empire, Israel the people confronted a very difficult and critical moment. But the crisis was not so much political and legal as it was spiritual, though, to be sure, it bore deep consequences for both politics and the Jews' standing in law. The political triumph of Christianity presented to Judaism a considerable challenge.

First, the claim of Christians that Jesus was, and is, the Christ, had now to find a hearing on the part of Jews. Second, the Christians maintained that the Jews' sages taught traditions with no standing in the revelation of Sinai. Third, the Christians alleged that they now

[3]Labriolle, in J. R. Palanque et al., *The Church in the Christian Roman Empire* I: *The Church and the Arian Crisis* (N.Y.: 1953), p. 242.
[4]How Judaism responded to the challenge of the success of Islam presents a quite different set of questions. But the Judaism that met that challenge had reached its definition in the fourth century and in response to Christianity. Its further success in coping with Islam demands attention in its own terms.

constituted the saved, the Israel of whom Scripture had spoken. Israel "after the flesh" did not. Fourth, the claim of Israel that the future bore salvation and vindication for God's people came under considerable doubt. Christians addressed Jews with both issues, and, by the end of the century, the challenge carried with it the authority of the state. If the Messiah is yet to come, then why does Jesus, enthroned as Christ, now rule the world? Christians asked Israel that question; but, of greater consequence, Israel asked itself.

One other event of the fourth century, besides the triumph of Christianity, demands attention: the ascension to the Roman throne of Julian, a pagan. For the brief spell of his reign, from 361 to 33, Christianity lost that most favored position that had so astonished the Church earlier in the century. To understand its impact, we have to bear in mind that the political shift in the status of Christianity came as a shock to Christians as much as to pagans and Jews. Christians at the court of Constantine (as Jerome reminds us) remembered days, not long past, of suffering in mines and prisons. So the shift which we now know would be permanent and enduring, did not win the confidence of the Christians. Things were still chancy and could change. Their insecurity rested on sound basis, for the throne had (miraculously) turned Christian, and could just as suddenly turn again. And that is precisely what happened just a half century after Constantine's legalization of the Christian Church—specifically, when, in 362–363 the pagan, Julian, regained the throne and turned the empire away from Christianity.

The impact on Judaism, for its part, proved considerable. As part of his policy to humiliate the Church, Julian further invited the Jews to rebuild the Temple. The success of that project would call into question the prediction attributed by the Gospels to Jesus that no stone would remain on stone, that the temple would never be rebuilt. But the project proved a fiasco, and Julian was killed in battle against Iran. Consequently, the succeeding emperors, Christians all, restored the throne to Christ (as they would put it) and secured for the Church and Christianity the control of the State through law. So—and Chrysostom so argued in 386–387, in the aftermath of Julian's brief reign—the destruction of the Temple in 70 now has proved definitive. Three hundred years later, the Temple was supposed to be rebuilt, but God prevented it. In the aftermath of Julian's reign, the Christians, regaining the throne, took severe measures to prevent the recurrence of pagan rule. They acted out of a realistic insecurity. The vigorous repression of paganism after Julian's apostasy expressed Christians' quite natural fear that such a thing might happen again. Bickerman states matters powerfully:

> Julian was yesterday, the persecutors the day before yesterday. Ambrose knew some magistrates who could boast of having spared Christians. At Antioch the Catholics had just endured the persecution of Valens ... and unbelievers of every sort dominated the capital of Syria. The army,

composed of peasants and barbarians, could acclaim tomorrow another Julian, another Valens, even another Diocletian. One could not yet, as Chrysostom says somewhere, force [people] to accept the Christian truth; one had to convince them of it.[5]

Although matters remained in doubt, the main fact stood firm. In the beginning of the fourth century Rome was pagan; in the end, Christian. In the beginning Jews in the land of Israel administered their own affairs. In the end their institution of self-administration lost the recognition it had formerly enjoyed. In the beginning Judaism enjoyed entirely licit status, and the Jews, the protection of the state. In the end Judaism suffered abridgement of its former liberties, and the Jews, abridgement of theirs. In the beginning the Jews lived in the land of Israel, and in some numbers. In the end they lived in Palestine, as a minority. Constantine and his mother built churches and shrines all over the country, but especially in Jerusalem, so the land of Israel received yet another name, for another important group, now becoming the Holy Land.

To turn to the broader perspective, from the beginning of the fourth century, we look backward over an uninterrupted procession of philosophers and emperors, Aristotle and Plato and Socrates and Alexander and Caesar upon Caesar. From the end of the fourth century we look forward to Constantinople, Kiev and Moscow, in the east, to Christian Rome, Paris and London, to cathedrals and saints, to an empire called holy and Roman and a public life infused with Christian piety and Christian sanctity, to pope after pope after pope. Before Constantine's conversion in 312, Christianity scarcely imagined a politics; its collective life was lived mostly in private. Afterward Christianity undertook to govern, shaped the public and political institutions of empires, and, through popes and emperors alike, defined the political history of the world for long centuries to come.

It follows that the third and final crisis in the formative history of Judaism derived from a political and religious change as catastrophic as the first and the second ones, of 586 and 70 respectively. The issues that demanded attention were these: what hope for Israel now—or ever? What meaning for Israel in history now—or at the end of time? The events of the day made urgent these essentially theological questions. For, as in 586 and in 70, theological issues and political dilemmas worked together to define the settings in which Judaic systems took shape. The outcome of the crisis of the fourth century was the Judaism that would predominate from that time to the present: the fully spelled out world view of the dual Torah, oral and written, and of the way of life of Israel as a holy people attaining sanctification in the here and now so as to reach salvation at the end of time. So we come to the critical moment, when Judaism as we know it reached the definition it would have for

[5]Robert Wilken, *Chrysostom and the Jews* (Oxford: Oxford University Press, 1982), pp. 32–33.

1,500 years, and, in matters of politics and culture and the institutions of society, Christianity too would emerge as it would build the West.

What, specifically, marks the emergence of the Judaic system of the dual Torah? In terms of scriptures, two enormous developments emerged:

1. an enormous commentary to the Mishnah, and
2. a set of immense commentaries to important books of the written Torah, the Scriptures—specifically, the books of Genesis and Leviticus.

These documents mark shifts in the symbolic system and structure of the Judaism then taking shape. The particular changes responded to the critical challenge of the political triumph of Christianity.

Let us be specific about the points of challenge and systemic response in the Judaism of the dual Torah. The symbolic system of Christianity, with Christ triumphant, with the cross as the now-regnant symbol, with the canon of Christianity now defined and recognized as authoritative, called forth from the sages of the Land of Israel a symbolic system strikingly responsive to the crisis:

1. The coming of the Messiah set as the teleology of the system of Judaism as they defined that system.
2. The symbol of the Torah expanded to encompass the whole of human existence as the system limned that existence.
3. The canon of Sinai broadened to take account of the entirety of the sages' teachings, as much as it had to encompass the written Torah everyone acknowledged as authoritative.

The contrast between the sages' system as revealed in writings closed in the later second and third century, in particular the Mishnah and its closely allied documents, and the system that emerged in the writings of the later fourth and fifth centuries tells the tale. The story becomes clear when we focus upon the single most striking shift: the development of the talmudic doctrine of the Messiah at the end of time and of the meaning of history.[6] That doctrine came to full expression for the first time in the pages of the Talmud of the land of Israel, which reached closure around A.D. 400, at the end of the first Christian century in the history of the West.

2. SYSTEM: THE TALMUDS' JUDAISM OF SALVATION THROUGH SANCTIFICATION

The Judaism that would emerge in the fourth-century documents took the position that, through sanctification, Israel would make itself worthy of salvation in the coming of the Messiah. Hence we speak of a "Judaism of

[6]In Chapter 6 we take up the revision of the symbol of the Torah.

salvation through sanctification." To understand the impact of the events of the fourth century, with their powerful challenge of a messianic character, we must rehearse the place of the category of salvation and the figure of the Messiah prior to the period at hand.

As we have noted, the Mishnah presented no doctrine of the Messiah, and its Judaic system stressed sanctification to the near exclusion of issues of salvation, history, the end of time, and the coming of the Messiah. That, of course, represents a surprising development. The character of the Israelite Scriptures, with their emphasis upon historical narrative as a mode of theological explanation, leads us to expect all Judaisms to evolve as deeply messianic religions. With all prescribed actions pointed toward the coming of the Messiah at the end of time, and all interest focused upon answering the historical-salvific questions (how long?), Judaism from late antiquity to the present day presents no surprises. Its liturgy evokes historical events to prefigure salvation; prayers of petition repeatedly turn to the speedy coming of the Messiah; and the experience of worship invariably leaves the devotee expectant and hopeful. Just as rabbinic Judaism is a deeply messianic religion, secular extensions of Judaism have commonly proposed secularized versions of the focus upon history and have shown interest in the purpose and denouement of events. Teleology—the statement of the purpose of the system and its goals—again appears as an eschatology, a doctrine of the end of time, embodied in messianic symbols.

Yet, as we realize, for a brief moment, a vast and influential document presented a kind of Judaism in which history did not define the main framework by which the issue of teleology took a form other than the familiar eschatological one, and in which historical events were absorbed, through their trivialization in taxonomic structures, into an ahistorical system. In the kind of Judaism in this document, messiahs played a part. But these "anointed men" had no historical role. They undertook a task quite different from that assigned to Jesus by the framers of the Gospels. They were merely a species of priest, falling into one classification rather than another. When we see the shift from the Mishnah, in the second century, to the doctrine of the Talmud and related writings, in the fourth, we realize how great an impact was made by the crisis of the messianic triumph of Jesus as Christ, ruler of the world of Rome.

For its part, the Mishnah presents no doctrine of the Messiah or large view of history. It contains no sustained reflection whatever on the nature and meaning of the destruction of the Temple in A.D. 70, an event which surfaces only in connection with some changes in the law explained as resulting from the end of the cult. The Mishnah pays no attention to the matter of the end time. The word *salvation* is rare; *sanctification*, commonplace. More strikingly, the framers of the Mishnah are virtually silent on the teleology of the system; they never tell us why we should do what the Mishnah tells us, much less what will happen if we do.

Incidents in the Mishnah are preserved either as narrative settings for the statement of the law, or, occasionally, as precedents. Historical events are classified and turned into entries on lists. But incidents in any case come few and far between. True, events do make an impact. But it is always for the Mishnah's own purpose and within its own taxonomic system and rule-seeking mode of thought. The Mishnah manages to provide an immense account of Israel's life without explicitly telling us about such matters as the Messiah and the meaning of history.

The Messiah in the Mishnah does not stand at the forefront of the framers' consciousness. The issues encapsulated in the myth and person of the Messiah are scarcely addressed. Messiah is a category, a classification of priest as much as a particular figure, a one-time person in history made up of one-time, singular events. More important, the Messiah theme does not define the purpose and goal of the system framed by the Mishnah. Theirs is a goal (a "teleology") in which history and the end of time play no role (hence, no "eschatology") and, it must follow, the Messiah theme, so characteristic of theories of the goal of history at the end of time, serves no useful purpose.

The authorship of the Mishnah therefore created a system in which, to begin with, the teleology had nothing to do with eschatology, and, it must follow, the figure of the Messiah played no part. That is why the framers of the Mishnah do not resort to speculation about the Messiah as a historical-supernatural figure. So far as that kind of speculation provides the vehicle for reflection on salvific issues, or in mythic terms, narratives on the meaning of history and the destiny of Israel, we cannot say that the Mishnah's philosophers take up those encompassing categories of being: Where are we heading? What can we do about it? This does not mean that questions found urgent in the aftermath of the destruction of the Temple and the disaster of Bar Kokhba failed to attract the attention of the Mishnah's sages. But they treated history in a different way, offering their own answers to its questions. To these we now turn.

History means not merely events, but how events serve to teach lessons, reveal patterns, tell what to do and what will happen tomorrow. The framers of the Mishnah explicitly refer to very few events, treating those they do mention with a focus quite separate from the unfolding events themselves. They rarely create narratives; historical events do not supply organizing categories or taxonomic classifications. We find no tractate devoted to the destruction of the Temple, no complete chapter of the Mishnah detailing the events of Bar Kokhba, nor even a sustained celebration of the events of the sages' own historical lives. When things that have happened are mentioned, it is neither to narrate nor to interpret and draw lessons from the events. It is either to illustrate a point of law or to pose a problem of the law—always *en passant*, never in a pointed way. The Mishnah absorbs into its encompassing system *all* events, small and large. With them the sages accomplish what they accomplish in everything else: a vast labor of taxonomy, an immense construction of the order and rules governing the classification of everything on earth and in heaven. The disruptive character of history—one-time events of ineluctable significance—scarcely impresses the philosophers. They find no difficulty in showing that what appears unique and beyond classification has in fact happened before and so falls within the range of trustworthy rules and known procedures. Once history's components, one-time events, lose their distinctiveness, then history as a didactic intellectual construct, as a source of lessons and rules, also loses all pertinence.

So lessons and rules come from sorting things out and classifying them from the procedures and modes of thought of the philosopher seeking regularity. To this labor of taxonomy, the historian's way of selecting data and arranging them into patterns of meaning to teach lessons proves inconsequential. One-time events are not important. The world is composed of nature and supernature. The laws that count are those to be discovered in heaven and, in heaven's creation and counterpart, on earth. Keep those laws and things will work out. Break them, and the result is predictable: Calamity of whatever sort will supervene in accordance with the rules. But just because it is predictable, a catastrophic happening testifies to what has always been and must always be, in accordance with reliable rules and within categories already discovered and well explained. That is why the lawyer-philosophers of the mid second century produced the Mishnah—to explain how things *are*. Within the framework of well-classified rules, there could be messiahs, but no single Messiah.

If the end of time and the coming of the Messiah do not serve to explain, for the Mishnah's system, why people should do what the Mishnah says, then what alternative teleology does the Mishnah's first apologetic, Avot, provide? Only when we appreciate the clear answers given in that document, brought to closure at ca. 250, shall we grasp how remarkable is the shift, which took place in later documents of the rabbinic canon, to a messianic framing of the issues of the Torah's ultimate purpose and value. Let us see how the framers of Avot, in the aftermath of the creation of the Mishnah, explain the purpose and goal of the Mishnah: an ahistorical, nonmessianic teleology. The first document generated by the Mishnah's heirs took up the work of completing the Mishnah's system by answering questions of purpose and meaning. Whatever teleology the Mishnah as such would ever acquire would derive from Avot.

Avot agreed with the prior sixty-two tractates of the Mishnah: history proved no more important here than it had before. With scarcely a word about history and no account of events at all, Avot manages—as we saw in Chapter 3—to provide an ample account of how the Torah came down to its own day. Accordingly, the passage of time as such plays no role in the explanation of the origins of the document, nor is the Mishnah presented as eschatological. Occurrences of great weight ("history") are never invoked. How, then, does the tractate tell the story of Torah, narrate the history of God's revelation to Israel, encompassing both Scripture and Mishnah? The answer is that Avot's framers manage to do their work of explanation without telling a story or invoking history at all. They pursue a different way of answering the same question, by exploiting a nonhistorical mode of thought and method of legitimation. And that is the main point: teleology serves the purpose of legitimation, and hence is accomplished in ways other than explaining how things originated or assuming that historical fact explains anything.

Disorderly historical events entered the system of the Mishnah and found their place within the larger framework of the Mishnah's orderly world. But to claim that the Mishnah's framers merely ignored what was happening would be incorrect. They worked out their own way of dealing with historical events, the disruptive power of which they not only conceded but freely recognized. Further, the Mishnah's authors did not intend to compose a history book or a work of prophecy or apocalypse. Even if they had wanted to narrate the course of events, they could hardly have done so through the medium of the Mishnah. Yet the Mishnah presents its philosophy in full awareness of the issues of historical calamity confronting the Jewish nation. So far as the philosophy of the document confronts the totality of Israel's existence, the Mishnah, by definition, also presents a philosophy of history.

The Mishnah's subordination of historical events contradicts the emphasis of a thousand years of Israelite thought. The biblical histories, the ancient prophets, the apocalyptic visionaries all had testified that events themselves were important. Events carried the message of the living God. Events constituted history, pointed toward, and so explained, Israel's destiny. An essentially ahistorical system of timeless sanctification, worked out through construction of an eternal rhythm which centered on the movement of the moon and stars and seasons, represented a life chosen by few outside the priesthood. Furthermore, the pretense that what happens matters less than what is testified against palpable and memorable reality. Israel had suffered enormous loss of life. The Talmud of the land of Israel takes these events seriously and treats them as unique and remarkable. The memories proved real. The hopes evoked by the Mishnah's promise of sanctification of a world in static perfection did not, for they had to compete with the grief of an entire century of mourning.

The most important change is the shift in historical thinking adumbrated in the pages of the Talmud of the land of Israel, a shift from focus upon the Temple and its supernatural principles to close attention to the people Israel and its natural, this-worldly history. Once Israel, holy Israel, had come to form the counterpart to the Temple and its supernatural life, that other history—Israel's—would stand at the center of things. Accordingly, a new sort of memorable event came to the fore in the Talmud of the Land of Israel. Let us give this new history appropriate emphasis. It was the story of Israel's suffering: remembrance of that suffering, on the one side, and an effort to explain events of such tragedy, on the other. So a composite "history" constructed out of the Yerushalmi's units of discourse which were pertinent to consequential events would contain long chapters on what happened to Israel, the Jewish people, and not only, or mainly, what had earlier occurred in the Temple.

The components of the historical theory of Israel's sufferings were manifold. First and foremost, history taught moral lessons. Historical events entered into the construction of a teleology for the Yerushalmi's system of Judaism as a whole. What the law demanded reflected the consequences of wrongful action on the part of Israel. So, again, Israel's own deeds defined the events of history. Rome's role, like Assyria's and Babylonia's, depended upon Israel's provoking divine wrath as it was executed by the great empire. This mode of thought comes to simple expression in what follows.

Y. ERUBIN 3:9

[IV B]   R. Ba, R. Hiyya in the name of R. Yohanan: "Do not gaze at me because I am swarthy, because the sun has scorched me. *My mother's sons were angry with me, they made me keeper of the vineyards; but, my own vineyard, I have not kept!* [Song 1:6]. What made me guard the vineyards? It is because of not keeping my own vineyard.

[C]   What made me keep two festival days in Syria? It is because I did not keep the proper festival day in the Holy Land.

[D]   "I imagined that I would receive a reward for the two days, but I received a reward only for one of them.

[E]   "Who made it necessary that I should have to separate two pieces of dough-offering from grain grown in Syria? It is because I did not separate a single piece of dough-offering in the Land of Israel."

Israel had to learn the lesson of its history to also take command of its own destiny.

But this notion of determining one's own destiny should not be misunderstood. The framers of the Talmud of the land of Israel were not telling the Jews to please—that is, manipulate—God by keeping commandments in order to thereby gain control of their own destiny. To the contrary, the paradox of the Yerushalmi's system lies in the fact that Israel can free itself of control by other nations only by humbly agreeing to accept God's rule. The nations—Rome, in the present instance—rest on one side of the balance, while God rests on the other. Israel must then choose between them. There is no such thing for Israel as freedom from both God and the nations, total autonomy and independence. There is only a choice of masters, a ruler on earth or a ruler in heaven.

With propositions such as these the framers of the Mishnah would certainly have concurred. And why not? For the fundamental affirmations of the Mishnah about the centrality of Israel's perfection in stasis—sanctification—readily prove congruent to the attitudes at hand. Once the Messiah's coming had become dependent upon Israel's condition and not upon Israel's actions in historical time, then the Mishnah's system will have imposed its fundamental and definitive character upon the Messiah myth. An eschatological teleology framed through that myth, then, would prove wholly appropriate to the method of the larger system of the Mishnah.

What makes a messiah a false messiah is not his claim to save Israel, but his claim to save Israel without the help of God. The meaning of the true Messiah is Israel's total submission, through the Messiah's gentle rule, to God's yoke and service. God is not to be manipulated through Israel's humoring of heaven in rite and cult. The notion of keeping the commandments so as to please heaven and persuade God to do what Israel wants is totally incongruent to the text at hand. Keeping the commandments as a mark of submission, loyalty, humility before God is the rabbinic system of salvation. So Israel does not "save itself." Israel never controls its own destiny, either on earth or in heaven. The only choice is whether to cast one's fate into the hands of cruel, deceitful men, or to trust in the living God of mercy and love. We shall now see how this critical position is spelled out in the setting of discourse about the Messiah in the Talmud of the land of Israel.

Bar Kokhba, above all, exemplifies arrogance against God. He lost the war because of that arrogance. In particular, he ignored the authority of sages.

Y. TAANIT 4:5

[X/J]   Said R. Yohanan, "Upon orders of Caesar Hadrian, they killed eight hundred thousand in Betar."

[K]   Said R. Yohanan, "There were eighty thousand pairs of trumpeteers surrounding Betar. Each one was in charge of a number of troops. Ben Kozeba was there and he had two hundred thousand troops who, as a sign of loyalty, had cut off their little fingers.

[L]   "Sages sent word to him, 'How long are you going to turn Israel into a maimed people?'

[M]   "He said to them, 'How otherwise is it possible to test them?'

[N]   "They replied to him, 'Whoever cannot uproot a cedar of Lebanon while riding on his horse will not be inscribed on your military rolls.'

[O]   "So there were two hundred thousand who qualified in one way, and another two hundred thousand who qualified in another way."

[P]   When he would go forth to battle, he would say, "Lord of the world! Do not help and do not hinder us! 'Hast thou not rejected us, O God? Thou dost not go forth, O God, with our armies'"[Ps. 60:10].

[Q]   Three and a half years did Hadrian besiege Betar.

[R]   R. Eleazar of Modiin would sit on sackcloth and ashes and pray every day, saying "Lord of the ages! Do not judge in accord with strict judgment this day! Do not judge in accord with strict judgment this day!"

[S]   Hadrian wanted to go to him. A Samaritan said to him, "Do not go to him until I see what he is doing, and so hand over the city [of Betar] to you. [Make peace... for you.]"

[T]   He got into the city through a drain pipe. He went and found R. Eleazar of Modiin standing and praying. He pretended to whisper something in his ear.

[U]   The townspeople saw [the Samaritan] do this and brought him to Ben Kozeba. They told him, "We saw this man having dealings with your friend."

[V]   [Bar Kokhba] said to him, "What did you say to him, and what did he say to you?"

[W]   He said to [the Samaritan], "If I tell you, then the king will kill me, and if I do not tell you, then you will kill me. It is better that the king kill me, and not you.

[X]   "[Eleazar] said to me, 'I should hand over my city.' ['I shall make peace... ,]"

[Y]   He turned to R. Eleazar of Modiin. He said to him, "What did this Samaritan say to you?"

[Z]   He replied, "Nothing."

[AA]   He said to him, "What did you say to him?"

[BB]   He said to him, "Nothing."

[CC]   [Ben Kozeba] gave [Eleazar] one good kick and killed him.

[DD]   Forthwith an echo came forth and proclaimed the following verse:

[EE]   "Woe to my worthless shepherd, who deserts the flock! May the sword smite his arm and his right eye! Let his arm be wholly withered, his right eye utterly blinded! [Zech. 11:17].

[FF]   "You have murdered R. Eleazar of Modiin, the right arm of all Israel, and their right eye. Therefore may the right arm of that man wither, may his right eye be utterly blinded!"

[GG]   Forthwith Betar was taken, and Ben Kozeba was killed.

We notice two complementary themes. First, Bar Kokhba treats heaven with arrogance, asking God merely to keep out of the way. Second, he treats an especially revered sage with a parallel arrogance. The sage had the power to preserve Israel. Bar Kokhba destroyed Israel's one protection. The result was inevitable.

The Messiah, the centerpiece of salvation history and hero of the tale, now emerged as a critical figure. The historical theory of this passage in the fourth-century document at hand is stated simply. In the authors' view, Israel had to choose between wars, either the war fought by Bar Kokhba or the "war for Torah." "Why had they been punished? It was because of the weight of the war, for they had not wanted to engage in the struggles over the meaning of the Torah" (Y. Ta. 3:9 XVI I). Those struggles, which were ritual arguments about ritual matters, promised the only victory worth winning. Then Israel's history would be written in terms of wars over the meaning of the Torah and the decision of the law. Now we must wonder how this doctrine of the Messiah differs from the fundamental conviction of the authorship of the Mishnah. True, the skins are new, but the wine is very old. For while we speak of sages and learning, the message is the familiar one. It is Israel's history that works out and expresses Israel's relationship with God. The critical dimension of Israel's life, therefore, is salvation; the definitive trait, a movement in time from now to then. It follows that the paramount and organizing category is history and its lessons. In the Yerushalmi we witness, among the Mishnah's heirs, a striking reversion to biblical convictions about the centrality of history in the definition of Israel's reality.

The heavy weight of prophecy, apocalyptic, and biblical historiography, with their emphasis upon salvation and on history as the indicator of Israel's salvation, stood against the Mishnah's quite separate thesis of what truly mattered. The Mishnah does not call upon the symbol of the Messiah in order to express its doctrine of the purpose and goal of matters. What, from the viewpoint of the authorship of the Mishnah, demanded description and analysis and required interpretation? It was the category of sanctification, for eternity. The true issue framed by history and apocalypse was how to move toward the foreordained end of salvation, how to act in time to reach salvation at the end of time. The Mishnah's teleology beyond time and its capacity to posit an eschatology without a place for a historical Mishnah take a position beyond that of the entire antecedent sacred literature of Israel. Only one strand, the priestly one, had ever taken so extreme a position on the centrality of sanctification and the peripheral nature of salvation. Wisdom had stood in between, with its own concerns, drawing attention both to what happened and to what endured. But to Wisdom what finally mattered was not nature or supernature, but rather abiding relationships in historical time.

The Talmud of Babylonia, at the end, carried forward the innovations we have seen in the Talmud of the land of Israel. In the view expressed here, the principal result of Israel's loyal adherence to the Torah and its religious duties will be Israel's humble acceptance of God's rule. That humility, under all conditions, makes God love Israel.

B. HULLIN 89A

"It was not because you were greater than any people that the Lord set his love upon you and chose you" [Deut. 7:7]. The Holy One, blessed be He, said to Israel, "I love you because even when I bestow greatness upon you, you humble yourselves before me. I bestowed greatness upon Abraham, yet he said to me, *'I am but dust and ashes'* [Gen. 18:27]; upon Moses and Aaron, yet they said, *'But I am a worm and no man'* [Ps. 22:7]. But with the heathens it is not so. I bestowed greatness upon Nimrod, and he said, *'Come, let us build us a city'* [Gen. 11:4]; upon Pharaoh, and he said, *'Who are they among all the gods of the countries?'* [2 Kings 18:35]; upon Nebuchadnezzar, and he said, *'I will ascend above the heights of the clouds'* [Isa. 14:14]; upon Hiram, king of Tyre, and he said, *'I sit in the seat of God, in the heart of the seas'* [Ezek. 28:2]."

The essence of the matter, then, is Israel's subservience to God's will, as expressed in the Torah and embodied in the teachings and lives of the great sages. When Israel fully accepts God's rule, then the Messiah will come. Until Israel subjects itself to God's rule, the Jews will be subjugated to pagan domination. Since the condition of Israel governs, Israel itself holds the key to its own redemption. But this it can achieve only by throwing away the key!

The paradox must be crystal clear: Israel acts to redeem itself through the opposite of self-determination—namely, by subjugating itself to God. Israel's power lies in its negation of power. Its destiny lies in giving up all pretense at deciding its own destiny. So weakness is the ultimate strength; forebearance, the final act of self-assertion; passive resignation, the sure step toward liberation. (The parallel for this paradox is in the person of the crucified Christ.) Israel's freedom is engraved on the tablets of the commandments of God: To free be is to freely obey. That is not the meaning associated with these words in the minds of others who, like the sages of the rabbinical canon, declared their view of what Israel must do to secure the coming of the Messiah.

The passage, praising Israel for its humility, completes the circle begun with the description of Bar Kokhba as arrogant and boastful. Gentile kings are boastful; Israelite kings are humble. So, in all, the Messiah myth deals with a concrete and limited consideration of the national life and character. The theory of Israel's history and destiny as it was expressed within that myth interprets matters in terms of a single criterion. At the end of time, God would send a (or the) Messiah to "save" Israel. That conception stands at the center of their system; it shapes and is shaped by their system. In context, the Messiah expresses the system's meaning and so makes it work.

When constructing a systematic account of their Judaism, the philosophers of the Mishnah did not make use of the Messiah myth in the construction of a teleology for their system. They found it possible to present a statement of goals for their projected life of Israel that was entirely separate from appeals to history and eschatology. Since they certainly knew, and even alluded to, long-standing and widely held convictions on eschatological subjects, beginning with those in Scripture, the framers thereby testified that, knowing the larger repertoire, they made choices different from others before and after them. Their document accurately and ubiquitously expresses these choices, both affirmative and negative. The appearance of a messianic eschatology fully consonant with the larger characteristic of the rabbinic system—with its stress on the viewpoints and prooftexts of Scripture, its interest in what was happening to Israel, its focus upon the national-historical dimension of the life of the group—indicates that the encompassing rabbinic system stands essentially autonomous of the prior, mishnaic system.

True, what had gone before was absorbed and fully assimilated. But the rabbinic system first appearing in the Talmud of the Land of Israel is different in the aggregate from the mishnaic system. It represents more than a negative response to its predecessor, however. The rabbinic system of the two Talmuds took over the fundamental convictions of the Mishnaic world view about the importance of Israel's constructing for itself a life beyond time. The rabbinic system then transformed the Messiah myth in its totality into an essentially ahistorical force. If people wanted to reach the end of time, they had to rise above time—that is, history—and stand off at the side of great movements of political and military character. That is the message of the Messiah myth as it reaches full exposure in the rabbinic system of the two Talmuds. At its foundation, it is precisely the message of teleology without eschatology expressed by the Mishnah and its associated documents. Accordingly, we cannot claim that the rabbinic or talmudic system in this regard constitutes a reaction against the mishnaic one. We must conclude, quite to the contrary, that in the Talmuds and their associated documents we see the restatement in classical-mythical form of the ontological convictions that had informed the minds of the second-century philosophers. The new medium contained the old and enduring message: Israel must turn away from time and change, submit to whatever happens, so as to win for itself the only government worth having—that is, God's rule, accomplished through God's anointed agent, the Messiah.

3. A SAMPLE CHAPTER OF THE YERUSHALMI

We turn from the overview of the system of the fourth-century writings to examine the character of the writings themselves. We shall deal with the Yerushalmi, also known as the Talmud of the Land of Israel; we shall then deal with the two great documents of biblical exegesis, the one to Genesis, the other to Leviticus, which, each in its way, shows us a profound response to a deep crisis confronting the Jewish people. What is important in the Talmud of the Land of Israel is its overall character. We see, in the passage before us, how that Talmud takes up the same passage of the Mishnah, then of the Tosefta, that we already know. The passages in which the Talmud cites the Mishnah are printed in boldface type; so too the Tosefta (which is, in any event, identified). When the Talmud cites Scripture, the cited verse is printed in italics.

M. SANHEDRIN 2:1

2.1

A. **A high priest judges, and [others] judge him;**

B. **gives testimony, and [others] give testimony about him;**

C. **performs the rite of removing the shoe [Deut. 25:7-9], and [others] perform the rite of removing the shoe with his wife.**

D. **[Others] enter levirate marriage with his wife, but he does not enter into levirate marriage,**

E. **because he is prohibited to marry a widow.**

F. **[If] he suffers a death [in his family], he does not follow the bier.**

G. **"But when [the bearers of the bier] are not visible, he is visible; when they are visible, he is not.**

H. **"And he goes with them to the city gate," the words of R. Meir.**

I. **R. Judah says, "He never leaves the sanctuary.**

J. **"since it says, 'Nor shall he go out of the sanctuary' [Lev. 21:12]."**

I. A. It is understandable that he judges others.

B. But as to others judging him, [it is appropriate to his station?]

C. Let him appoint a mandatory.

D. Now take note: What if he has to take an oath?

E. Can the mandatory take an oath for his client?

F. Property cases involving [a high priest]—in how large a court is the trial conducted?

G. With a court of twenty-three judges.

H. Let us demonstrate that fact from the following:

I. **A king does not sit in the Sanhedrin, nor do a king and a high priest join in the court session for intercalation [T. San. 2:15].**

J. [In this regard,] R. Haninah and R. Mana—one of them said, "The king does not take a seat on the Sanhedrin, on account of suspicion [of influencing the other judges].

K. "Nor does he take a seat in a session for intercalation, because of suspicion [that it is in the government's interest to intercalate the year].

L. "And a king and a high priest do not take a seat for intercalation, for it is not appropriate to the station of the king [or the high priest] to take a seat with seven judges."

M. Now look here:

N. If it is not appropriate to his station to take a seat with seven judges, is it not an argument *a fortiori* that he should not [be judged] by three?

O. That is why one must say, Property cases involving him are tried in a court of twenty-three.

II. A. [What follows is verbatim at M. Hor. 3:1:] Said R. Eleazar, "A high priest who sinned—they administer lashes to him, but they do not remove him from his high office."

B. Said R. Mana, "It is written, 'For the consecration of the anointing oil of his God is upon him: I am the Lord' [Lev. 21:12]."

C.   [Here omitted:] ("That is as if to say: 'Just as I [stand firm] in my high office, so Aaron [stands firm] in his high office.'")

D.   [Here omitted:] (Said R. Abun, "'*He shall be holy to you [for I the Lord who sanctify you am holy]*' [Lev. 21:8].")

E.   "That is as if to say, 'Just as I [stand firm] in my consecration, so Aaron [stands firm] in his consecration.'"

F.   R. Haninah Ketobah, R. Aha in the name of R. Simeon b. Laqish: "An anointed priest who sinned—they administer lashes to him [by the judgment of a court of three judges].

G.   "If you rule that it is by the decision of a court of twenty-three judges [that the lashes are administered], it turns out that his ascension [to high office] is descent [to public humiliation, since if he sins he is publicly humiliated by a sizable court]."

III. A.   R. Simeon b. Laqish said, "A ruler who sinned—they administer lashes to him by the decision of a court of three judges."

B.   What is the law as to restoring him to office?

C.   Said R. Haggai, "By Moses! If we put him back into office, he will kill us!"

D.   R. Judah the Patriarch heard this ruling [of R. Simeon b. Laqish's] and was outraged. He sent a troop of Goths to arrest R. Simeon b. Laqish. [R. Simeon b. Laqish] fled to the Tower, and, some say, it was to Kefar Hittayya.

E.   The next day R. Yohanan went up to the meetinghouse, and R. Judah the Patriarch went up to the meetinghouse. He said to him, "Why does my master not state a teaching of Torah?"

F.   [Yohanan] began to clap with one [20a] hand [only].

G.   [Judah the Patriarch] said to him, "Now do people clap with only one hand?"

H.   He said to him, "No, nor is Ben Laqish here [and just as one cannot clap with one hand only, so I cannot teach Torah if my colleague, Simeon b. Laqish, is absent]."

I.   [Judah] said to him, "Then where is he hidden?"

J.   He said to him, "In a certain tower."

K.   He said to him, "You and I shall go out to greet him tomorrow."

L.   R. Yohanan sent word to R. Simeon b. Laqish, "Get a teaching of Torah ready, because the patriarch is coming over to see you."

M.   [Simeon b. Laqish] came forth to receive them and said, "The example which you [Judah] set is to be compared to the paradigm of your Creator. For when the All-Merciful came forth to redeem Israel [from Egypt], he did not send a messenger or an angel, but the Holy One, blessed be He, himself came forth, as it is said, '*For I will pass through the Land of Egypt that night*' [Ex. 12:12]—and not only so, but he and his entire retinue.

N.   [Here omitted:] (["'*What other people on earth is like thy people Israel, whom God went to redeem to be his people*' [2 Sam. 7:23].] 'Whom God went' (sing.) is not written here, but 'Whom God went' (plural)[—meaning, he and all his retinue].")

O.   [Judah the Patriarch] said to him, "Now why in the world did you see fit to teach this particular statement [that a ruler who sinned is subject to lashes]?"

P.   He said to him, "Now did you really think that because I was afraid of you, I would hold back the teaching of the All-Merciful? [And lo, citing 1 Sam. 2:23f.,] R. Samuel b. R. Isaac said, '[*Why do you do such things? For I hear of your evil dealings from all the people.] No, my sons, it is no good report [that I hear the people of the Lord* spreading abroad]. [Here omitted:] (If a man sins against a man, God will mediate for him; but if a man sins against the Lord, who can intercede for him? But they would not listen to the voice of their father, for it was the will of the Lord to slay them' [1 Sam. 2:23–25.]. [When] the people of the Lord spread about [an evil report about a man], they remove him [even though he is the patriarch].")...

VI. A.   R. Yosé b. R. Bun in the name of R. Huna: "The following Mishnah saying [belongs] to R. Simeon: *"And from the sanctuary he will not go forth'* [Lev. 21:12]—with [the bearers of the bier] he does not go forth, but he does go forth after them."

      B.   **'When [the bearers of the bier] are not visible, he is visible, when they are visible, he is not. And he goes with them to the city gate," the words of R. Meir.**

      C.   **R. Judah says, "He never leaves the sanctuary, since it says, 'Nor shall he go out of the sanctuary' (Lev. 21:12)" [M. San. 2:1G-J].**

      D.   If he did go out, he should not come back.

      E.   R. Abbahu in the name of R. Eleazar: "The word 'mourning' applies only to the corpse alone, as it is written, *'And her gates shall lament and mourn'"* [Is. 3:26].

      F.   Hiyya bar Adda replied, "And is it not written, 'The fishermen shall mourn and lament'" [Is. 19:8]?

2.2

      A.   **And when he gives comfort to others —**

      B.   **the accepted practice is for all the people to pass one after another, and the appointed [prefect of the priests] stands between him and the people.**

      C.   **And when he receives consolation from others,**

      D.   **all the people say to him, "Let us be your atonement."**

      E.   **And he says to them, "May you be blessed by Heaven."**

      F.   **And when they provide him with the funeral meal,**

      G.   **all the people sit on the ground, while he sits on a stool.**

I. A.   [The statement at M. San. 2:2G] implies: A stool is not subject to the law of mourners' overturning the bed.

      B.   [But that is not necessarily so. For] the high priest [to begin with] is subject to that requirement of overturning the bed [and, it follows, no conclusion can be drawn from M.].

II. A.   It was taught: They do not bring out the deceased [for burial] at a time near the hour of reciting the *Shema,* unless they did so an hour earlier or an hour later, so that people may recite the *Shema* and say the Prayer.

      B.   And have we not learned: *When they have buried the dead and returned, [If they can begin the Shema and finish it before reaching the row of mourners, they begin it; but if they cannot, they do not begin it] [M. Ber. 3:2].* [Thus they do bring out the deceased for burial at a time quite close to that for reciting the *Shema.*]

      C.   Interpret [the cited pericope of Mishnah] to deal with a case in which the people thought that they had ample time for burying the corpse but turned out not to have ample time for that purpose [prior to the time for reciting the *Shema*].

      D.   It is taught: **The person who states the eulogy and all who are involved in the eulogy interrupt [their labor] for the purpose of reciting the *Shema,* but**

> **do not do so for saying the Prayer. M'SH W: Our rabbis interrupted for the purposes of reciting the *Shema* and saying the Prayer [T. Ber. 2:11].**

E. Now have we not learned, *If they can begin and finish . . . ?* [As above, B. Now here we have them interrupt the eulogy!]

F. The Mishnah refers to the first day [of the death, on which they are exempt from saying the *Shema*], and the Tosefta pericope to the second [day after death, on which they are liable to say the *Shema*].

G. Said R. Samuel bar Abedoma, "This one who entered the synagogue and found the people standing [and saying] the prayer, if he knows that he can complete the Prayer before the messenger of the congregation [who repeats the whole in behalf of the congregation] will begin to answer, 'Amen,' [to the Prayer of the community], he may say the Prayer, and if not, he should not say the Prayer."

H. To which "Amen" is reference made?

I. Two Amoras differ in this regard.

J. One said, "To the *Amen* which follows, 'The Holy God.'"

K. And the other said, "to the *Amen* which follows, 'Who hears prayer' on an ordinary day."

III. A. It was taught: **R. Judah says, "If there is only a single row [of mourners], those who are standing as a gesture of respect are liable to say [the *Shema*], and those who are standing as a gesture of mourning are exempt [from the obligation to say the *Shema*]. If they proceed to the eulogy, those who see the face [of the mourners] are exempt [from having to say the *Shema*,] and those who do not see their face are liable [T. Ber. 2:11]."**

B. Note that which we have learned: *When he gives comfort to others, the accepted practice is for all the people to pass after one another, and the appointed [prefect of the priests] stands between him and the people* [M. San. 3:3A–B].

C. This is in accord with the earlier practice [Mishnah] [to be cited below].

D. And as to that which we have learned: *[Of those who stand in the row of mourners], the ones on the inner line are exempt from reciting the Shema, and the ones on the outer row are liable* [M. Ber. 3:2]—

E. this is in accord with the later Mishnah [to be cited below].

F. Said R. Haninah, "At first [the former Mishnah = B], the families would stand and the mourners would pass before them. R. Yosé ordained that the families would pass and the mourners would stand still [the later Mishnah = D].

G. **Said R. Samuel of Sofafta, "The matters were restored to their original condition."**

2.3

A. **The king does not judge, and [others] do not judge him;**

B. **does not give testimony, and [others] do not give testimony about him;**

C. **does not perform the rite of removing the shoe, and others do not perform the rite of removing the shoe with his wife;**

D. **does not enter into levirate marriage, not [do his brothers] enter levirate marriage with his wife.**

E. **R. Judah says, "If he wanted to perform the rite of removing the shoe or to enter into levirate marriage, his memory is a blessing."**

F.   **They said to him, "They pay no attention to him if he expressed the wish to do so."**

G.   **[Others] do not marry his widow.**

H.   **R. Judah says, "A king may marry the widow of a king.**

I.   **"For so we find in the case of David, that he married the widow of Saul,**

J.   **"For it is said, *'And I gave you your master's house and your master's wives into your embrace'"* [2 Sam. 12:8].**

I. A.   *[The king] does not judge [M. San. 2:3A].* And has it not been written: *"[So David reigned over all Israel;] and David administered justice and equity to all his people"* [2 Sam. 8:15].

    B.   And yet do you say [that the king does not judge]?

    C.   [From this verse of Scripture, we draw the following picture:] He would indeed judge a case, declaring the innocent party to be innocent, the guilty party to be guilty. But if the guilty party was poor, he would give him [the funds needed for his penalty] out of his own property. Thus he turned out doing justice for this one [who won the case] and doing charity for that one [who had lost it].

    D.   Rabbi says, "[If] a judge judged a case, declaring the innocent party to be innocent, and the guilty party to be guilty, [the cited verse of Scripture indicates that] the Omnipresent credits it to him as if he had done an act of charity with the guilty party, for he has taken out of the possession of the guilty party that which he has stolen."

II. A.   **And [others] do not judge him [M. San. 2:3A].** This is in line with the verse [in the Psalm of David], *"From thee [alone] let my vindication come!"* [Ps. 17:2].

    B.   R. Isaac in the name of rabbi: "King and people are judged before Him every day, as it is said, ' . . . and may he do justice for his servant and justice for his people Israel, as each day requires' [1 King 8:59]."

III. A.   **R. Judah says, "If he wanted to perform the rite of removing the shoe or to enter into levirate marriage, his memory is a blessing" [M. San. 2:3E].**

    B.   They said to him, "If you rule in this way, you turn out to diminish the honor owing to the king."

IV. A.   **Others do not marry the widow [M. San. 2:3G]** or the woman divorced by a king.

    B.   This is by reason of that which is said: *"So [David's concubines] were shut up until the day of their death, living as if in widowhood"* [2 Sam. 20:3].

    C.   R. Yudah bar Pazzi in the name of r. Pazzi in the name of R. Yohanan: "This teaches that David [treating them as forbidden though in law they were not] would have them dressed and adorned and brought before him every day, and he would say to his libido, 'Do you lust after something forbidden to you?' By your life! I shall now make you lust for something which is permitted to you."

    D.   Rabbis of Caesarea say, "They were in fact forbidden [20b] to hand [and it was not merely that he treated the women whom Absalom had raped as forbidden to him, but the law deemed them prohibited].

    E   "For if a utensil belonging to an ordinary man used by an ordinary man is prohibited for use of a king, a utensil belonging to a king which was used by an ordinary man—is not an argument *a fortiori* that the king should be forbidden to make use of it?"

V. A.   R. Judah says, "The king may marry the widow of a king. For we find in the case of David that he married widows of Saul, for it is said, *'And I gave you your master's house and your master's wives into your embrace'"* [2 Sam. 12:8] [M. San. 2:3H–J].

B.   This refers to Rispah, Abigail, and Bath Sheba.

C.   [The reference to Abigail, 1 Sam. 25, calls to mind Nabral and his origins:] Hezron had three sons, as it is written, *"The sons of Hezron that were born to him: Yerahmeel, Ram, and Kelubai"* [1 Chron. 2:9]

D.   The first [son] was Yerahmeel, but he married a gentile woman to be crowned through her [royal ancestry], as it is written, *"Yerahmeel also had another wife, whose name was Atarah [crown]"* [1 Chron. 2:26].

E.   *"She was the mother of Onam"* [1 Chron. 2:26], for she brought mourning *(aninah)* into his household.

F.   *"Ram was the father of Amminadab, and Amminadab was the father of Nahshon, [prince of the sons of Judah]. Nahshon was the father of Salma, Salma of Boaz, [Boaz of Obed, Obed of Jesse]"* [1 Chron. 2:10–12]. And Boaz married Ruth.

G.   Lo, Nadab came from Kelubai.

H.   Nabal said, "In all Israel there is no son better than I."

I.   This is in line with that which is written, *"And there was a man in Maon, whose business was in Carmel. The man was very rich"* [1 Sam. 25:2].

J.   *Now he was a Kelubaite* (1 Sam. 25:3), for he came from Kelubai.

K.   *"David heard in the wilderness that Habal was shearing [his sheep. So David sent ten young men; and David said to the young men, 'Go up to Carmel, and go to Nabal, and greet him in my name]. And thus shall you salute the living one: 'Peace be to you, [and peace be to your house, and peace be to all that you have]'"* [1 Sam. 25:4–6].

L.   Said R. Yusta bar Shunam, "They became a whole camp."

M.   *"And Nabal answered David's servants, ['Who is David?']"* [1 Sam. 25:10].

N.   How do we know that *in capital cases they begin from the side* [the youngest members of the court] [M. San. 4:2]?

O.   Samuel the Elder taught before R. Aha: *"'And David said to him men, [Gird every man his sword, and every man girded on his sword, and David also girded on his sword'"* [1 Sam. 25:13]. David thus is the last to express his opinion.]

P.   *"'And he railed at them'* [1 Sam. 25:14]—what is the meaning of 'And he railed at them'?

Q.   "He incited them with words." [But see QH].

R.   *"Now therefore know this and consider what you should do; [for evil is determined against our master and against all his house, and he is so ill-natured that one cannot speak to him"* [1 Sam. 25:17].

S.   *"And as she rode on the ass . . . behold, David and his men came down toward her;] and she met them"* [1 Sam. 25:20].

T.   She showed her thigh, and they followed out of desire for her.

U.   *"' . . . she met them'*—all of them had [involuntary] ejaculations" (PM).

V.   *"Now David said, 'Surely in vain have I guarded [all that this fellow has in the wilderness . . . and he has returned me evil for good. God do so to the enemies of*

David . . . if by morning I leave so much as] one who pisses against the wall of all who belong to him'" [1 Sam. 25:21–22].

W.   [This reference to one who pisses on a wall is to a dog.] Now what place is therefore referring to a dog, who pisses on the wall? The meaning is that even a dog will get no pity.

X.   *"When Abigail saw David, [she made haste, and alighted from the ass, and fell before David on her face, and bowed to the ground]"* [1 Sam. 25:23].

Y.   She said to him, "My lord, David, as to me, what have I done? And my children—what have they done? My cattle—what have they done?"

Z.   He said to her, "It is because [Nabal] has cursed the kingdom of David."

AA.   She said to him, "And are you [now] a king?"

BB.   He said to her, "And has not Samuel anointed me as king?"

CC.   She said to him, "Our lord Saul's coinage still is in circulation."

DD.   *"But I your handmaid . . . "* [1 Sam. 25:25]—this teaches that he demanded to have sexual relations with her.

EE.   Forthwith she removed her stained [sanitary napkin] and showed it to him [indicating that she was in her menses and forbidden to have sexual relations on that account].

FF.   He said to her, "Can one examine menstrual stains at night?"

GG.   They said to him, "And let your ears hear what your mouth speaks. They do not examine sanitary napkins by night—and do they judge capital cases by night [as David was judging Nabal]!"

HH.   He said to her, "The trial concerning him was complete while it was still day."

II.   She said to him, *"[And when the Lord was done to my lord according to all the good that he has spoken concerning you . . .] my lord shall have no causes of grief, [for pangs of conscience, for having shed blood without cause]'"* [1 Sam. 25:30–31].

JJ.   Said R. Eliezer, "There were indeed doubts [riddles] there."

KK.   R. Levi was reviewing this pericope. R. Zeira told the associates, "Go and listen to R. Zeira, for it is not possible that he will lay out the pericope without saying something fresh about it."

LL.   Someone went in and told them that that was not so.

MM.   R. Zeira heard and said, "Even in matters of biblical stores there is the possibility of saying something fresh:

NN.   "'. . . have no doubts . . .'—that is, there were indeed causes [riddles] there."

OO.   [Continuing Abigail's speech to David:] *"When word of your cause of grief goes forth, people will say about you, "You are a murdered* [1 Sam. 25:31], and you are destined to fall (ibid.) into sin, specifically to err through the wife of a man. It is better that there should be but one such case, and not two.

PP.   "A much greater sin is going to come against you than this one. Do not bring this one along with the one which is coming.

QQ.   *"For having shed blood"* [1 Sam. 25:31]—"You are going to rule over all Israel, and people will say about you, 'He was a murderer.'

RR.   "And that which you say, 'Whoever curses the dominion of the house of David is subject to the death penalty,'

SS.   "but you still have no throne."

TT.   *"[And when the Lord has dealt well with my lord], then remember your handmaid"* [1 Sam. 25:31].

UU.   This indicates that she treated herself as available [to David by referring to herself as his handmaid], and since she treated herself as available, Scripture itself treated her as diminished.

VV.   For in every other passage you read, *"Abigail,"* but in this one: *"And David said to Abigail"* [1 Sam. 25:32].

WW.   *"And David said . . ., 'Blessed be your discretion, and blessed be you, who have kept me this day from bloodguilt'"* [1 Sam. 25:33]—in two senses, in the sense of the blood of menstruation, and in the sense of bloodshed [for she kept him from both kinds of bloodguilt].

2.4

A.   **[If the king] suffers a death in his family, he does not leave the gate of his palace.**

B.   **R. Judah says, "If he wants to go out after the bier, he goes out,**

C.   **"for thus we find in the case of David, that he went out after the bier of Abner,**

D.   **"since it is said, *'And King David followed the bier'"* [2 Sam. 3:31].**

E.   **They said to him, "This action was only to appease the people."**

F.   **And when they provide him with the funeral meal, all the people sit on the ground, while he sits on a couch.**

I.   A.   There is a Tanna who teaches that the women go first [in the mourning procession], and the men after them.

B.   And there is a Tanna who teaches that the men go first, and the women afterward.

C.   The one who said that the women go first invokes as the reason that they caused death to come into the world.

D.   The one who said that men go first invokes the reason that it is to preserve the honor of Israelite women, so that people should not stare at them.

E.   Now is it not written, *"And King David followed the bier"* [2 Sam. 3:31]? *They said to him, "This action was only to appease the people"* [M. San. 2:4D–E].

F.   Once he appeased the women, he went and appeased the men [in the view of A].

G.   Or: Once he appeased the men, he went and appeased the women [in the view of B].

III.   A.   *"And David returned [to bless his household. But Michal the daughter of Saul came out to meet David, and said, 'How the king of Israel honored himself today, uncovering himself today before the eyes of his servants' maids, as one of the vulgar fellows shamelessly uncovers himself!']"* [2 Sam. 6:20].

B.   What is the meaning of "one of the vulgar fellows"?

C.   Said R. Ba bar Kahana, "The most vulgar of them all—this is a dancer!"

D.   She said to him, "Today the glory of father's house was revealed."

E.   They said about Saul's house that [they were so modest] that their heel and their toe never saw [their privy parts].

F.   This is in line with that which is written, *"And he came to the sheepfolds [by the way, where there was a cave; and Saul went in to relieve himself]"* [1 Sam. 24:3].

G.   R. Bun bar R. Eleazar: "It was a sheepfold within yet another sheepfold."

H.   *"And Saul went in to relieve himself' ["cover his feet"]: [David] saw him lower his garments slightly and excrete slightly [as needed].*

I.   [David] said, *"Cursed by anyone who lays a hand on such modesty."*

J.   This is in line with that which he said to him, *"Lo, this day your eyes have seen [how the Lord gave you today into my hand in the cave; and some bade me kill you, but it spared you]"* [1 Sam. 24:10].

K.   It is not written, *"I spared you,"* but *"it spared you"*—that is, "Your own modesty is what spared you."

L.   And David said to Michal, *"But by the maids of whom you have spoken, by them I shall be held in honor"* [2 Sam. 6:22].

M.   For they are not handmaidens ('amahot), but mothers ('immahot).

N.   And how was Michal punished? *"And Michal the daughter of Saul had no child to the day of her death"* [2 Sam. 6:23].

O.   And is it now not written, *". . . and the sixth was Ithream of Eglah, David's wife"* [2 Sam. 3:5]?

P.   She lowed like a cow (Eglah) and expired [giving birth on the day of her death].

Q.   You have no Israelite who so lowered himself in order to do religious deeds more than did David.

R.   On what account did he lower himself for the sake of religious deeds?

S.   For the people were staring at the ark and dying, as it is written, *"And he slew some of the men of Beth Shemesh, [because they looked into the ark of the Lord; he slew seventy men, and fifty thousand men, of them, and the people mourned because the Lord had made a great slaughter among the people]"* [1 Sam. 6:19].

T.   R. Haninah and R. Mana: one said, *"'And he smote of the people seventy men'*—this refers to the Sanhedrin.

U.   *"'And fifty thousand men'*—for they were comparable in worth to fifty thousand men."

V.   And one of them said, *"'He smote of the people seventy men'*—this is the Sanhedrin.

W.   *"'And fifty thousand'*—of the ordinary people as well."

X.   It is written, *"A song of ascents of David: O Lord, my heart is not lifted up"* [Ps. 131:1]—'when Samuel anointed me."

Y.   *"My eyes are not raised too high"* [Ps. 131:1]—"when I slew Goliath."

Z.   *"And I do not occupy myself with things too great or too marvelous for me]"* [Ps. 131:1] "when I brought the ark up."

AA.   "Or too wondrous for me"—" when they put me back on my throne."

BB.   *"But I have calmed and quieted my soul, like a child quieted at its mother's breast"* [Ps. 1131:2]—'Like a child which gives up goes down from its mother's belly, so my soul is humbled for me."

2.5

A.   **[The king] calls out [the army to wage] an optional war [fought by choice] on the instructions of a court of seventy-one.**

B.   **He [may exercise the right of eminent domain in order to] open a road for himself, and [others] may not stop him.**

C.   **The royal road has no required measure.**

D. **all the people plunder and lay before him [what they have grabbed], and he takes the first portion.**

I. A. [The rule of M. San. 2:5A is in line with] that which is written, "At his word they shall go out, and at his word they shall come in, [both he and all the people of Israel with him, the whole congregation]" [Num. 27:21].

II. A. *He [may exercise the right of eminent domain in order to] open a road for himself and others may not stop him [... and he takes the first portion] [M. San. 2:5B–D].*

   B. This is in line with that which is written, *"And the people drove those cattle before him, and said, 'This is David's spoil'"* [1 Sam. 30:20].

III. A. *"He was with David at Pas-dammim, [when the Philistines were gathered there for battle. There was a plot of ground full of barley, and the men fled from the Philistines. But he took his stand in the midst of the plot and defended it, and slew the Philistines; and the Lord saved them by a great victory]"* [1 Chron. 11:13–14]. [Note also 2 Sam. 23:11f.: *"And next to him was Shamah, the son of Agee the Hararite. The Philistines gathered together at Lehi, where there was a plot of ground full of lentils; and the men fled from the Philistines. But he took his stand in the midst of the plot and defended it, and slew the Philistines; and the Lord wrought a great victory."*]

   B. R. Yohanan said, "It was a field as red as blood [so the place name is taken literally]."

   C. And R. Samuel said, "[It was so called] for from that place the penalties ceased [as will be explained below]."

   D. *"When the Philistines were gathered [there for battle, there was a plot of ground full of barley."* R. Jacob of Kepar Hanan said, "They were lentils, but their buds were as fine as those of barley [which accounts for the divergence between 1 Chron. 11:12 and 2 Sam. 23:11]."

   E. Said R. Levi, "This refers to the Philistines, who came standing up straight like barley, but retreated bent over like lentils."

   F. One Scripture says, *"There was a plot of ground full of barley"* [1 Chron. 11:13], and it is written, *"... full of lentils"* [2 Sam. 23:11].

   G. [20c] R. Samuel bar Nahman said, "The event took place in a single year, and there were two fields there, one of barley, the other of lentils."

   H. [To understand the following, we must refer to 2 Sam. 23:15-16: *"And David longed and said, 'O that someone would give me water to drink from the well of Bethlehem which is by the gate!' And the three mighty men broke through the host of the Philistines and drew water out of the well of Bethlehem that was by the gate."* Now "water" here is understood to mean "learning," "gate" the rabbinical court, and David is thus understood to require instruction. At issue is the battlefield in which the Philistines had hidden themselves, that is, as at Pas-dammim. What troubled David now is at issue.] David found it quite obvious that he might destroy the field of grain and pay its cost (DMYM).

   I. Could it be obvious to him [that he might destroy the field and *not* pay its cost to its Israelite owners]? [It is not permissible to rescue oneself by destroying someone else's property, unless one pays compensation. So that cannot be at issue at all.]

   J. [If he did have to pay, as he realized, then what he wanted to know "at the gate" was] which of them to destroy, and for which of the two to pay compensation [since he did not wish to destroy both fields such as, at G, Samuel posits were there].

   K. [These are then the choices] between the one of lentils and the one of barley.

L.   The one of lentils is food for man, and the one of barley is food for beast. The one of lentils is not liable, when turned into flour, for a dough offering, and the one of barley is liable, when turned into flour, for dough offering. As to lentils, the *omer* is not taken therefrom; as to barley the *omer* is taken therefrom. [So these are the three choices before David, and since there were two fields, he wanted to know which to burn and for which to pay compensation.]

M.   [This entire picture of the character of the battlefield is rejected by rabbis,] for rabbis say there was one field, but the incident took place [twice, in a period of] two years [and hence, in one year, it was planted with one crop, in the other year, the other].

N.   David then should have learned from the rule prevailing in the preceding year. But they do not derive a rule from one year to the next.

O.   One verse states, *"They took their stand in the midst of the plot and defended it"* [1 Chron. 11:14].

P.   And the other Scripture states, *"... and he defended it"* [2 Sam. 23:12].

Q.   What this teaches is that he restored the field to its owner, and it was as precious to him as a field planted with saffron.

IV. A.   It is written, *"And David said longingly, 'O that some one would give me water to drink from the well of Bethlehem [which is by the gate']"* [1 Chron. 11:17].

B.   R. Hiyya bar Ba said, "He required a teaching of law."

C.   *"Then the three mighty men broke through [the camp of the Philistines]"* [1 Chron. 11:18].

D.   Why three? Because the law is not decisively laid down by fewer than three.

E.   *"But David would not drink of it; [he poured it out to the Lord, and said, 'Far be it from me before my God that I should do this. Shall I drink the lifeblood of these men? For at the risk of their lives they brought it']"* [1 Chron. 11:18-19].

F.   David did not want the law to be laid down in his own name.

G.   "He poured it out to the Lord"—establishing [the decision] as [an unattributed] teaching for the generations [so that the law should be authoritative and so be cited anonymously].

H.   *He may exercise the right of eminent domain in order to open a road for himself, and others may not stop him.*

I.   Bar Qappara said, "It was the festival of Sukkot, and the occasion was the water offering on the altar, and it was a time in which high places were permitted [before the centralization of the cult in Jerusalem]. [So the view that David required a legal teaching is not accepted; it was literally water which David wanted and got.]"

J.   *"And three mighty men broke through ..."*—Why three? One was to kill [the Philistines]; the second was to clear away the bodies; and the third [avoiding the corpse uncleanness] was to bring the flask for water in a state of cultic cleanness.

K.   One version of the story states, *"... He poured it out to the Lord ..."* [1 Chron. 11:18].

L.   And the other version of the story states, *"He spilled it ..."* [2 Sam. 23:16].

M.   The one which states "spilled" supports the view of R. Hiyya bar Ba [who treats the story as figurative], and the one which stated, "poured it out to the Lord" supports the picture of Bar Qappara [who treats it as a literal account].

N.   Huna in the name of R. Yosé, "David required information on the laws covering captives."

O.   R. Simeon b. Rabbi says, "What he thirsted after was the building of the house for the sanctuary [the Temple]."

2.6

A.   **"He should not multiply wives to himself" [Deut. 17:17]—only eighteen.**

B.   **R. Judah says, "He may have as many as he wants, so long as they do not entice him [to abandon the Lord]" [Deut. 17:17].**

C.   **R. Simeon says, "Even if there is only one who entices him [to abandon the Lord]—lo, this one should not marry her."**

D.   **If so, why is it said, *"He should not multiply wives to himself"*?**

E.   **Even though they should be like Abigail [1 Sam. 25:3].**

F.   ***"He should not multiply horse to himself" [Deut. 17:16]—only enough for his chariot.***

G.   ***"Neither shall he greatly multiply to himself silver and gold" [Deut. 17:17]—only enough to pay his army.***

H.   ***"And he writes out a scroll of the Torah for himself" [Deut. 17:18]—***

I.   **When he goes to war, he takes it out with him; when he comes back, he brings it back with him; when he is in session in court, it is with him; when he is reclining, it is before him.**

J.   **As it is said, *"And it shall be with him, and he shall read in it all the days of his life" [Deut. 17:19].***

K.   **[Others may] not (1) ride on his horse, (2) sit on his throne, (3) handle his scepter.**

L.   **And [others may] (4) not watch him while he is getting a haircut, or (5) while he is nude, or (6) in the bathhouse,**

M.   **since it is said, *"You shall surely set him as king over you" [Deut. 17:15]—that reverence for him will be upon you.***

I.   A.   R. Kahana: "[The limitation to eighteen wives] is by reason of the following: *'And the sixth, Ithream, of Eglah, David's wife. These were born to David in Hebron'* [2 Sam. 3:5]. And what is stated further on? *'...I would add to you as much more...'* [2 Sam. 12:8]. [This indicates that there would be yet two more groups of six wives, eighteen in all.]"

    B.   *"He should not multiply horses to himself"* [Deut. 17:16], only enough for his chariot [M. San. 2:6F].

    C.   This is in line with the following: *"And David hamstrung all the chariot horses, but left enough for a hundred chariots"* [2 Sam. 8:4].

    D.   *"Neither shall he greatly multiply to himself silver and gold"* [Deut. 17:17]—only enough to pay his army [M. San. 2:6G].

    E.   R. Joshua b. Levi said, "But that provides solely for the wages for a given year alone [and not wages for several consecutive years]."

II.   A.   Said R. Aha, "Said Solomon, *'I said of laughter, it is mad'* (Qoh. 2:2)]. 'Three things the attribute of justice ridiculed and I profaned:

    B.   *"'He should not multiply wives to himself'* [Deut. 17:17].

    C.   "And it is written, *'Now King Solomon loved many foreign women'"* [1 Kings 11:1]. [This pericope resumes below, I.]

D. R. Simeon b. Yohai said, "He loved them literally, that is, he fornicated with them."

E. Hananiah, nephew of R. Joshua, says, "[He actually married them and violated the precept,] *'You shall not marry with them'* [Deut. 7:3]."

F. R. Yosé says, "It was to draw them to the teachings of Torah and to bring them under the wings of the Indwelling Presence of God."

G. R. Eliezer says, "It was by reason of the following verse: 'Did not Solomon king of Israel sin on account of such women? . . . *nevertheless foreign women made even him to sin'* [Neh. 13:26]."

H. It turns out that R. Simeon b. Yohai, Hananiah, and R. Eliezer maintain one viewpoint, and R. Yosé differs from all three of them.

I. *"He should not multiply horses to himself '* [Deut. 17:16].

J. "And it is written, *'Solomon had forty thousand stalls of horses for his chariots and twelve thousand horsemen'* [1 Kings 4:26].

K. "They were unemployed, [there being peace in Solomon's days].

L. "But one who is not a king is permitted in these [that is, having many wives and horses, and much gold and silver].

M. "And it is written, *'And the king made silver to be in Jerusalem as stones'* " [1 Kings 10:27].

N. Was none of them stolen?

O. Said R. Yosé b. Haninah, "They were stones of a measure of ten cubits or eight cubits, and so they were [too large to be so stolen]."

P. R. Simeon b. Yohai taught, "Even the weights in the time of Solomon were not of silver but of gold."

Q. What is the Scriptural basis for this statement? *"None was of* silver; it was accounted as nothing in the days of Solomon" [1 Kings 10:21].

R. It is written, *"I said of laughter, 'It is mad'"* [Qoh. 2:2].

S. Said the Holy One, blessed be He, to Solomon, "What is this crown [doing] on your head? Get off my throne."

T. R. Yosé b. Hanina said, "At that moment an angel came down and took the appearance of Solomon and removed Solomon from his throne and took the seat in his stead."

U. Solomon went around the synagogues and schoolhouses, saying, *"I, Qohelet, have been king over Israel in Jerusalem"* [Qoh. 1:12].

V. But they showed him the king sitting in his basilica, and [said to him,] "Do you say, 'I Qohelet'?" And they beat him with reeds and placed before him a dish of grits.

W. At that moment he wept and said, *"This was my portion from all my labor"* [Qoh. 2:10].

X. There are those who say they beat him with a staff, and there are those who say they beat him with a reed, and some say that they beat him with a belt of knotted rope.

Y. Now who caused Solomon's downfall [= was his adversary]?

Z. Said R. Joshua b. Levi, "It was the *yud* in the word, 'increase' (YRBH) which served as his adversary."

AA. R. Simeon b. Yohai taught, "The book of Deuteronomy went up and spread itself out before the Holy one, blessed be He.

BB.   "It said before him, 'Lord of the world! You have written in your Torah that any covenant part of which is null is wholly nullified.'

CC.   "Now lo, Solomon wishes to uproot a *yud* [as above] of mine,'

DD.   "Said to him the Holy One, blessed be He, 'Solomon and a thousand like him will be null, but not one word of yours will be nullified,'"

EE.   R. Huna in the name of R. Aha: "The *yud* which the Holy One, blessed be He, removed from our matriarch, Sarah, [when her name was changed from Sarai,] half of it was given to Sarah, and half of it was given to Abraham.

FF.   R. Hoshaiah taught, "The *yud* went up and prostrated itself before the Holy One, blessed be He, and said, 'Lord of the world! You have uprooted me from the name of that righteous woman!'

GG.   "The Holy One, blessed be He, said to him, 'Go forth. In the past you were set in the name of a woman, and at the end of the name [Sarai]. By your life, I am going to put you in the name of a male, and at the beginning of the name'"

HH.   This is in line with that which is written, *"And Moses called Hoshea b. Nun, 'Joshua'"* [Num. 13:16].

III. A.   *And he writes for himself a scroll of the Torah* [Deut. 17:18]—

   B.   **for his own use, that he not have to make use of the one of his fathers, but rather of his own [T. San. 4:7].**

   C.   And they correct his scroll by comparing it to the scroll of the Temple courtyard, on the authority of the Sanhedrin of seventy-one members.

   D.   *When he goes forth to war, it goes with him,* as it is said, *"And it shall be with him, and he shall read in it all the days of his life"* (Deut. 17:19) [Cf. M. San. 2:6I–J].

   E.   **Lo, it is a matter of an argument *a fortiori*: Now if a king of Israel, who is taken up with the needs of israel, is told, *"And he shall read in it all the days of his life,"* an ordinary person, how much the more so [must he read in the Torah all the days of his life].**

   F.   **Along these same lines, concerning Joshua it is written, *"This book of the law shall not depart out of your mouth, but you shall meditate on it day and night"* [Joshua 1:8].**

   G.   **Lo, it is a matter of an argument *a fortiori*: Now if Joshua, who is taken up with the needs of Israel, is told, "You shall meditate in it day and night," an ordinary person, how much more so [must he meditate in the Torah all the days of his life] [T. San. 4:8–9].**

IV. A.   A king of Israel: *Others may not ride on his horse, sit on his throne, or handle his crown, scepter* [M. San. 2:6K], or any other of his possessions.

   B.   And when he does, all of them are to be burned in the presence of his corpse, as it is said, *"You shall die in peace. And as spices were burned for your fathers, the former kings who were before you, so men shall burn spices for you and lament for you"* [Jer. 34:5].

   C.   **And others may not see him while he is nude, or when he is getting a haircut, or in the bathhouse [M. San. 2:6L].**

   D.   This is in line with the following verse: *"Your eyes will see the king in his beauty"* [Is. 33:17].

   E.   R. Haninah went up to R. Yudan the Patriarch. He came out to greet him, dressed in his undershirt.

F. He said to him, *"Go and put on your woolen cloak, on the grounds of 'Your eyes will see the king in his beauty'"* [Is. 33:17].

G. R. Yohanan went up to call on R. Yudan the Patriarch. He came forth to receive him in a shirt made of cotton.

H. He said to him, "Go back and put on your cloak of wool, on the grounds of: 'Your eyes will see the king in his beauty.'"

I. When R. Yohanan was leaving, [R. Yudan the Patriarch] said to him, "Bring refreshment for the mourner [bring good cheer]."

J. He said to him, "Send and get Menahem, the cake baker, for it is written, *'The teaching of kindness is on her tongue'* [Prov. 31:26]."

K. As he was leaving, [Yohanan] saw R. Haninah bar Sisi chopping wood.

L. He said to him, "Rabbi, this occupation is not consonant with your status."

M. He said to him, "And what shall I do? For I have no one who serves me as a disciple."

N. He said to him, "If you have no one to serve you as a disciple, you should not accept upon yourself appointment [to a court]."

V. A. Yosé Meoni interpreted the following verse in the synagogue in Tiberias: *"Hear this, o priests!'* [Hos. 5:1]: Why do you not labor in the Torah? Have not the twenty-four priestly gifts been given to you?

B. "They said to him, 'Nothing at all has been given to us.'

C. [20d] *"And give heed, O House of Israel!'* [Hos. 5:1].

D. "'Why do you not give the priests the twenty-four gifts concerning which you have been commanded at Sinai?'

E. "They said to him, 'The king takes them all.'

F. *"Hearken, O house of the king! For the judgment pertains to you'* (Hos. 5:1).

G. "To you have I said, 'And this shall be the priests' due from the people, from those offering a sacrifice . . .: *they shall give to the priest the shoulder, the two cheeks, and the stomach'* [Deut. 18:3].

H. "I am going to take my seat with them in court and to make a decision concerning them and blot them [the kings] out of the world."

I. R. Yudan the Patriarch heard [about this attack on the rulers] and was angry.

J. [Yosé] feared and fled.

K. R. Yohanan and R. Simeon b. Saqish went up to make peace with [the Patriarch].

L. They said to him, "Rabbi, he is a great man."

M. He said to them, "Is it possible that everything which I ask of him, he will give to me?"

N. They said to him, "Yes." [So Yosé was called back.]

O. [The Patriarch] said to [Yosé], "What is the meaning of that which is written: 'For their mother has played the harlot' [Hos. 2:5]?

P. "Is it possible that our matriarch, Sarah, was a whore?"

Q. He said to him, "As is the daughter, so is her mother.

R. "As is the mother, so is the daughter.

S. "As is the generation, so is the patriarch.

T. "As is the patriarch, so is the generation.

U. "As is the altar, so are its priests."

V. Kahana said likewise: "As is the garden, so is the gardener."

W. He said to them, "It is not enough for him that he dishonors me one time not in my presence, but also in my presence he does so these three times [Q–T]!"

X. He said to him, "What is the meaning of that which is written, *'Behold, everyone who uses proverbs will use this proverb about you, 'Like mother, like daughter'* [Ez. 16:44].

Y. "Now was our matriarch, Leah, a whore?

Z. "As it is written, *'And Dinah went out'* [Gen. 34:1] [like a whore, thus reflecting on her mother]"

AA. He said to him, 'It is in accord with that which is written, *'And Leah went out to meet him'* [Gen. 30:16]

BB. "They compared one going out to the other [and Leah went out to meet her husband, and Dinah learned from this that it was all right to go out, so she went out to meet the daughters of the land, but got raped]." [This was an acceptable reply to Yudan.]

VI. A. R. Hezekiah was going along the way. A Samaritan met him. He said to him, "Rabbi, are you the rabbi of the Jews?"

B. He said to him, "Yes."

C. He said to him, "Note what is written, *'You will surely set a king over you'* [Deut. 17:15].

D. "It is not written 'I shall set . . .,' but *'You* shall set . . .,' for you yourself set him over you.

We note, beginning back with the Talmud to Mishnah tractate Sanhedrin 2:1, that we start with a simple comment on the substance of the law before us, unit I. We proceed, II, with thematically relevant materials. Then comes an important story, which moves from the exegesis of the Mishnah to the consideration of deeds of the sages, illustrative of the rule and the enforcement thereof. I have skipped some of the intervening material, since our principal interest is in the overall character of the document. What is striking in unit VI is the citation and amplification of the Mishnah's rule. The same pattern recurs in the discussion of M. 2:2, with the rule at hand compared to a relevant rule in another passage of the Mishnah and the Tosefta. It is interesting to see how sages' reading of the story of Pas Dammim expresses their commitment to study of the Torah, which they impute, of course, to David. The upshot of this view of David, who is the prototype of the Messiah, is simple. The Messiah (of course) will be a sage, and the rule of sages now prefigures the coming rule of the Messiah. That implicit point is, in fact, the most striking assertion of the passage before us.

The Raising of Lazarus,
manuscript passage and
illumination from the Rossano
Gospels. (The Vatican Library.)

Opening of the tractate
"Kiddushin" from the Babylonian
Talmud printed by Daniel
Bomberg in Venice, 1520—523.
The center text is Rashi's
commentary on the text, and
the *tosafot* on the left and
bottom. (From *Encyclopedia Judaica*,
Vol. 15, p. 757.)

4. SCRIPTURE (WRITTEN): A SAMPLE CHAPTER OF GENESIS RABBAH

In the fourth century, the sages produced the great works on Genesis, in Genesis Rabbah, and on Leviticus, in Leviticus Rabbah, which answered the questions of salvation, of the meaning and end of Israel's history, that the Mishnah and its continuator writings did not take up. Why in the fourth century in particular? Because, as we have seen, the historical crisis precipitated by Christianity's takeover of the Roman Empire and its government demanded answers from Israel's sages: What does it mean? What does history mean? Where are we to find guidance to the meaning of our past—and our future? Sages looked, then, to Genesis, maintaining that the story of the creation of the world and the beginning of Israel would show the way toward the meaning of history and the salvation of Israel. They further looked to Leviticus, and, in Leviticus Rabbah, they accomplished the link between the sanctification of Israel through its cult and priesthood, which is the theme of the book of Leviticus, and the salvation of Israel, which is the concern of the commentators to that book. What they did was to place Israel, the people, at the center of the story of Leviticus, applying to the life of the people of Israel those rules of sanctification that, when observed, would prepare Israel, holy Israel, for salvation. So, in a nutshell, the framers of Leviticus Rabbah imparted to the book of Leviticus the message, in response to the destruction of the Temple, that the authors of the Mishnah had addressed 200 years earlier: Israel's holiness endures. Sanctifying the life of Israel now will lead to the salvation of Israel in time to come: Sanctification and salvation, the natural world and the supernatural, the rules of society and the rules of history all become one in the life of Israel.

Let us now spell out the message of the compilers of Genesis Rabbah, the commentary to the book of Genesis produced in the late fourth or early fifth century, in the time of the third and last crisis in the formation of Judaism. In the book of Genesis, as the sages who composed Genesis Rabbah see things, God set forth to Moses the entire scope and meaning of Israel's history among the nations and salvation at the end of days. They read Genesis not as a set of individual verses, one by one, but as a single and coherent statement, whole and complete. Here, in a few words, is a restatement of the conviction of the framers of Genesis Rabbah about the message and meaning of the book of Genesis:

> We now know what will be in the future. How do we know it? Just as Jacob had told his sons what would happen in time to come, just as Moses told the tribes their future, so we may understand the laws of history if we study the Torah. And in the Torah, we turn to beginnings: the rules as they were laid out at the very start of human history. These we find in the book of Genesis, the story of the origins of the world and of Israel.

The Torah tells us not only what happened but why. The Torah permits us to discover the laws of history. Once we know those laws, we may also peer into the future and come to an assessment of what is going to happen to us—and, especially, of how we shall be saved from our present existence. Because everything exists under the aspect of a timeless will, God's will, and all things express one thing, God's program and plan. In the Torah we uncover the workings of God's will. Our task as Israel is to accept, endure, submit, and celebrate.

The framers' conviction is that what Abraham, Isaac, and Jacob did shaped the future history of Israel. If, therefore, we want to discover the meaning of events now and tomorrow, we look back at yesterday. But the interest is not merely in history as a source of lessons. It is history as the treasury of truths about the here and now and especially about tomorrow: The same rules apply. What the patriarchs did supplies the model, the message, the meaning for what we should do. The sages of the Jewish people, in the Land of Israel, came to Genesis with the questions of their own day because, they maintained, the world reveals not chaos but order, and God's will works itself out not once but again and again. If we can find out how things got going, we also can find meaning in today and method in where we are heading. That is why they looked to a reliable account of the past and searched out the meaning of their own days. Bringing to the stories of Genesis that conviction that the book of Genesis told not only the story of yesterday but also the tale of tomorrow, the sages whose words are before us in this anthology transformed a picture of the past into a prophesy for a near tomorrow. What made Israel's sages look longingly at the beginnings of the world and of Israel? The reason, as we have seen, was that in their own day they entertained deep forebodings about Israel's prospects. Now to the document itself.

In Genesis Rabbah, sages read the book of Genesis as if it portrayed the history of Israel and Rome—and Rome in particular. Now Rome plays a role in the biblical narrative, with special reference to the counterpart and opposite of the patriarchs, first Ishmael, then Esau, and, always, Edom. For that is the single obsession binding sages of the document at hand to common discourse with the text before them. Why Rome in the form it takes in Genesis Rabbah? And why the obsessive character of the sages' disposition of the theme of Rome? If their picture were merely of Rome as tyrant and destroyer of the Temple, we should have no reason to link the text to the problems of the age of redaction and closure. But now it is Rome as Israel's brother, counterpart, and nemesis, Rome as the one thing standing in the way of Israel's, and the world's, ultimate salvation. So the stakes are different, and much higher.

Let us begin with a simple example of how ubiquitous is the shadow of Ishmael/Esau/Edom/Rome. Wherever sages reflect on future history, their minds turn to their own day. They found the hour difficult, because Rome, now Christian, claimed that very birthright and blessing that they understood to be theirs alone. Christian Rome posed a threat without precedent. Now another dominion, besides Israel's, claimed the rights and blessings that sustained Israel. Wherever in Scripture they turned, sages found comfort in the iteration that the birthright, the blessing, the Torah, and the hope—all belonged to them and to none other. Here is a striking statement of that constant proposition.

LIII:XII

1. A. "[So she said to Abraham, 'Cast out this slave woman with her son, for the son of this slave woman shall not be heir with my son Isaac.'] And the thing was very displeasing to Abraham on account of his son" [Gen. 21:11]:

   B. That is in line with this verse: "And shuts his eyes from looking upon evil" [Is. 33:15]. [Freedman, p. 471, n. 1: He shut his eyes from Ishmael's evil ways and was reluctant to send him away.]

2. A. "But God said to Abraham, 'Be not displeased because of the lad and because of your slave woman; whatever Sarah says to you, do as she tells you, for through Isaac shall your descendants be named'" [Gen. 21:12]:

   B. Said R. Yudan bar Shillum, "What is written is not 'Isaac' but 'through Isaac.' [The matter is limited, not through all of Isaac's descendants but only through some of them, thus excluding Esau.]"

3. A. R. Azariah in the name of Bar Hutah: "The use of the B, which stands for two, indicates that he who affirms that there are two worlds will inherit both worlds [this age and the age to come]."

   B. Said R. Yudan bar Shillum, "It is written, 'Remember his marvelous works that he has done, his signs and the judgments of his mouth' [Ps. 105:5]. I have given a sign, namely, it is one who gives the appropriate evidence through what he says. Specifically, he who affirms that there are two worlds will be called 'your seed.'

   C. "And he who does not affirm that there are two worlds will not be called 'your seed.'"

Number 1 makes "the matter" refer to Ishmael's misbehavior, not Sarah's proposal, so removing the possibility of disagreement between Abraham and Sarah. Numbers 2, 3 interpret the limiting particle, "in," that is, *among* the descendants of Isaac will be found Abraham's heirs, but not all the descendants of Isaac will be heirs of Abraham. Number 2 explicitly excludes Esau—that is Rome; and Number 3 makes the matter doctrinal in the context of Israel's inner life. As the several antagonists of Israel stand for Rome in particular, so the traits of Rome, as sages perceived them, characterized the biblical heroes. Esau provided a favorite target. From the womb Israel and Rome contended.

LXIII:VI

1. A. "And the children struggled together [within her, and she said, 'If it is thus, why do I live?' So she went to inquire of the Lord. And the Lord said to her, 'Two nations are in your womb, and two peoples, born of you, shall be divided; the one shall be stronger than the other, and the elder shall serve the younger'] " [Gen. 25:22–23]:

B. R. Yohanan and R. Simeon b. Laqish:

C. R. Yohanan said, "[Because the word, 'struggle,' contains the letters for the word, 'run,'] this one was running to kill that one and that one was running to kill this one."

D. R. Simeon b. Laqish: "This one releases the laws given by that one, and that one releases the laws given by this one."

2. A. R. Berekhiah in the name of R. Levi said, "It is so that you should not say that it was only after he left his mother's womb that [Esau] contended against [Jacob].

B. "But even while he was yet in his mother's womb, his fist was stretched forth against him: 'The wicked stretch out their fists [so Freedman] from the womb'" [Ps. 58:4].

3. A. "And the children struggled together within her:"

B. [Once more referring to the letters of the word "struggled," with special attention to the ones that mean, "run,"] they wanted to run within her.

C. When she went by houses of idolatry, Esau would kick, trying to get out: "The wicked are estranged from the womb" [Ps. 58:4].

D. When she went by synagogues and study-houses, Jacob would kick, trying to get out: "Before I formed you in the womb, I knew you" [Jer. 1:5].

4. A. "...and she said, 'If it is thus, why do I live?'"

B. R. Haggai in the name of R. Isaac: "This teaches that our mother, Rebecca, went around to the doors of women and said to them, 'Did you ever have this kind of pain in your life?'"

C. "[She said to them,] 'If thus:' 'If this is the pain of having children, would that I had not gotten pregnant.'"

D. Said R. Huna, "If I am going to produce twelve tribes only through this kind of suffering, would that I had not gotten pregnant."

5. A. It was taught on Tannaite authority in the name of R. Nehemiah, "Rebecca was worthy of having the twelve tribes come forth from her. That is in line with this verse:

B. "'Two nations are in your womb, and two peoples, born of you, shall be divided; the one shall be stronger than the other, and the elder shall serve the younger. When her days to be delivered were fulfilled, behold, there were twins in her womb. The first came forth red, all his body like a hairy mantle, so they called his name Esau. Afterward his brother came forth . . .' [Gen. 25:23–24].

C. "'Two nations are in your womb': thus two.

D. "'and two peoples': thus two more, hence four.

E. "'. . . the one shall be stronger than the other': two more, so six.

F. "'. . . and the elder shall serve the younger': two more, so eight.

G. "'When her days to be delivered were fulfilled, behold, there were twins in her womb': two more, so ten.

H. "'The first came forth red': now eleven.

J. "'Afterward his brother came forth': now twelve."

K. There are those who say, "Proof derives from this verse: 'If it is thus, why do I live?' Focusing on the word for 'thus,' we note that the two letters of that word bear the numerical value of seven and five respectively, hence, twelve in all."

6. A. "So she went to inquire of the Lord":

B. Now were there synagogues and houses of study in those days [that she could go to inquire of the Lord]?

C. But is it not the fact that she went only to the study of Eber?

D. This serves to teach you that whoever receives an elder is as if he receives the Presence of God.

Numbers 1-3 take for granted that Esau represents Rome, and Jacob, Israel. Consequently the verse underlines the point that there is natural enmity between Israel and Rome. Esau hated Israel even while he was still in the womb. Jacob, for his part, revealed from the womb those virtues that would characterize him later on, eager to serve God as Esau was eager to worship idols. The text invites just this sort of reading. Numbers 4 and 5 relate Rebecca's suffering to the birth of the twelve tribes. Number 6 makes its own point, independent of the rest and tacked on. In the next passage Rome appears as a pig, an important choice for symbolization, as we shall see in Leviticus Rabbah as well:

LXV:I

1. A. "When Esau was forty years old, he took to wife Judith, the daughter of Beeri, the Hittite, and Basemath the daughter of Elon the Hittite; and they made life bitter for Isaac and Rebecca" [Gen. 26:34–35]:

   B. "The swine out of the wood ravages it, that which moves in the field feeds on it" [Ps. 80:14].

   C. R. Phineas and R. Hilqiah in the name of R. Simon: "Among all of the prophets, only two of them spelled out in public [the true character of Rome, represented by the swine], Asaf and Moses.

   D. "Asaf: 'The swine out of the wood ravages it.'

   E. "Moses: 'And the swine, because he parts the hoof' [Deut. 14:8].

   F. Why does Moses compare Rome to the swine? Just as the swine, when it crouches, puts forth its hoofs as if to say, 'I am clean,' so the wicked kingdom steals and grabs, while pretending to be setting up courts of justice.

   G. "So Esau, for all forty years, hunted married women, ravished them, and when he reached the age of forty, he presented himself to his father, saying, 'Just as father got married at the age of forty, so I shall marry a wife at the age of forty.'

   H. 'When Esau was forty years old, he took to wife Judith, the daughter of Beeri, the Hittite, and Basemath the daughter of Elon the Hittite.'"

How long would Rome rule, when would Israel succeed? The important point is that Rome was next to last, Israel last. Rome's triumph brought assurance that Israel would be next—and last:

LXXV:IV

2. A. "And Jacob sent messengers before him":

   B. To this one [Esau] whose time to take hold of sovereignty would come before him [namely, before Jacob, since Esau would rule, then Jacob would govern].

   C. R. Joshua b. Levi said, "Jacob took off the purple robe and threw it before Esau, as if to say to him, 'Two flocks of starlings are not going to sleep on a single branch' [so we cannot rule at the same time].'"

3. A. "...to Esau his brother":

   B. Even though he was Esau, he was still his brother.

Esau remains Jacob's brother, but Esau—Rome—rules before Jacob will. The application to contemporary affairs cannot be missed, both in the recognition of the true character of Esau—a brother!—and in the interpretation of the future of history.

To conclude: Genesis Rabbah reached closure, people generally agree, toward the end of the fourth century. That century marks the beginning of the West as we have known it. Why so? Because in the fourth century, from the conversion of Constantine and over the next hundred years, the Roman empire became Christian—and with it, the West. So the fourth century marks the first century of the history of the West in that form in which the West would flourish for the rest of time, to our own day. Accordingly, we should not find surprising sages' recurrent references, in the reading of Genesis, to the struggle of two equal powers, Rome and Israel, Esau and Jacob, Ishmael and Isaac. The world-historical change, marking the confirmation in politics and power of the Christians' claim that Christ was king over all humanity, demanded from sages an appropriate and, to Israel, persuasive response.

5. SCRIPTURE (WRITTEN): A SAMPLE CHAPTER OF LEVITICUS RABBAH

Reading one thing in terms of something else, the authors of Leviticus Rabbah systematically adopted for themselves the reality of the Scripture, its history and doctrines. They looked for the rules and laws, the regularities of the history that Scripture portrayed. Like social scientists, they tested theses of history, social rules, against the facts presented by "reality"—for them, Scripture. In so doing they transformed that history from a sequence of one-time events, leading from one place to some other, into an ever-present mythic world. No longer was there one Moses, one David, one set of happenings of a distinctive and never-to-be-repeated character. Now whatever happens, of which the thinkers propose to take account, must enter and be absorbed into that established and ubiquitous pattern and structure founded in Scripture. It is not that biblical history repeats itself.   Rather, biblical history no longer constitutes history as a story of things that happened once, long ago, and pointed to some one moment in the future. Rather it becomes an account of things that happen every day—hence, an ever-present mythic world.

In Leviticus Rabbah, Scripture as a whole does not dictate the order of discourse, let alone its character.   In this document they chose in Leviticus itself a verse here, a phrase there.   These then presented the pretext for propositional discourse commonly quite out of phase with the cited passage.   The verses that are quoted ordinarily shift from the meanings they convey to the implications they contain, speaking about something, anything, other than what they seem to be saying.   So the "as if" frame of mind brought to Scripture brings renewal to Scripture, seeing everything with fresh eyes.   And the result of the new vision was a reimagining of the social world envisioned by the document at hand—the everyday world of Israel in its Land in that difficult time.   For what the sages now proposed was a reconstruction of existence along the lines of the ancient design of Scripture as they read it.   Thus, from a sequence of one-time and linear events, everything that happened was turned into a repetition of known and already-experienced paradigms, hence, once more, a mythic being.   The source and core of the myth, of course, derive from Scripture—Scripture reread, renewed, reconstructed along with the society that revered Scripture.

So the mode of thought that dictated the issues and the logic of the document, telling the thinkers to see one thing in terms of something else, addressed Scripture in particular and collectively.   And thinking as they did, the framers of the document saw Scripture in a new way, just as they saw their own circumstance afresh, rejecting their world in favor of Scripture's, reliving Scripture's world in their own terms.   That, incidentally, is why they did not write history, an account of what was happening and what it meant.   It was not that they did not recognize or appreciate important changes and trends reshaping their nation's life. They could not deny that reality.   In their apocalyptic reading of the dietary and leprosy laws, they made explicit their close encounter with the history of the world as they knew it.   But they had another mode of responding to history: They treated history as if it were already known and readily understood.   Whatever happened had already happened. Scripture dictated the contents of history, laying forth the structures of time, the rules that prevailed and were made known in events.   Self-evidently, these same thinkers projected into Scripture's day the realities of their own, turning Moses and David into rabbis, for example. But that is how people think in that mythic, enchanted world in which, to begin with, reality blends with dream, and hope projects onto future and past alike how people want things to be.

Let us turn, now, from these somewhat abstract observations to a concrete account of what happened, in particular, when the thinkers at hand undertook to reimagine reality—both their own and Scripture's. Exactly how did they think about one thing in terms of another, and what did they choose, in particular, to recognize in this rather complex process of juggling unpalatable present and unattainable myth? To state the answer in advance, when they read the rules of sanctification of the priesthood, they heard the message of the salvation of all Israel. Leviticus became the story of how Israel, purified from social sin and sanctified, would be saved. Let us turn, then, to the classifications of rules that sages located in the social laws of Leviticus. The first, and single paramount, category takes shape within the themes associated with the national life of Israel. The principal lines of structure flow along the fringes: Israel's relationships with others. These are (so to speak) horizontal, with the nations, and vertical, with God. But, from the viewpoint of the framers of the document, the relationships form a single, seamless web, for Israel's vertical relationships dictate the horizontals as well; when God wishes to punish Israel, the nations come to do the work.

The relationships that define Israel, moreover, prove dynamic, not static, in that they respond to the movement of the Torah through Israel's history. When the Torah governs, then the vertical relationship is stable and felicitous, the horizontal one secure, and, when not, God obeys the rules and the nations obey God. The recurrent messages of Leviticus Rabbah may be stated in a single paragraph. God loves Israel, so gave them the Torah, which defines their life and governs their welfare. Israel is alone in its category *(sui generis)*, so what is a virtue to Israel is a vice to the nation, life-giving to Israel, poison to the gentiles. True, Israel sins, but God forgives that sin, having punished the nation on account of it. Such a process has yet to come to an end, but it will culminate in Israel's complete regeneration.

Meanwhile, Israel's assurance of God's love lies in the many expressions of special concern for even the humblest and most ordinary aspects of the national life: the food the nation eats, the sexual practices by which it procreates. These life-sustaining, life-transmitting activities draw God's special interest, as a mark of his general love for Israel. Israel, then, is supposed to achieve its life in conformity with the marks of God's love. Moreover, these indications signify also the character of Israel's difficulty—namely, subordination to the nations in general, but to the fourth kingdom, Rome, in particular. Both food laws and skin diseases stand for the nations. There is yet another category of sin, also collective and generative of collective punishment, and that is social. The moral character of Israel's life, the treatment of people by one another, the practice of gossip and small-scale thuggery—these, too, draw down divine penalty. The nation's fate therefore corresponds to its moral condition. The moral condition, however, emerges not only from the current generation. Israel's richest hope lies in the merit of the ancestors, thus in the Scriptural record of the merits attained by the founders of the nation, those who originally brought it into being and gave it life. Let us now consider a sample chapter of this complex and profound document.

XIII:V

1. A.   Said R. Ishmael b. R. Nehemiah, "All the prophets foresaw what the pagan kingdoms would do [to Israel].

   B.   "The first man foresaw what the pagan kingdoms would do [to Israel].

   C.   "That is in line with the following verse of Scripture: 'A river flowed out of Eden [to water the garden, and there it divided and became four rivers]' [Gen. 2:10]. [The four rivers stand for the four kingdoms, Babylonia, Media, Greece, and Rome]."

2. A.   R. Tanhuma said it, [and] R. Menahema [in the name of] R. Joshua b. Levi: "The Holy One, blessed be He, will give the cup of reeling to the nations of the world to drink in the world to come.

   B.   "That is in line with the following verse of Scripture: 'A river flowed out of Eden' [Gen. 2:10], the place from which justice [DYN] goes forth."

3. A.   "[There it divided] and became four rivers" [Gen. 2:10]—this refers to the four kingdoms.

   B.   "The name of the first is Pishon (PSWN); [it is the one which flows around the whole land of Havilah, where there is gold; and the gold of that land is good; bdellium and onyx stone are there]" [Gen. 2:11–12].

   C.   This refers to Babylonia, on account [of the reference to Babylonia in the following verse:] "And their [the Babylonians'] horsemen spread themselves (PSW)" [Hab. 1:8].

   D.   [It is further] on account of [Nebuchadnezzar's being] a dwarf, shorter than ordinary men by a handbreadth.

   E.   "[It is the one which flows around the whole land of Havilah" [Gen. 2:11].

   F.   "This [reference to the river's flowing around the whole land] speaks of Nebuchadnezzar, the wicked man, who came up and surrounded the entire Land of Israel, which places its hope in the Holy One, blessed be He.

   G.   That is in line with the following verse of Scripture: "Hope in God, for I shall again praise him" (Ps. 42:5).

   H.   "Where there is gold" [Gen. 2:11]—this refers to the words of Torah, "which are more to be desired than gold, more than much fine gold" [Ps. 19:11].

   I.   "And the gold of that land is good" [Gen. 2:12].

   J.   This teaches that there is no Torah like the Torah that is taught in the Land of Israel, and there is no wisdom like the wisdom that is taught in the Land of Israel.

   K.   "Bdellium and onyx stone are there" [Gen. 2:12]—Scripture, Mishnah, Talmud, and lore.

4. A.   "The name of the second river is Gihon; [it is the one which flows around the whole land of Cush]" [Gen. 2:13].

   B.   This refers to Media, which produced Haman, that wicked man, who spit out venom like a serpent.

   C.   It is on account of the verse: "On your belly will you go" [Gen. 3:14].

   D.   "It is the one which flows around the whole land of Cush" [Gen. 2:13].

E. [We know that this refers to Media, because it is said:] "Who rules from India to Cush" [Est. 1:1].

5. A. "And the name of the third river is Tigris (HDQL), [which flows east of Assyria] [Gen. 2:14].

B. This refers to Greece [Syria], which was sharp (HD) and speedy (QL) in making its decrees, saying to Israel, "Write on the horn of an ox that you have no portion in the God of Israel."

C. "Which flows east (QDMT) of Assyria" [Gen. 2:14].

D. Said R. Huna, "In three aspects the kingdom of Greece was in advance (QDMH) of the present evil kingdom [Rome]: in respect to ship-building, the arrangement of camp vigils, and language."

E. Said R. Huna, "Any and every kingdom may be called 'Assyria' (ashur), on account of all of their making themselves powerful at Israel's expense."

F. Said R. Yose b. R. Hanina, "Any and every kingdom may be called Nineveh (NNWH), on account of their adorning (NWY) themselves at Israel's expense."

G. Said R. Yose b. R. Hanina, "Any and every kingdom may be called Egypt (MSRYM), on account of their oppressing (MSYRYM) Israel."

6. A. "And the fourth river is the Euphrates (PRT)" [Gen. 2:14].

B. This refers to Edom [Rome], since it was fruitful (PRT), and multiplied through the prayer of the elder [Isaac at Gen. 27:39].

C. Another interpretation: It was because it was fruitful and multiplied, and so cramped his world.

D. Another explanation: Because it was fruitful and multiplied and cramped his son.

E. Another explanation: Because it was fruitful and multiplied and cramped his house.

F. Another explanation: "Parat"—because in the end, "I am going to exact a penalty from it."

G. That is in line with the following verse of Scripture: "I have trodden (PWRH) the winepress alone" [Is. 63:3].

7. A. [Gen. R. 42:2:] Abraham foresaw what the evil kingdoms would do [to Israel].

B. "[As the sun was going down,] a deep sleep fell on Abraham; and lo, a dread and great darkness fell upon him]" [Gen. 15:12].

C. "Dread" ('YMH) refers to Babylonia, on account of the statement, "Then Nebuchadnezzer was full of fury (HMH)" [Dan. 3:19].

D. "Darkness" refers to Media, which brought darkness to Israel through its decrees: "to destroy, to slay, and to wipe out all the Jews" [Est. 7:4].

E. "Great" refers to Greece.

F. Said R. Judah b. R. Simon, "The verse teaches that the kingdom of Greece set up one hundred twenty-seven governors, one hundred and twenty-seven hyparchs and one hundred twenty-seven commanders."

G. And rabbis say, "They were sixty in each category."

H. R. Berekhiah and R. Hanan in support of this position taken by rabbis: "'Who led you through the great terrible wilderness, with its fiery serpents and scorpions and thirsty ground where there was no water]' [Deut. 8:15].

I. "Just as the scorpion produces eggs by sixties, so the kingdom of Greece would set up its administration in groups of sixty."

J.   "Fell on him" [Gen. 15:12].

K.   This refers to Edom, on account of the following verse: "The earth quakes at the noise of their [Edom's] fall" [Jer. 49:21].

L.   There are those who reverse matters.

M.   "Fear" refers to Edom, on account of the following verse: "And this I saw, a fourth beast, fearful, and terrible" [Dan. 7:7].

M.   "Darkness" refers to Greece, which brought gloom through its decrees. For they said to Israel, "Write on the horn of an ox that you have no portion in the God of Israel."

O.   "Great" refers to Media, on account of the verse: "King Ahasuerus made Haman [the Median] great" [Est. 3:1].

P.   "Fell on him" refers to Babylonia, on account of the following verse: "Fallen, fallen is Babylonia" [Is. 21:9].

8. A.   Daniel foresaw what the evil kingdoms would do [to Israel].

B.   "Daniel said, I saw in my vision by night, and behold, the four winds of heaven were stirring up the great sea. And four great beasts came up out of the sea, [different from one another. The first was like a lion and had eagles' wings. Then as I looked, its wings were plucked off . . . And behold, another beast, a second one, like a bear . . . After this I looked, and lo, another, like a leopard . . . After this I saw in the night visions, and behold, a fourth beast, terrible and dreadful and exceedingly strong; and it had great iron teeth]" [Dan. 7:3–7].

C.   If you enjoy sufficient merit, it will emerge from the sea, but if not, it will come out of the forest.

D.   The animal that comes up from the sea is not violent, but the one that comes up out of the forest is violent.

E.   Along these same lines: "The boar out of the wood ravages it" [Ps. 80:14].

F.   If you enjoy sufficient merit, it will come from the river, and if not, from the forest.

G.   The animal that comes up from the river is not violent, but the one that comes up out of the forest is violent.

H.   "Different from one another" [Dan. 7:3].

I.   Differing from [hating] one another.

J.   This teaches that every nation that rules in the world hates Israel and reduces them to slavery.

K.   "The first was like a lion [and had eagles' wings]" [Dan. 7:4].

L.   This refers to Babylonia.

M.   Jeremiah saw [Babylonia] as a lion. Then he went and saw it as an eagle.

N.   He saw it as a lion: "A lion has come up from his thicket" [Jer. 4:7].

O.   And [as an eagle:] "Behold, he shall come up and swoop down as the eagle" [Jer. 49:22].

P.   People said to Daniel, "What do you see?"

Q.   He said to them, "I see the face like that of a lion and wings like those of an eagle: 'The first was like a lion and had eagles' wings. Then, as I looked, its wings were plucked off, and it was lifted up from the ground [and made to stand upon two feet like a man and the heart of a man was given to it]' [Dan. 7:4].

R.   R. Eleazar and R. Ishmael b. R. Nehemiah:

S.   R. Eleazar said, "While the entire lion was smitten, its heart was not smitten.

T. "That is in line with the following statement: 'And the heart of a man was given to it' [Dan. 7:4]."

U. And R. Ishmael b. R. Nehemiah said, "Even its heart was smitten, for it is written, 'Let his heart be changed from a man's' [Dan. 4:17].

X. "And behold, another beast, a second one, like a bear. [It was raised up one side; it had three ribs in its mouth between its teeth, and it was told, Arise, devour much flesh]" [Dan. 7:5].

Y. This refers to Media.

Z. Said R. Yohanan, "It is like a bear."

AA. It is written, "similar to a wolf" (DB); thus, "And a wolf was there."

BB. That is in accord with the view of R. Yohanan, for R.Yohanan said, "'Therefore a lion out of the forest [slays them]' [Jer. 5:6]—this refers to Babylonia.

CC. "'A wolf of the deserts spoils them' [Jer. 5:6] refers to Media.

DD. "'A leopard watches over their cities' [Jer. 5:6] refers to Greece.

EE. "'Whoever goes out from them will be savaged' [Jer. 5:6] refers to Edom.

FF. "'Why so? 'Because their transgressions are many, and their backslidings still more' [Jer. 5:6]."

GG. "After this, I looked, and lo, another, like a leopard [with four wings of a bird on its back; and the beast had four heads; and dominion was given to it]" [Dan. 7:6].

HH. This [leopard] refers to Greece, which persisted impudently in making harsh decrees, saying to Israel, "Write on the horn of an ox that you have no share in the God of Israel."

II. "After this I saw in the night visions, and behold, a fourth beast, terrible and dreadful and exceedingly strong; [and it had great iron teeth; it devoured and broke in pieces and stamped the residue with its feet. It was different from all the beasts that were before it; and it had ten horns]" [Dan. 7:7].

JJ. This refers to Edom [Rome].

KK. Daniel saw the first three visions on one night, and this one he saw on another night. Now why was that the case?

LL. R. Yohanan and R. Simeon b. Laqish:

MM. R. Yohanan said, "It is because the fourth beast weighed as much as the first three."

NN. And R. Simeon b. Laqish said, "It outweighed them."

OO. R. Yohanan objected to R. Simeon b. Laqish, "'Prophesy, therefore, son of man, clap your hands [and let the sword come down twice; yea, thrice. The sword for those to be slain; it is the sword for the great slaughter, which encompasses them]' [Ez. 21:14–15]. [So the single sword of Rome weighs against the three others]."

PP. And R. Simeon b. Laqish, how does he interpret the same passage? He notes that [the threefold sword] is doubled [Ez. 21:14], [thus outweighs the three swords, equally twice their strength].

9. A. Moses foresaw what the evil kingdoms would do [to Israel].

B. "The camel, rock badger, and hare" [Deut. 14:7]. [Compare: "Nevertheless, among those that chew the cud or part the hoof, you shall not eat these: the camel, because it chews the cud but does not part the hoof, is unclean to you. The rock badger, because it chews the cud but does not part the hoof, is unclean to you. And the hare, because it chews the cud but does not part the hoof, is unclean to you, and the pig, because it parts the hoof and is cloven-footed, but does not chew the cud, is unclean to you" (Lev. 11:4–8).]

C. The camel (GML) refers to Babylonia, [in line with the following verse of Scripture: "O daughter of Babylonia, you who are to be devastated!] Happy will be he who requites (GML) you, with what you have done to us" [Ps. 147:8].

D. "The rock badger" [Deut. 14:7]—this refers to Media.

E. Rabbis and R. Judah b. R. Simon.

F. Rabbis say, "Just as the rock badger exhibits traits of uncleanness and traits of cleanness, so the kingdom of Media produced both a righteous man and a wicked one."

G. Said R. Judah b. R. Simon, "The last Darius was Esther's son. He was clean on his mother's side and unclean on his father's side."

H. "The hare" [Deut 14:7]—this refers to Greece. The mother of King Ptolemy was named "Hare" [in Greek: lagos].

I. "The pig" [Deut. 14:7]—this refers to Edom [Rome].

J. Moses made mention of the first three in a single verse and the final one in a verse by itself [Deut. 14:7, 8]. Why so?

K. R. Yohanan and R. Simeon b. Laqish.

L. R. Yohanan said, "It is because [the pig] is equivalent to the other three."

M. And R. Simeon b. Laqish said, "It is because it outweighs them."

N. R. Yohanan objected to R. Simeon b. Laqish, "'Prophesy, therefore, son of man, clap your hands [and let the sword come down twice, yea thrice]'" [Ez. 21:14].

O. And how does R. Simeon b. Laqish interpret the same passage? He notes that [the threefold sword] is doubled [Ez. 21:14].

10. A. [Gen. R. 65:1:] R. Phineas and R. Hilqiah in the name of R. Simon: "Among all the prophets, only two of them revealed [the true evil of Rome], Assaf and Moses.

B. "Assaf said, 'The pig out of the wood ravages it' [Ps. 80:14].

C. "Moses said, 'And the pig, [because it parts the hoof and is cloven-footed but does not chew the cud]' [Lev. 11:7].

D. "Why is [Rome] compared to a pig?

E. "It is to teach you the following: Just as, when a pig crouches and produces its hooves, it is as if to say, 'See how I am clean [since I have a cloven hoof],' so this evil kingdom takes pride, seizes by violence, and steals, and then gives the appearance of establishing a tribunal for justice."

F. There was the case of a ruler in Caesarea, who put thieves, adulterers, and sorcerers to death, while at the same time telling his counsellor, "That same man [I] did all these three things on a single night."

11. A. Another interpretation: "The camel" [Lev. 11:4].

B. This refers to Babylonia.

C. "Because it chews the cud [but does not part the hoof]" [Lev. 11:4].

D. For it brings forth praises [with its throat] of the Holy One, blessed be He. [The Hebrew words for "chew the cud"—bring up cud—are now understood to mean "give praise." GRH is connected with GRWN, throat, hence, "bring forth [sounds of praise through] the throat."

E. R. Berekhiah and R. Helbo in the name of R. Ishmael b. R. Nahman: "Whatever [praise of God] David [in writing a psalm] treated singly [item by item], that wicked man [Nebuchadnezzar] lumped together in a single verse.

F. "'Now I, Nebuchadnezzar, praise and extol and honor the King of heaven, for all his works are right and his ways are just, and those who walk in pride he is able to abase' [Dan. 4:37].

G. "'Praise'—'O Jerusalem, praise the Lord' [Ps. 147:12].

H. "'Extol'—'I shall extol you, O Lord, for you have brought me low' [Ps. 30:2].

I. "'Honor the king of heaven'—'The Lord reigns, let the peoples tremble! He sits enthroned upon the cherubim, let the earth quake' [Ps. 99:1].

J. "'For all his works are right'—'For the sake of thy steadfast love and thy faithfulness' [Ps. 115:1].

K. "'And his ways are just'—'He will judge the peoples with equity' [Ps. 96:10].

L. "'And those who walk in pride'—'The Lord reigns, he is robed in majesty, the Lord is robed, he is girded with strength' [Ps. 93:1].

M. "'He is able to abase'—'All the horns of the wicked he will cut off'" [Ps. 75:11].

N. "The rock badger" [Lev. 11:5]—this refers to Media.

O. "For it chews the cud"—for it gives praise to the Holy One, blessed be He: "Thus says Cyrus, king of Persia, 'All the kingdoms of the earth has the Lord, the God of the heaven, given me'" [Ezra 1:2].

P. "The hare"—this refers to Greece.

Q. "For it chews the cud"—for it gives praise to the Holy One, blessed be He.

R. Alexander the Macedonian, when he saw Simeon the Righteous, said, "Blessed be the God of Simeon the Righteous."

S. "The pig" (Lev. 11:7)—this refers to Edom.

T. "For it does not chew the cud"—for it does not give praise to the Holy One, blessed be He.

U. And it is not enough that it does not give praise, but it blasphemes and swears violently, saying, "Whom do I have in heaven, and with you I want nothing on earth" [Ps. 73:25)]

12. A. Another interpretation [of GRH, cud, now with reference to GR, stranger]:

B. "The camel" [Lev. 11:4]—this refers to Babylonia.

C. "For it chews the cud" [now: brings up the stranger]—for it exalts righteous men: "And Daniel was in the gate of the king" [Dan. 2:49].

D. "The rock badger" [Lev. 11:5]—this refers to Media.

E. "For it brings up the stranger"—for it exalts righteous men: "Mordecai sat at the gate of the king" [Est. 2:19].

F. "The hare" [Lev. 11:6]—this refers to Greece.

G. "For it brings up the stranger"—for it exalts the righteous.

H. When Alexander of Macedonia saw Simeon the Righteous, he would rise up on his feet. They said to him, "Can't you see the Jew, that you stand up before this Jew?"

I. He said to them, "When I go forth to battle, I see something like this man's visage, and I conquer."

J. "The pig" [Lev. 11:7]—this refers to Rome.

K. "But it does not bring up the stranger"—for it does not exalt the righteous.

L.   And it is not enough that it does not exalt them, but it kills them.

M.   That is in line with the following verse of Scripture: "I was angry with my people, I profaned my heritage; I gave them into your hand, you showed them no mercy; on the aged you made your yoke exceedingly heavy" [Is. 47:6].

N.   This refers to R. Aqiba and his colleagues.

13. A.   Another interpretation [now treating "bring up the cud" (GR) as "bring along in its train" (GRR)]:

B.   "The camel" [Lev. 11:4]—this refers to Babylonia.

C.   "Which brings along in its train"—for it brought along another kingdom after it.

D.   "The rock badger" [Lev. 11:5]—this refers to Media.

E.   "Which brings along in its train"—for it brought along another kingdom after it.

F.   "The hare" [Lev. 11:6]—this refers to Greece.

G.   "Which brings along in its train"—for it brought along another kingdom after it.

H.   "The pig" [Lev. 11:7]—this refers to Rome.

I.   "Which does not bring along in its train"—for it did not bring along another kingdom after it.

J.   And why is it then called "pig" (HZYR)? For it restores (MHZRT) the crown to the one who truly should have it [namely, Israel, whose dominion will begin when the rule of Rome ends].

K.   That is in line with the following verse of Scripture: "And saviors will come up on Mount Zion to judge the Mountain of Esau [Rome], and the kingdom will then belong to the Lord" [Ob. 1:21].

To stand back and consider this vast apocalyptic vision of Israel's history, we first review the message of the construction as a whole. This comes in two parts—first the explicit, then the implicit. As to the former, the first claim is that God had told the prophets what would happen to Israel at the hands of the pagan kingdoms, Babylonia, Media, Greece, Rome. These are further represented by Nebuchadnezzar, Haman, Alexander for Greece, Edom or Esau, interchangeably, for Rome. The same vision came from Adam, Abraham, Daniel, and Moses. The same policy toward Israel—oppression, destruction, enslavement, alienation from the true God—emerged from all four.

How does Rome stand out? First, it was made fruitful through the prayer of Isaac on behalf of Esau. Second, Edom is represented by the fourth and final beast. Rome is related through Esau, as Babylonia, Media, and Greece are not. The fourth beast was seen in a vision separate from the first three. It was worst of all and outweighed the rest. In the apocalypticizing of the animals of Lev. 11:4–8/Deut. 14:7—the camel, rock badger, hare, and pig—the pig, standing for Rome, again emerges as different from the others and more threatening than the rest. Just as the pig pretends to be a clean beast by showing the cloven hoof, but in fact is an unclean one, so Rome pretends to be just but in fact governs by thuggery. Edom does not pretend to praise God but only blasphemes. It does not exalt the righteous but kills them. These symbols concede nothing to Christian monotheism and biblicism. Of greatest importance, while all the other beasts bring further ones in their wake, the pig does not: "It does not bring another kingdom after it." It will restore the crown to the one who will truly deserve it, Israel. Esau will be judged by Zion, so Obadiah 1:21. Now, how has the symbolization delivered an implicit message? It is in the treatment of Rome as distinct from, but essentially equivalent to, the former kingdoms. This seems a stunning way of saying that the now-Christian empire in no way requires differentiation from its pagan predecessors. Nothing has changed, except matters have gotten worse. Beyond Rome, standing in a straight line with the others, lies the true shift in history, the rule of Israel and the cessation of the dominion of the (pagan) nations.

To conclude, Leviticus Rabbah came to closure, it is generally agreed, around A.D. 400—that is, approximately a century after the Roman Empire in the east had begun to become Christian, and half a century after the last attempt to rebuild the Temple in Jerusalem had failed—a tumultuous age indeed. Accordingly, we have had the chance to see how distinctive and striking are the ways in which, in the text at hand, the symbols of animals that stand for the four successive empires of humanity and point towards the messianic time serve for the framers' message.

6. JUDAISM CONFRONTS CHRISTIANITY

Jews and Christians alike believed in the Israelite Scriptures, and so understood that major turnings in history carried a message from God. That message bore meaning for questions of salvation and the Messiah, the identification of God's will in Scripture, the determination of who is Israel and what it means to be Israel, and similar questions of a profoundly historical and social character. So it is no wonder that the enormous turning represented by the advent of a Christian empire should have precipitated deep thought on these issues, important as they are in the fourth-century thought of both Judaic sages and Christian theologians. The specification of the message at hand, of course, would produce long-term differences between the Christianity of the age and the Judaism of the time.

Prior to the time of Constantine, the documents of Judaism that earlier reached closure—the Mishnah, tractate Avot, the Tosefta—scarcely took cognizance of Christianity and did not deem the new faith to be much of a challenge. If the scarce and scattered allusions do mean to refer to Christianity at all, then sages regarded it as an irritant, an exasperating heresy among Jews, who should have known better. But, then, neither Jews nor pagans took much interest in Christianity in the new faith's first century and a half. The authors of the Mishnah framed a system to which Christianity bore no relevance whatsoever; theirs were problems presented in an altogether different context. For their part, pagan writers were indifferent to Christianity, not mentioning it until about 160. Only when Christian evangelism enjoyed some solid success, toward the later part of that century, did pagans compose apologetic works attacking Christianity. Celsus stands at the start, followed by Porphyry in the third century. But by the fourth century, pagans and Jews alike knew that they faced a formidable, powerful enemy. Pagan writings speak explicitly and accessibly. The answers sages worked out for the intellectual challenge of the hour do not emerge equally explicitly and accessibly. But they are there, and, when we ask the right questions and establish the context of discourse, we clearly hear the answers in the Talmud of the Land of Israel, Genesis Rabbah, and Leviticus Rabbah, as clearly as we hear pagans' answers in the writings of Porphyry and Julian, not to mention the Christians' answers in the rich and diverse writings of the fourth-century fathers, such as Eusebius, Jerome, John Crysostom, and Aphrahat, to mention just four. So, as Rosemary Radford Ruether first pointed out, the fourth century was the first century of Christianity and Judaism as the West would know them both.[7]

Historians of Judaism take as dogma the view that Christianity never made any difference to Judaism. They see Judaism as the faith of a "people that dwells apart"; Judaism went its splendid, solitary way, exploring paths untouched by Christians. Christianity, people hold, was born in the matrix of Judaism; but Judaism, beginning to now, officially ignored the new "daughter" religion and followed its majestic course in aristocratic isolation. As we have seen, though, the Judaism expressed by the writings of the sages of the Land of Israel in the fourth century—the age of Constantine—not only responded to issues raised for Israel by the political triumph of Christianity but did so in a way that, intellectually at least, made possible the entire future history of Judaism in Europe and beyond.

It follows that the impact of the third crisis was definitive. The importance of the age of Constantine in the history of Judaism derives from a simple fact. It was at this time that important Judaic documents undertook to deal with agenda defined, for both Judaism and Christianity, by the triumph of Christianity. Important Christian thinkers reflected on issues presented by the political revolution in the status of Christianity. Issues of the rewriting of human history, the restatement of the challenge and claim of Christ the King as Messiah against the continuing "unbelief" of Israel (phrased from the Christian viewpoint, Jews would refer to their continuing belief in God's power to save the world at the end of time), the definition of who is Israel—these make their appearance in Christian writings of the day. And these issues

---

[7]Neusner, *Studies in Religion* (1972), 2:1–10.

derive from the common agenda of both Judaism and Christianity—namely, the Holy Scriptures of Ancient Israel, received in Judaism as the written half of the One Whole Torah of Moses, our Rabbi, and in Christianity as the Old Testament.

The sages of the fourth century replied to the Christian challenge in a system that held its own within Israel, the Jewish people, from that time on. They turned back to Scripture, rereading the two books that mattered: first, the one on the Creation of the world and of the children of Israel, Genesis; second, the one on the sanctification of Israel. So they proposed to explain history by rereading the book of Genesis. There they found the lesson that what happened to the patriarchs in the beginning signals what would later happen to their children. And Jacob then is Israel now, just as Esau then is Rome now. And Israel remains Israel: bearer of the blessing. They explain the status and authority of the traditions—now 200 years old—of the Mishnah and related writings by assigning to them a place in the Torah. Specifically, in the canonical documents of the period at hand we find for the first time clear reference to the notion that when God revealed the Torah to Moses at Sinai, part of the Torah was in the medium of writing, the other part, in the medium of memory (oral). And, it would later be explained, the Mishnah (and much else) enjoyed the status of Oral Torah. They explain the Messiah claim of Israel in very simple terms. Israel indeed will receive the Messiah, but salvation at the end of time awaits the sanctification of Israel in the here and now. And that will take place through humble and obediant loyalty to the Torah.

Sages thus countered the claim that there is a new Israel in place of the old, and this they do by rereading the book of Genesis and of Leviticus, with their message of sanctification of Israel, and finding a typology of the great empires—Babylonia, Media, Greece, Rome. And the coming, the fifth and final sovereign, will be Israel's messiah. So, in all, the points important to Christianity in the advent of Constantine and the Christian empire—history vindicates Christ, the New Testament explains the Old, the Messiah has come and his claim has now been proved truthful, and the old Israel is done for and will not have a messiah in the future—were all countered, for the Jews in a self-evidently valid manner, by the writings of the fourth-century sages. The rabbinic system, which laid stress on the priority of sanctification as the condition of salvation, on the dual media by which the Torah came forth from Sinai, on the messinaic dimension of Israel's everyday life, and on the permanence of Israel's position as God's first love—that system came to first articulate expression in the Talmud of the land of Israel and related writings—there, and not in the Mishnah and in its compansions. And the reason is clear: The system responded to a competing system, one heir of the ancient Israelite Scripture answering another heir and its claims. The siblings would struggle, like Esau and Jacob, for the common blessing. For the Jewish people, the system of the fourth-century sages would endure for millennia as self-evidently right and persuasive. The Judaism of the sages of the land of Israel who redacted the principal documents at hand therefore framed both a doctrine and an apologetic remarkably relevant to the issues presented to both Christianity and Judaism by the crisis of Christianity's worldly triumph.

The success of the Judaism shaped in this place, in this time, is clear. Refined and vastly restated in the Talmud of Babylonia, 200 years later, the system of Judaism worked out here and now enjoyed the status of self-evidence among Jews confronted with Christian governments and Christian populations over the next 1,500 years. So far as ideas matter in bonding a group—the success among the people of Israel in Europe, west and east alike, of the Judaism defined in the fourth-century writings of the sages of the land of Israel derives from the power and persuasive effect of the ideas of that Judaism. Coming to the surface in the writings of the age, particularly the Talmud of the land of Israel, Genesis Rabbah, and Leviticus Rabbah, that Judaism therefore secured for despairing Israel a long future of hope and confident endurance.

Why the common set of questions? Because, as we have noted, Jews and Christians alike believed in the Israelite Scriptures, and so understood that major turnings in history carried a message from God. The specification of the message at hand, of course, would produce long-term differences between the Christianity and the Judaism of the time. But the shared program brought the two religions into protracted confrontation on an intersecting set of questions. The struggle between the one and the other—a struggle that would continue until our own time—originated in the simple fact that, to begin with, both religions agreed on pretty much everything that mattered. They differed on little, and so made much of that little. Scripture taught them both that vast changes in the affairs of empires came about because of God's will. History proved principles of theology. In that same Torah, prophets promised the coming of the Messiah, who would bring salvation. Who was, and is, that Messiah, and how shall we know? And that same Torah addressed a particular people, Israel, promising that people the expression of God's favor and love. But who is Israel, and who is not Israel? So Scripture defined the categories that were shared in common. Scripture filled those categories with deep meaning. That is why it was possible for a kind of dialogue—made up, to be sure, of two monologues on the same topics—to commence. The dialogue continued for centuries because the conditions that had precipitated it, specifically the rise to political dominance of Christianity and the subordination of Judaism, remained constant for 1,500 years.

8. THE OUTCOME OF THE THIRD AND FINAL CRISIS: THE JUDAISM OF THE DUAL TORAH

The Judaic system that emerged from the encounter with triumphant Christiantiy in the fourth century chose as its generative symbol the Torah, meaning "the one whole Torah of Moses, our rabbi." Judaism is the religion of the Torah—that is, of instruction of God's will, revealed by God to Israel through Moses at Mount Sinai. The definition of the Torah of Sinai encompasses more than the Pentateuch, or even the entirety of the Hebrew Bible or "Old Testament." In this view of Judaism, the Torah came to Moses in two media—one in writing, that is, the Scriptures; the other in the medium of memory, or, orally. Thus Judaism comprises "the written Torah," and "the oral Torah." Judaism, therefore, is the religion of the dual Torah, and Judaists, people who believe in and practice Judaism, are those who accept and follow the religion of the "one whole Torah of Moses, our rabbi."

But what of the Judaism of the dual Torah in relationship to the life of Israel, the Jewish people, over time? That Judaism of the dual Torah endured and flourishes today as the religion of a small group of people. In the formulation of the sages of the Mishnah and the Talmud, the Torah confronted the challenge of the Cross of Christianity and, later, the sword and crescent of Islam as well. Within Israel, the Jewish people, the Torah triumphed. If we understand how rabbinic Judaism met the crisis of Christianity in its triumphant form, as ruler of the world from the time of Constantine in the fourth century, we also will grasp why Judaism as the rabbis defined it succeeded through history from that time to this. For when Christianity arose to define the civilization of the West, Judaism met and overcame it greatest crisis. And it held. As a result, Jews remained within the system. They continued for the entire history of the West to see the world through the world view and conduct life in accord with the way of life of the Torah as the rabbis explained it.

To state matters simply, with the triumph of Christianity through Constantine and his successors in the West, Christianity's explicit claims, now validated in world-shaking events of the age, demanded a reply. The sages of the Talmud provided it. At those very specific points at which the Christian challenge met head-on old Israel's world view, sages' doctrines responded. What did Israel's sages have to present as the Torah's answer to the cross? It was the Torah. This took three forms. The Torah was defined in the doctrine, first, of the status, as oral and memorized revelation, of the Mishnah, and, by implication, of other rabbinical writings.   The Torah, moreover, was presented as the encompassing symbol of Israel's salvation.   The Torah, finally, was embodied in the person of the Messiah, who, of course, would be a rabbi. The Torah in all three modes confronted the cross, with its doctrine of the triumphant Christ, Messiah and king, ruler now of earth as of heaven.

What was the outcome?   A stunning success for that society for which, to begin with, sages, and, in sages' view, God, cared so deeply: eternal Israel after the flesh.   For Judaism in the rabbis' statement did endure in the Christian West, imparting to Israel the secure conviction of constituting that Israel after the flesh to which the Torah continued to speak. How do we know sages' Judaism won? Because when, in turn, Islam gained its victory, Christianity throughout the Middle East and North Africa gave way.   But sages' Judaism in those same vast territories retained the loyalty and conviction of the people of the Torah.   The cross would rule only where the crescent and its sword did not.   But the Torah of Sinai everywhere and always sanctified Israel in time and promised secure salvation for eternity.   So Israel believed then, as faithful Israel, those Jews who also are Judaists, believes today.   The entire history of Judaism, from the formative age to the present, is contained within these simple propositions.

5

why judaism flourished

1. THE TORAH AND THE HEART: THE UNION OF PRIVATE ATTITUDE AND PUBLIC POLICY

In the definitive writings of Judaism, "our sages of blessed memory," who defined the Judaism of the dual Torah of Scripture and the Mishnah and explained and expanded both into the enduring religious world view and way of life for Israel, the Jewish people, taught what Israel is supposed to feel. And, as we shall see, the lessons that they taught proved remarkably congruent to the requirements of Israel's public policy. A defeated and subordinated nation made a virtue of humility, accommodation, acceptance, good will. As a result, peoples heartfelt feelings and the behavior required by their political circumstance exhibited a striking correspondence. That union between the inner life and the community's political situation gave to the Judaic system of the dual Torah enormous power both for the individual and for the nation. It imparted that same trait of self-evidence to the everyday life of the community that was enjoyed by the world view of the Judaic system as a whole.

The doctrine of virtue or appropriate attitude, moreover, persisted pretty much unchanged from the beginning of the writing of the rabbis' part of the Torah to the end of late antiquity and beyond. The repertoire of approved and disapproved feelings remained constant through the half millennium of the unfolding of the canon of Judaism from the Mishnah through the Talmud of Babylonia. The emotions encouraged by Judaism in its formative age, such as humility, forbearance, accommodation, and a spirit of conciliation, corresponded exactly to the political and social requirements of the Jews' condition in that time. The same repertoire of emotions persisted with no material change through the unfolding of the writings of the sages of that formative age because of the constancy of the Jews' political and social condition. The affective rules therefore formed an integral part of the way of life and world view put forward to make sense of the existence of a social group. In this way, the Judaic system of the dual Torah linked the deepest personal emotions to the cosmic fate and transcendent faith of that social group of which each individual formed a part. Emotions lay down judgments, they derive from rational cognition. The individual Israelite's innermost feelings, the microcosm, correspond to the public and historic condition of Israel, the macrocosm.

What Judaism teaches the private person to feel links her or his heart to what Judaism states about the condition of Israel in history and of God in the cosmos. All form one reality, in supernatural world and nature, in time and in eternity. In the innermost chambers of deepest feelings, the Israelite therefore lives out the public history and destiny of the people, Israel. The genius of Judaism, the reason for its resilience and endurance, lies in its power to teach Jews to feel in private what they also must think in public about the condition of both self and nation. The world within, and the world without are so bonded that one is never alone. The individual's life is lived always with the people.

The notion of the centrality of human feelings in the religious life of Israel presents no surprises. Scripture is explicit on both sides of the matter. The human being is commanded to love God. In the biblical biography of God, the tragic hero, God, will despair, love, hope, feel disappointment or exultation. The biblical record of God's feelings and God's will concerning the feelings of humanity—wanting human love, for example—leaves no room for doubt. Nor does the Judaism that emerges from late antiquity ignore or propose to obliterate the datum that *"the merciful God wants the heart."* The Judaism of the rabbis of late antiquity makes explicit that God always wants the heart. God commands that humanity love God with full heart, soul, mind, and might. That is the principal duty of humanity. So without the rabbinic canon and merely on the basis of knowledge that that canon begins in the written Torah of Scripture, the facts about the critical place of religious affections in Israel's religion would still prove clear and one-sided. Just as the sages framed matters of the written Torah in a fresh and original way, all the time stating in their own language and categories the teachings of the written Torah, so here too, we ask where, when, how, and for what purpose did rabbinical authorships draw upon the legacy of the written Torah in concluding, as they did, that "the Merciful God wants the heart."

2. EMOTION AS TRADITION

An epitome of the sages' treatment of emotions yields a simple result. Early, middle, and late, a single doctrine and program dictated what people had to say on how Israel should tame its heart. So far as the unfolding components of the canon of Judaism portray matters, emotions therefore form part of an iron tradition. That is, a repertoire of rules and relationships handed on from the past, always intact and ever unimpaired, governed the issue. The labor of the generations meant to receive the repertoire and recipe for feeling proved one of only preserving and maintaining that tradition. As successive documents came to closure, we see each one adding its improvements while leaving the structure basically the same. Like a cathedral that takes a thousand years to build but, through the construction and not only at the end, always looks uniform and antique, so the view of the affective life over centuries remained not only cogent but essentially uniform. A brief survey makes the matter clear.

While the Mishnah casually refers to emotions—tears of joy, tears of sorrow—where feelings matter, it is always in a public and communal context. For one important example, when there is an occasion of rejoicing, one form of joy is not to be confused with some other, nor one context of sorrow with another. Accordingly, marriages are not to be held on festivals (M. M.Q. 1:7). Likewise mourning is not to take place then (M. M.Q. 1:5, 3:7–9). When emotions play a role, it is because of the affairs of the community at large—rejoicing on a festival, or mourning on a fast day (M. Suk. 5:1–4), for example. Emotions are to be kept in hand, as in the case of the relatives of the executed felon (M. San. 6:6). If I had to specify the single underlying principle affecting all forms of emotion, for the Mishnah it is that feelings must be kept under control, never fully expressed without reasoning about the appropriate context. Emotions must always lay down judgments. We see in most of those cases in which emotions play a systemic role, and not merely a tangential one, that the basic principle is the same. We can, and must, so frame our feelings as to accord with the appropriate rule. In only one case does emotion play a decisive role in settling an issue, and that has to do with whether or not a farmer was happy that water came upon his produce or grain. That case underscores the conclusion just now drawn. If one feels a particular sentiment, it is a matter of judgment, and it therefore invokes the law's penalties. In this system, therefor, emotions are treated not as spontaneous, but as significant aspects of one's judgment.

Tractate Avot presents the single most comprehensive account of religious affections. The reason is that, in that document above all, how we feel defines a critical aspect of virtue. The issue proves central, not peripheral. The doctrine emerges fully exposed. A simple catalogue of permissible feelings comprises humility, generosity, self-abnegation, love, conciliation, and eagerness to please. A list of impermissible emotions includes envy, ambition, jealousy, arrogance, unwavering adherence to one's opinion, self-centeredness, grudgingness, and vengefulness. People should aim at eliciting from others acceptance and good will and should avoid confrontation, rejection, and humiliation of the other. This they do through conciliation and through relinquishing their own claims and rights. So both catalogues form a harmonious and uniform whole, aiming at the cultivation of the humble and malleable person, one who accepts everything and resents nothing. True, these virtues, in this tractate as in the system as a whole, derive from knowledge of what really counts, which is what God wants. But God favors those who please others. The virtues appreciated by human beings prove identical to the ones to which God responds. And what single virtue of the heart encompasses the rest? Restraint, the source of self-abnegation and humility, serves as the anecdote for ambition, vengefulness, and, above all, arrogance. It is restraint of one's own interest that enables one to deal generously with others, humility about oneself that generates a liberal spirit towards others.

So the emotions prescribed in tractate Avot turn out to provide variations of a single feeling, which is the sentiment of the disciplined heart, whatever affective form it may take. And where does the heart learn its lessons, if not in relationship to God? "Make his wishes yours, so that he will make your wishes his" (Avot 2:4). Applied to relationships between human beings, this inner discipline of the emotional life will yield exactly those virtues of conciliation and self-abnegation, humility and generosity of spirit, that the framers of tractate Avot spell out in one example after another. Imputing to Heaven exactly those responses felt on earth—that is, "Anyone from whom people take pleasure, God takes pleasure" (Avot 3:10)—makes the point at the most general level.

When the authors or compilers of the Tosefta finished their labor of amplification and complement, they had succeeded in adding only a few fresh and important developments of established themes. What is striking is, first, the stress upon the communal stake in the individual's emotional life. Still more striking is the Tosefta's authors' explicit effort to invoke an exact correspondence between public and private feelings. In both realms emotions are to be tamed, kept in hand and within accepted proportions. Public sanctions for inappropriate, or disproportionate, emotions entail feelings, for instance, of shame. It need hardly be added that feeling shame for improper feelings once again underscores the social, judgmental character of those feelings. Shame is public; guilt, private. People are responsible for how they feel as much as for how, in word or deed, they express feeling. Hence an appropriate penalty derives from the same aspect of social life—that is, affective life.

I cannot imagine a more stunning tribute to the power of feeling than the allegation, surfacing in the Tosefta, that the Temple was destroyed because of vain hatred. That sort of hatred, self-serving and arrogant, stands against the feelings of love that characterize God's relationship to Israel. Accordingly, it was improper affections that destroyed the relationship embodied in the Temple cult of old. Given the critical importance accorded to the Temple cult, sages could not have made more vivid their view that a private person's feelings shape the public destiny of the entire nation. So the issues came to expression in high stakes. But the basic position of the authors of the Mishnah, inclusive of their first apologists in Avot, seems entirely consistent. What Tosefta's authors accomplished is precisely what they claimed, which was to amplify, supplement, and complement established principles and positions.

Emotions not taken up earlier in the pages of the Yerushalmi did not come under discussion. Principles introduced earlier enjoyed restatement and extensive exemplification. Some principles of proper feelings might even generate secondary developments of one kind or another. But nothing not present at the outset drew sustained attention later. The system proved essentially complete in the earliest statement of its main points. Everything that followed for 400 years served to reenforce and restate what to begin with had emerged loud and clear. What, then, do the authors or compilers of the Yerushalmi contribute? Temper marks the ignorant person; restraint and serenity, the learned one. In general, we note, where the Mishnah introduces into its system issues of the affective life, the Yerushalmi's authors and compilers will take up those issues. But they rarely create them on their own and never say much new about those they do treat. What we find is instruction to respect public opinion and cultivate social harmony. What is most interesting in the Yerushalmi is the recognition that there are rules descriptive of feelings, as much as of other facts of life. These rules tell us how to dispose of cases in which feelings make a difference. The fact is, therefore, that the effects of emotions, as much as of opinions or deeds, come within the rule of law. It must follow, in the view of sages, that affective life once more proves an aspect of society. People are assumed to frame emotions, as much as opinions, in line with common and shared judgments. In no way do emotions form a special classification, one expressive of what is private, spontaneous, individual, and beyond the law and reason.

The Bavli—that is, the Talmud of Babylonia, a document, much like the Yerushalmi, produced ca. A.D. 600—carried forward with little change the now-traditional program of emotions, listing the same ones catalogued earlier and no new ones. The authors said about those feelings what had been said earlier. A leader must be someone acceptable to the community. God then accepts him too. People should be ready to give up quarrels and forgive. The correspondence of social and personal virtues reaches explicit statement. The community must forebear, the individual must forgive. Communal tolerance for causeless hatred destroyed the Temple; individual vendettas yield miscarriages. The two coincide. In both cases people nurture feelings that express arrogance. Arrogance is what permits the individual to express emotions without discipline, and arrogance is what leads the community to undertake what it cannot accomplish.

A fresh emphasis portrayed in the Bavli favored mourning and disapproved of rejoicing. We can hardly maintain that that view came to expression only in the latest stages in the formation of the canon. The contrary is the case. The point remains consistent throughout. Excessive levity marks arrogance; deep mourning characterizes humility. So many things come down to one thing. The nurture of an attitude of mourning should mark both the individual and the community, both in mourning for the Temple, but also mourning for the condition of nature, including the human condition, signified in the Temple's destruction.

A mark of humility is humble acceptance of suffering. This carried forward the established view that suffering now produces joy later. The ruin of the Temple, for example, served as a guarantee that just as the prophetic warnings came to realization, so too would prophetic promises of restoration and redemption. In the realm of feelings, the union of opposites came about through the same mode of thought. Hence God's love comes to fulfillment in human suffering, and one who joyfully accepts humiliation or suffering will enjoy the appropriate divine response of love.

Another point at which the authors of the Bavli introduce a statement developing a familiar view derives from the interpretation of how to love one's neighbor. It is by imposing upon one's neighbor the norms of the community, rebuking the other for violating accepted practice. The emotion of love thus takes on concrete social value in reenforcing the norms of the community. Since the verse at hand invites exactly that interpretation, we can hardly regard as innovative the Bavli's paragraph on the subject. Stories about sages rang the changes on the themes of humility, resignation, restraint, and perpetual good will. A boastful sage loses his wisdom; a humble one retains it. Since it is wisdom about which a sage boasts, the matching of apposites conforms to the familiar mode of thought.

The strikingly fresh medium for traditional doctrines in the Bavli takes the form of prayers composed by sages. Here the values of the system came to eloquent expression. Sages prayed that their souls may be as dust for everyone to tread upon. They asked for humility in spirit, congenial colleagues, good will, good impulses. They asked God to be cognizant of their humiliation, to spare them from disgrace. The familiar affective virtues and sins, self-abnegation as against arrogance, made their appearance in liturgical form as well. Another noteworthy type of material, also not new, in which the pages of the Bavli prove rich,

Adam and Eve from Cemetery of Peter and Marcellinus,
Rome. (Vatican Department of Antiquities, Vatican City.)

portrayed the deaths of sages. One dominant motif is uncertainty in the face of death, a sign of humility and self-abnegation.

The basic motif—theological as much as affective—encompassing all materials is simple. Israel is estranged from God and therefore should exhibit the traits of humility and uncertainty, acceptance and conciliation. When God recognizes in Israel's heart, as much as in the nation's deeds and deliberation, the proper feelings, God will respond by ending that estrangement which marks the present age. So the single word encompassing the entire affective doctrine of the canon of Judaism is *alienation*. No contemporary who has survived the Holocaust can miss the psychological depth of the system which joins the human condition to the fate of the nation and the world, and links the whole to the broken heart of God.

We therefore find ourselves with the idea that if one wants something, one should aspire to its opposite. Things are never what they seem. To be rich, accept what you have. To be powerful, conciliate your enemy. To be endowed with public recognition in which to take pride, express humility. So, too, the doctrine of the emotional life expressed in law, scriptural interpretation, and tales of sages alike turns out to be uniform and simple. Emotions well up uncontrolled and spontaneous. Anger, vengeance, pride, arrogance—these humans feel by nature. So feelings, as much as affirmations and actions, must become what by nature they are not. If one wants riches, seek the opposite. If one wants honor, pursue the opposite. But how do you seek the opposite of wealth? It is by accepting what you have. And how pursue humility, if not by doing nothing to aggrandize oneself? So the life of the emotions, in conformity to the life of reflection and of concrete deed, will consist in the transformation of what things *seem* into what they *ought* to be. No contemporary psychologists or philosophy can fail to miss the point. Here we have an example of the view—whether validated by the facts of nature or not—that emotions constitute constructs, and feelings lay down judgments. So the heart belongs, together with the mind, to the human being's power to form reasoned viewpoints. Coming from sages, intellectuals to their core, such an opinion surely coheres with the context and circumstance of those who hold it.

3. SEEING THINGS AS IF THEY WERE NOT WHAT THEY SEEM

This theory of the emotional life, persistent through the unfolding of the canonical documents of Judaism, fits into a larger way of viewing the world. How shall we describe this mode of thought? We might call it an *as-if* way of seeing things. That is to say, it is *as if* a common object or symbol represented an uncommon one. Nothing says what it means. Everything important speaks elliptically and symbolically. All statements carry deeper meaning, which inheres in other statements altogether. So, too, each emotion bears a negative and a positive charge, as each matches and balances the other: humility, arrogance, love, hate. If natural to the heart is a negative emotion, then one has the power to sanctify that negative, sinful feeling and turn it into a positive, holy emotion. Ambition, then, must be tamed, so transformed into humility; hatred and vengeance must change into love and acceptance.

What we see in the surveyed doctrine of emotions is an application of a large-scale, encompassing exercise in analogical thinking—something is like something else, stands for, evokes, or symbolizes that which is quite outside itself. It may be the opposite of something else, in which case it conforms to the exact opposite of the rules that govern that something else. The reasoning is analogical or it is contrastive, and the fundamental logic is taxonomic. The taxonomy rests on those comparisons and contrasts we should call metonymic and parabolic. In that case, what lies on the surface misleads. What lies beneath or beyond the surface—there is the true reality. How shall we characterize people who see things this way? They constitute the opposite of ones who call a thing as it is. They have become accustomed to perceiving more—or less—than is at hand. Perhaps that is a natural mode of thought for the Jews of this period (and not then alone), so long used to calling themselves God's first love, yet now seeing others with greater worldly reason claiming that same advantaged relationship. Not in mind only, but still more, in the politics of the world, the people that remembered its origins along with the very creation of the world and founding of humanity, that recalled how it alone served, and serves, the one and only God, for hundreds of years had confronted a quite different existence.

The radical disjuncture between the way things were and the way Scripture said things were supposed to be (and would some day become) surely imposed on Jews an unbearable tension. It was one thing for the slave born to slavery to endure. It was another for the free man sold into slavery to accept that same condition. The vanquished people, the broken-hearted nation that had in 586 and again in 70 lost its city and its Temple, that had, moreover, in the fourth century produced another nation from its midst to take over its Scripture and much else, could not bear too much reality. That defeated people, in its intellectuals, as represented in the sources we have surveyed, then found refuge in a mode of thought that trained vision to see things other than as the eyes perceived them. Among the diverse ways by which the weak and subordinated accommodate to their circumstance, the one of iron-willed pretense in life is most likely to yield the mode of thought at hand: Things never are, because they cannot be, what they seem. The uniform tradition on emotions persisted intact because the social realities of Israel's life proved permanent, until, in our own time, they changed. I need not repeat the simple observation that the affective program of the canon, early, middle, and late, fits tightly in every detail with this doctrine of an ontological teleology in eschatological disguise. Israel is to tame its heart so that it will feel that same humility within that Israel's world view and way of living demand in life at large. Submit, accept, conciliate, stay cool in emotion as much as in attitude, inside and outside—and the Messiah will come.

4. FORBEARANCE OR AGGRESSION

The profound program of emotions, the sages' statement of how people should feel and why they should take charge of their emotions, remained quite constant. No one can imagine that Jews in their hearts felt the way sages said they should. The repertoire of permissible and forbidden feelings can hardly have defined the broad range of actual emotions, whether private or social, of the community of Israel. In fact, we have no evidence about how people really felt. We see only a picture of what sages thought they should, and should not, feel. Writings that reveal stunning shifts in doctrine, teleology, and hermeneutical method lay form from beginning to end the one picture of the ideal Israelite. It is someone who accepts, forgives, conciliates, makes the soul "like dirt beneath other peoples' feet." An age of total war, such as our own, may find it difficult to appreciate the virtues of submission to the will of others, first one's neighbors in the community, second, the world beyond. These kinds of people bear such uncomplimentary sobriquets as milk-toast, "wimp," or merely coward.   Ours is an age that admires the strong-minded individual, the uncompromising hero, the warrior, whether on the battlefield or in the intellect.

Why sages counseled a different kind of courage we need hardly ask. Given the situation of Israel, vanquished on the battlefield, broken in the turning of history's wheel, we need hardly wonder why wise men advised conciliation and acceptance. Exalting humility made sense, there being little choice. Whether or not these virtues found advocates in other contexts for other reasons, in the circumstance of the vanquished nation, for the people of broken heart, the policy of forbearance proved instrumental, entirely appropriate to both the politics and social condition at hand. If Israel had produced a battlefield hero, the nation could not give him an army. If Jewry cultivated the strong-minded individual, it sentenced such a person to a useless life of ineffective protest. The nation required not strong-minded leadership but consensus. The social virtues of conciliation, moreover, reenforced the bonds that joined the nation lacking frontiers, the people without a politics of its own; for all there was to hold Israel together to sustain its life as a society, would have to come forth out of sources of inner strength. Bonding emerged mainly from within. So consensus, conciliation, self-abnegation, and humility, the search for acceptance without the group—these in the literary culture at hand defined appropriate emotions because they dictated wise policy and shrewd politics.

Israel could survive only on the sufferance of others. Israel would therefore nurture not merely policies of subordination and acceptance of diminished status among nations; Israel also would develop, in its own heart, the requisite emotional structure. The composition of individuals' hearts would then comprise the counterpart virtues. A policy of acceptance of the rule of others dictated affections of conciliation to the will of others. A defeated people meant to endure defeat would have to get along by going along. How to persuade each Jew to accept what all Jews had to do to endure? Persuade the heart, not only the mind. Then each one privately would feel what everyone publicly had, in any case, to think. This would account for the persistence of sages' wise teachings on temper, their sagacious counsel on conciliating others and seeking the approval of the group. Society, in the canonical writings, set the style for the self's deepest sentiments. So the approved feelings retained approval for so long because emotions, in the thought of the sages of the canon at hand, followed rules. Feelings laid down judgments. Affections therefore constituted not mindless effusions but deliberate constructions. Whether or not the facts then conformed to sages' view (or now with the mind of psychology, philosophy, and anthropology) we do not know. But the sages' view did penetrate deeply into what had to be. And that is so, whether or not what had to be would ever correspond with what was.

The sages of the formative age of Judaism proposed for Israel the formation of exactly that type of personality which could, and did, endure the condition and circumstance of the Exile. In rejecting the heroic model of Bar Kokhba for the Messiah-general's arrogance and affirming the very opposite, the sages who defined Judaism in the first seven centuries A.D., and whose heirs expanded and developed the system they had defined, made the right choice. Life in exile, viewed as living in other peoples' countries and not in their own land, meant for Israel, as Judaism conceived Israel, a long span of endurance, a test of patience to end only with the end of time. That life in exile required Israel to live in accord with the will of others. Under such circumstances the virtues of the independent citizen—sharing command of affairs of state, the gifts of innovation, initiative, independence of mind—proved beside the point. From the end of the second revolt against Rome in 135 to the creation of the State of Israel in 1948, Israel, the Jewish people, faced a different task.

The human condition of Israel therefore defined a different heroism, one filled with patience, humiliation, self-abnegation. To turn survival into endurance, pariah status into an exercise in Godly living, the sages' affective program served full well. Israel's hero saw power in submission, wealth in the gift of gratitude, wisdom in the confession of ignorance. Like the cross, ultimate degradation was made to stand for ultimate power. Like Jesus on the cross, so Israel in exile served God through suffering. True, the cross would represent a scandal to the nations and foolishness to some Jews. But Israel's own version of the doctrine at hand endured and defined the nation's singular and astonishing resilience, for Israel did endure and endures today.

If, then, as a matter of public policy, the nurture of the personality of the Israelite as one of forbearance and self-abnegation proved right, within the community too the rabbis were not wrong. The Jewish people rarely enjoyed instruments of civil coercion capable of preserving social order and coherence. Governments at best afforded Jews limited rights over their own affairs. When, at the start of the fifth century, the Christian Roman government ended the existence of the patriarchate of the Jews of the land of Israel, people can well have recognized the parlous condition of whatever Jewish authorities might ever run things. A government in charge of itself and its subjects, a territorial community routinely able to force individuals to pay taxes and otherwise conform where necessary—these political facts of normality rarely marked the condition of Israel between 429 and 1948. What was left was another kind of power, civil obedience generated by force from within. The stress on pleasing others and conforming to the will of the group, so characteristic of sayings of sages, the emphasis that God likes people whom people like—these substitutes for the civil power of political coercion imparted to the community of Israel a different power of authority.

Both sources of power, the one in relationship to the public world beyond, the other in respect to the social world within, in the sages' rules gained force through the primal energy of emotion. Enough has been said to require little explication of that fact. A system that made humility a mark of strength and a mode of gaining God's approval, a social policy that imputed ultimate virtue to feelings of conciliation, restraint, and conformity to social norms had no need of the armies and police that it lacked. The heart would serve as the best defense, inner affections as the police who are always there when needed. The remarkable inner discipline of Israel through its exacting condition in history from the beginnings of the sages' system to today began in those feelings that laid down judgments, that construction of affections, coherent with beliefs and behavior, that met the match of misery with grandeur of soul. So the vanquished nation every day would overcome the one-time victors. Israel's victory would come through the triumph of the broken heart, now mended with the remedy of moderated emotion. That union of private feeling and public policy imparted to the Judaic system of the dual Torah its power, its status of self-evidence, for the long centuries during which Israel's condition persisted in the definition imparted by the events of the third crisis in the formation of Judaism.

6

the judaism of the dual torah in its formative age

1. THE ECOLOGY OF JUDAISM: A REPRISE

Judaism reached its complete statement in response to the crisis of Christian rule of the Roman Empire, and it flourished in the West so long as Christianity defined the politics of the state and of culture.   The ecological framework in which Judaism came into being, therefore, finds definition in the setting of the counterpart system of Christianity. Christian theologians and Judaic sages actually entered a confrontation on the same issues, defined in the same way, not in the first century but in the fourth.   And the reason for the confrontation was political and theological. By contrast, nothing prior to Constantine's time required a confrontation of any sort. In the first and early second centuries, moreover, the two groups did not talk about the same thing to begin with.

As we have noted, the paramount, if not sole, element of the heritage of ancient Israel to shape the later formative history of Judaism derived from the priestly conception that God wants Israel to live a holy life.   The Five Books of Moses, read in the synagogue every Sabbath morning, said precisely that as a principal point of emphasis. On the Christian side, one powerful motif derived from the prophetic and apocalyptic heritage of ancient Israel, with its promise that history had a beginning, middle, and end, that events mattered, and that, at the end of time, the Messiah would come and save the world. An important part of the early Church saw the primary classification of Jesus as the Christ, the Messiah. It follows that the definitive category for the builders of Judaism was sanctification, and, for the builders of Christianity, salvation. Each party in due course would absorb the other category into its system; as we have seen, sages did so by making sanctification the condition of salvation. But until the political revolution in the religious life of the two groups brought on by Constantine's government, neither party found it necessary to confront in a sharp and clear way the claims of the other.

In particular, Christians and Jews in the first century did not argue with one another. Each set of groups—the family of Christianities, the family of Judaisms—went its way, focusing upon its own program. When Christianity came into being, in the first century, one important strand of the Christian movement stressed issues of salvation, in the Gospels maintaining that Jesus was, and is, Christ, come to save the world and radically change history. At that same time, an important group within the diverse Judaic systems of the age, the Pharisees, who left an important legacy to the sages of the Mishnah, emphasized issues of sanctification, maintaining that the task of Israel is to attain that holiness of which the Temple was a singular embodiment. When, in the Gospels, we find the record of the Church placing Jesus into opposition with the Pharisees, we witness the confrontation of different people talking about different things to different people. But in the fourth century, by contrast, different people addressing different groups really did talk about exactly the same things. That is the point, therefore, at which the Judaic and Christian conflict reached the form in which, for fifteen hundred years, it would come to intellectual expression. People really did differ about the same issues. These issues—the meaning of history, the identity of the Messiah, and the definition of Israel, or of God's instrument for embodying in a social group God's will—would define the foundations of the dispute from then on. So we find for the first time a genuine confrontation: people differing about a shared agendum in exactly the same terms.

What about the moment at which Judaism in important documents did deal in a significant way with the existence of Christianity? It was in the fourth century. The issues presented to Jews by the triumph of Christianity inform the documents shaped in the Land of Israel in the period of that triumph. The three largest writings, the great commentary to Genesis called Genesis Rabbah, the Talmud of the Land of Israel, and the commentary to Leviticus called Leviticus Rabbah, as we have seen, systematically work out important components of the intellectual program of the age: the meaning of history, the Messianic crisis, the identification of Israel. These issues do not play an important role in prior components of the unfolding canon of Judaism—in particular, the

Mishnah and the Tosefta and Sifré to Numbers, all of which, it is generally held, reached closure before the fourth century. So the contrast in each case suggests that a new set of issues has compelled attention, in documents of the age, to questions neglected in earlier compilations. And these issues proved pressing for other intellectuals, the Christian ones, of the same period. On the basis of the confluence of discourse on precisely the same questions, in precisely the same terms, I think we may fairly argue that the two groups talked about the same things at the same time and so engaged in whatever genuine debate proved possible. So, in all, the fourth century in many ways marks the point of intersection of trajectories of the history of the two religions, Judaic and Christian.

In developing as it did in the fourth century, the religious world of the West—the world of Judaism and Christianity—saw the two systems change places. The one nurtured in active politics became apolitical, leaving the world of history. The other, born on the fringes of empire, took control of the government of the world. Judaism, prepared for one politics, now addressed a people without politics, and Christianity, born among the weak and subjugated, turned out to rule the world. The ecology of each drastically shifted. All Christianities—the set of related religious systems, world views, ways of life, addressed to a distinctive social group that took shape around the crucifixion and resurrection of Christ—took for granted a single fact. This world lay in the charge of others, not Christians. The Christian's duty in this life directed attention to the next. Imitating Christ for some required martyrdom, for others acts of eleemosynary kindness. For none could imagine what would actually take place: a Rome become Christian. The corresponding Judaisms—that is, the set of intersecting religious systems formed within Israel, the Jewish people, long centuries before the advent of the Christianities of the formative centuries—shared the opposite premise. It was that Israel constituted a this-worldly and political entity, whatever other ranges of existence beyond and within may have defined as vistas for consideration. So Christianities and Judaisms concurred, each on its own side of the line of politics and government, history and power: The one made no provision for rule, the other took it for granted. In the fourth century the two sets of systems changed positions. And, for the West, that has made all the difference.

2. THE SYMBOL OF "TORAH"

Judaism as we know it at the end of late antiquity reached its now familiar definition when "the Torah" lost its capital letter and definite article and ultimately became "torah." What for nearly a millennium had been a particular scroll or book thus came to serve as a symbol of an entire system. When a rabbi spoke of *torah*, he no longer meant only a particular object, a scroll and its contents. Now he used the word to encompass a distinctive and well-defined world view and way of life. Torah had come to stand for something one does. Knowledge of the Torah promised not merely information about what people were supposed to do, but ultimate redemption or salvation.

The Torah of Moses clearly occupied a critical place in all systems of Judaism from the closure of the Torah book, the Pentateuch, in the time of Ezra onward. But in late antiquity, for one group alone the book developed into an abstract and encompassing symbol, so that in the Judaism that took shape in the formative age, the first seven centuries A.D., everything was contained in that one thing. When we speak of *torah*, in rabbinical literature of late antiquity, we no longer denote a particular book, on the one side, or the contents of such a book, on the other. Instead, we connote a broad range of clearly distinct categories of noun and verb, concrete fact and abstract relationship alike. Torah stands for a kind of human being. It connotes a social status and a sort of social group. It refers to a type of social relationship. It further denotes a legal status and differentiates among legal norms. As symbolic abstraction, the word encompasses things and persons, actions and status, points of social differentiation and legal and normative standing, as well as "revealed truth." In all, the main points of insistence of the whole of Israel's life and history come to full symbolic expression in that single word. If people wanted to explain how they would be saved, they would use the word *Torah*. If they wished to sort out their parlous relationships with gentiles, they would use the word *Torah*. Torah stood for salvation and accounted for Israel's this-worldly condition and the hope, for both individual and national alike, of life in the world to come. For the kind of Judaism under discussion, therefore, the word *Torah* stood for everything. The Torah symbolized the whole, at once and entire. When, therefore, we wish to describe the unfolding of the definitive doctrine of Judaism in its formative period, the first exercise consists in paying close attention to the meanings imputed to a single word.

Every detail of the religious system at hand exhibits essentially the same point of insistence, captured in the simple notion of the Torah as the generative symbol, the total, exhaustive expression of the system as a whole. That is why the definitive ritual of the Judaism under study consisted in studying the Torah as the generative symbol, the total, exhaustive expression of the system as a whole. That is why the definitive myth explained that one who studied Torah would become holy, like Moses, "our rabbi," and like God, in whose image humanity was made and whose Torah provided the plan and the model for what God wanted of that humanity. As for Christians, it was in Christ God made flesh, so the framers of the system of Judaism at hand found in the Torah that image of God to which Israel should aspire, and to which the sage in fact conformed.

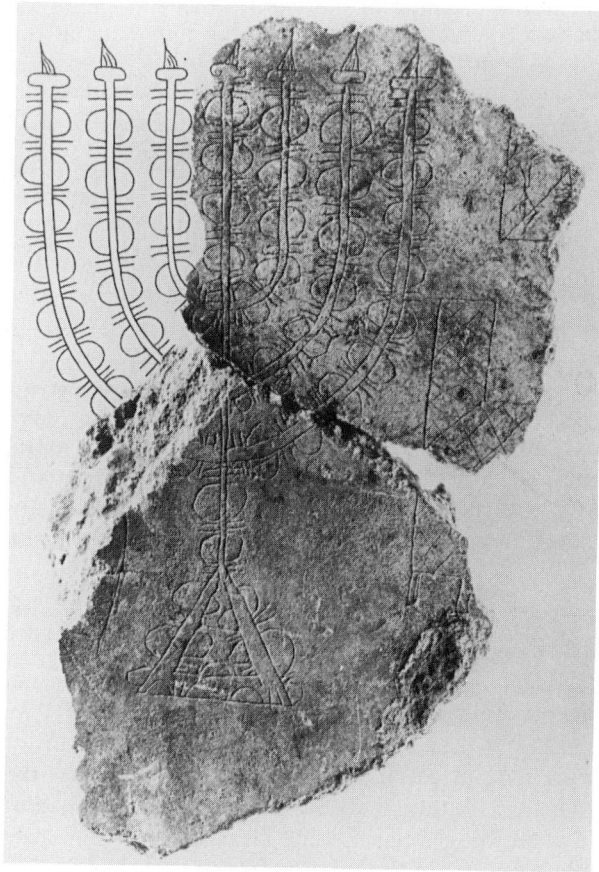

Earliest depiction of the menorah, found by an archaeological team of the Hebrew University. (Courtesy of the Consulate General of Israel, New York.)

The meaning of the several uses of the Torah, then, requires only brief explanation.

1. When the Torah refers to a particular thing, it is to a scroll containing divinely revealed words.

2. The Torah may further refer to revelation, not as an object but as a corpus of doctrine.

3. When one "does Torah," the disciple "studies" or "learns," and the master "teaches," Torah. Hence while the word *Torah* never appears as a verb, it does refer to an act.

4. The word also bears a quite separate sense: *torah* as category or classification or corpus of rules. For example, "the torah of driving a car" is a usage entirely acceptable to some documents. This generic usage of the word does occur.

5. The word *Torah* very commonly refers to a status, distinct from and above another status, as "teachings of Torah" as against "teachings of scribes." For the two Talmuds, that distinction is absolutely critical to the entire hermeneutic enterprise. But it is important even in the Mishnah.

6. Obviously, no account of the meaning of the word *Torah* can ignore the distinction between the two Torahs, written and oral. It is important only in the secondary stages of the formation of the literature.

7. Finally, the word *Torah* refers to a source of salvation, often fully worked out in stories about how the individual and the nation will be saved through Torah. In general, the sense of the word *salvation* is not complicated. It is simply salvation in the way in which Deuteronomy and the Deuteronomic historians understand it: Kings who do what God wants win battles; those who do not, lose. So, too, people who study and do Torah are saved from sickness and death, and the way Israel can save itself from its condition of degradation also is through Torah.

3. THE MISHNAH AND THE CONCEPTION OF THE ORAL TORAH

To understand the most important symbolic trait of Judaism in its formative age, the development of the notion of a dual Torah, written and oral, we have first of all to return to the tractate Avot and its picture of the chain of tradition that led from Sinai to the authorities of the Mishnah:

> Moses received Torah at Sinai and handed it on to Joshua, Joshua to elders, and elders to prophets. And prophets handed it on to the men of the great assembly. They said three things: Be prudent in judgment. Raise up many disciples. Make a fence for the Torah.

What we see is the claim that at Sinai Moses received not only the Scriptures—the Torah everyone knew, that is, the written Torah—but something beyond. This something falls into the classification of Torah, revelation, but is not contained within the written Torah. We know that because the sayings assigned to the authorities in the chain of tradition cite not Scripture, but wisdom of another source. In time to come, this other source of *torah* would be understood as a memorized Torah—that is, the other half of the "one whole Torah of Moses, our rabbi." Finally, the doctrine of the dual Torah would emerge whole and complete, encompassing all of the sayings of the recognized sages, not only in ancient times but also in the present day. Then the Judaic system of the dual Torah would encompass not revelation out of the past—"tradition"—but the revelation consisting in the Torah teaching of today's sage. That teaching did not derive from the past, from "tradition," and Judaism never constituted a traditional religion. That teaching derived from today's sage, teaching Torah. At that point Judaism as a living religion of everyday revelation from God to Israel would attain its full and complete definition: the religion of God's revelation, Torah in the here and now.

In the beginning, however, as we have already noted, the issue was joined with reference to the Mishnah in particular. The question of the standing and status of the Mishnah invoked the conception of revelation of an other-than-written character from Sinai. Upon its closure, the Mishnah gained an exalted political status as the constitution of Jewish government of the Land of Israel. Accordingly, the clerks who knew and applied its law had to explain the standing of that law—that is, its relationship to the law of the Torah. But the Mishnah provided no account of itself. Unlike biblical law codes, the Mishnah begins with no myth of its own origin. It ends with no doxology. Discourse commences in the middle of things and ends abruptly. What follows from such laconic mumbling is that the exact status of the document required definition entirely outside the framework of the document itself. The framers of the Mishnah gave no hint of the nature of their book, so the Mishnah reached the political world of Israel without a trace of self-conscious explanation or any theory of validation.

The one thing that is clear, alas, is negative. The framers of the Mishnah nowhere claimed, implicitly or explicitly, that what they have written forms part of the Torah, enjoys the status of God's revelation to Moses at Sinai, or even systematically carries forward secondary exposition and application of what Moses wrote down in the wilderness. Later, I think 200 years beyond the closure of the Mishnah, the need to explain the standing and origin of the Mishnah led some to posit two things. First, God's revelation of the Torah at Sinai encompassed the Mishnah as much as Scripture. Second, the Mishnah was handed on through oral formulation and oral transmission from Sinai to the framers of the document as we have it. These two convictions, fully exposed in the ninth-century letter of Sherira, an important rabbinical authority in Babylonia, in fact emerge from the references of both Talmuds to the dual Torah. One part is in writing, the other was oral and now is in the Mishnah.

As for the Mishnah itself, however, it contains not a hint that anyone has heard any such tale. The earliest apologists for the Mishnah, represented in Avot and the Tosefta alike, know nothing of the fully realized myth of the dual Torah of Sinai. It may be that the authors of those documents stood too close to the Mishnah to see the Mishnah's standing as a problem or to recognize the task of accounting for its origins. Certainly they never refer to the Mishnah as something out there, nor speak of the document as autonomous and complete. Only the two Talmuds reveal that conception—alongside their mythic explanation of where the document came from and why it should be obeyed. So the Yerushalmi marks the change. In any event, the absence of explicit expression of such a claim in behalf of the Mishnah requires little specification. It is just not there.

But the absence of an implicit claim demands explanation. When ancient Jews wanted to gain for their writings the status of revelation, of torah, or at least to link what they thought to what the Torah had said, they could do one of four things. They could sign the name of a holy man of old—for instance, Adam, Enoch, Ezra. They could imitate the Hebrew style of Scripture. They could claim that God had spoken to them. They could, at the very least, cite a verse of Scripture and impute to the cited passage their own opinion. These four methods—pseudepigraphy, stylistic imitation (hence, forgery), claim of direct revelation from God, and eisegesis—found no favor with the Mishnah's framers. To the contrary, they signed no name to their book. Their Hebrew was new in its syntax and morphology, completely unlike that of the Mosaic writings of the Pentateuch. They never claimed that God had anything to do with their opinions. They rarely cited a verse of Scripture as authority. It follows that, whatever the authors of the Mishnah said about their document, the implicit character of the book tells us that they did not claim God had dictated or even approved what they had to say. Why not? The framers simply ignored all the validating conventions of the world in which they lived. And, as I said, they failed to make explicit use of any others.

It follows that we do not know whether the Mishnah was supposed to be part of the Torah or to enjoy a clearly defined relationship to the existing Torah. We also do not know what else, if not the Torah, was meant to endow the Mishnah's laws with heavenly sanction. To state matters simply, we do not know what the framers of the Mishnah said they had made, nor do we know what the people who received and were supposed to obey the Mishnah thought they possessed.

A survey of the uses of the word *Torah* in the Mishnah, to be sure, provides us with an account of what the framers of the Mishnah, founders of what would emerge as rabbinic Judaism, understood by that term. But it will not tell us how they related their own ideas to the Torah, nor shall we find a trace of evidence of that fully articulated way of life—the use of the word Torah to categorize and classify persons, places, things, relationships, all manner of abstractions—that we find fully exposed in some later redacted writings. True, the Mishnah places a high value upon studying the Torah and upon the status of the sage. The following characteristic sayings speaks of a *mamzer*—that is, one born of parents who had no legal right to wed, a serious disability in a caste society such as the one at hand—as against an *am haares*, understood here simply as an ignorant person. A "*mamzer*-disciple of a sage takes priority over a high-priest *am haares*," as at M. Hor. 3:8. But that judgment, distinctive though it is, cannot settle the question. All it shows is that the Mishnah pays due honor to the sage. But if the Mishnah does not claim to constitute part of the Torah, then what makes a sage a sage is not mastery of the Mishnah in particular. What we have in hand merely continues the established and familiar position of the wisdom writers of old. Wisdom is important. Knowledge of the Torah is definitive. But to maintain that position, one need hardly profess the fully articulated Torah myth of rabbinic Judaism. Proof of that fact, after all, is the character of the entire wisdom literature prior to the Mishnah itself.

So the issue is clearly drawn. It is not whether we find in the Mishnah exaggerated claims about the priority of the disciple of a sage. We do find such claims. The issue is whether we find in the Mishnah the assertion that whatever the sage has on the authority of his master goes back to Sinai. We seek a definitive view that what the sage says falls into the classification of Torah, just as what Scripture says constitutes Torah from God to Moses. That is what distinguishes wisdom from the Torah as it emerges in the context of rabbinic Judaism. To state the outcome in advance: We do not find the Torah in the Mishnah, and the Mishnah is not part of the Torah.

When the authors of the Mishnah surveyed the landscape of Israelite writings down to their own time, they saw only Sinai—that is, what we now know as Scripture. Based on the documents they cite or mention, we can say with certainty that they knew the pentateuchal law. We may take for granted that they accepted as divine revelation also the Prophets and the Writings, to which they occasionally make reference. That they regarded as a single composition—that is, as revelation—the Torah, Prophets, and Writings appears from their references to the Torah as a specific "book," and to a Torah scroll. Accordingly, one important meaning associated with the word *Torah* was concrete in the extreme. The Torah was a particular book or sets of books, regarded as holy, revealed to Moses at Sinai. That fact presents no surprise, since the Torah scroll(s) had existed, it is generally assumed, for many centuries before the closure of the Mishnah in 200.

What is surprising is that everything from the formation of the canon of the Torah to their own day seems to have proved null in their eyes. Between the Mishnah and Mount Sinai lay a vast, empty plain. From the perspective of the Torah myth as they must have known it, from Moses and the prophets to before Judah the Patriarch, lay a great wasteland. So the concrete and physical meaning attaching to the word *Torah*—that is the Torah, the Torah revealed by God to Moses at Mount Sinai (including the books of the Prophets and the Writings)—bore a contrary implication. Beyond the Torah there was no torah. Besides the Pentateuch, Prophets, and Writings, not only did no physical scroll deserve veneration, but no corpus of writings demanded obedience. So the very limited sense in which the words *the Torah* were used passed a stern judgment upon everything else, all the other writings that we know circulated widely, in which other Jews alleged that God had spoken and said "these things."

The range of the excluded possibilities that other Jews explored demands no survey. But in a moment we shall take a passing glance at another Judaism of this same time and place. What other possibilities have been neglected? They encompass everything, not only the Gospels (by 200 long since in the hands of outsiders), but secret books, history books, psalms, wisdom writings, rejected works of prophecy—everything excluded from any biblical canon by whoever determined there should be a canon. If the library of the Essenes at Qumran tells us what might have been, then we must regard as remarkably impoverished the (imaginary) library that would have served the authors of the Mishnah: The Book of Books, but nothing else. We seldom see so stern, so austere a vision of what commands the status of holy revelation among Judaisms over time. The tastes of the Mishnah's authors express a kind of literary iconoclasm, but with a difference. The literary icons did survive in the churches of Christendom. But in their own society and sacred setting, the judgment of Mishnah's authors would prevail from its time to ours. Nothing in the Judaisms of the heritage from the Hebrew Scripture's time to the Mishnah's day would survive the implacable rejection of the framers of the Mishnah, unless under Christian auspices or buried in caves. So when we take up that first and simplest meaning associated with the word *Torah*, "the Torah," we confront a stunning judgment: this and nothing else, this alone, the thing alone of its kind and no other thing of similar kind.

We confront more than a closing off of old possibilities, ancient claims to the status of revelation. For, at the other end, out of the Torah as a particular thing, a collection of books, would emerge a new and remarkably varied set of meanings. Possibilities first generated by the fundamental meaning imputed to the word *Torah* would demand realization. How so? Once the choice for the denotative meaning of the Torah became canonical in the narrowest possible sense, the ranges of connotative meaning imputed to the Torah stretched forth to an endless horizon. So the one concrete meaning made possible many abstract ones, all related to that single starting point. Only at the end shall we clearly grasp, in a single tableau, the entire vista of possibilities. To begin with, it suffices to note that the Mishnah's theory of the Torah not only closed, but also opened, many paths.

4. TORAH AND AVOT

Avot draws into the orbit of Torah talk the names of authorities of the Mishnah. But Avot does not claim that the Mishnah forms part of the Torah. Nor, obviously, does the tractate know the doctrine of the two Torahs. Only in the Talmuds do we begin to find clear and ample evidence of that doctrine. Avot, moreover, does not understand by the word *Torah* much more than the framers of the Mishnah do. Not only does the established classification scheme remain intact, but the sense essentially replicates already familiar usages, producing no innovation. On the contrary, I find a diminution in the range of meanings.

Yet Avot in the aggregate does differ from the Mishnah. The difference has to do with the topic at hand. The other sixty-two

Ornament in the form of the Ark of the Covenant at the Catacombs, Beit–Shearim. Menorah sculpted in stone dates from the 2nd century. (Courtesy of the Consulate General of Israel, New York.)

tractates of the Mishnah contain Torah sayings here and there. But they do not fall within the framework of Torah discourse. They speak about other matters entirely. The consideration of the status of Torah rarely pertains to that speech. Avot, by contrast, says a great deal about Torah-study. The claim that Torah study produces direct encounter with God forms part of Avot's thesis about the Torah. That claim, by itself, will hardly have surprised Israelite writers of wisdom books over a span of many centuries, whether those assembled in the Essene commune at Qumran, on the one side, or those represented in the pages of Proverbs and in many of the Psalms, or even the Deuteronomistic circle, on the other.

A second glance at tractate Avot, however, produces a surprising fact. In Avot, Torah is instrumental. The figure of the sage, his ideals and conduct, forms the goal, focus and center. To state matters simply: Avot regards the study of Torah as what a sage does. The substance of Torah is what a sage says. That is so whether or not the saying relates to scriptural revelation. The content of the sayings attributed to sages endows those sayings with self-validating status. The sages usually do not quote verses of Scripture and explain them, nor do they speak in God's name. Yet, it is clear, sages talk Torah. What follows? It is this: If a sage says something, what he says is Torah. More accurately, what he says falls into the classification of Torah. Accordingly, as I said, Avot treats Torah learning as symptomatic, an indicator of the status of the sage, hence, as merely instrumental.

The simplest proof of that proposition lies in the recurrent formal structure of the document, the one thing the framers of the document never omit and always emphasize: (1) the name of the authority behind a saying, from Simeon the Righteous on downward, and (2) the connective-attributive "says." So what is important to the redactors is what they never have to tell us. Because a recognized sage makes a statement, what he says constitutes, in and of itself, a statement in the status of Torah. To spell out what this means, let us look at the opening sentences. "Moses received Torah," and it reached "the Men of the Great Assembly." "The three things" those men said bear no resemblance to anything we find in written Scripture. They focus upon the life of sagacity—prudence, discipleship, a fence around the Torah. And, as we proceed, we find time and again that, while the word *Torah* stands for two things, divine revelation and the act of study of divine revelation, it produces a single effect, the transformation of unformed man into sage. One climax comes in Yohanan ben Zakkai's assertion that the purpose for which a man (an Israelite) was created was to study Torah, followed by his disciples' specifications of the most important things to be learned in the Torah. All of these pertain to the conduct of the wise man, the sage.

We have to locate the document's focus not on Torah but on the life of sagacity (including, to be sure, Torah study). But what defines and delimits Torah? It is the sage himself. So we may simply state the tractate's definition of Torah: Torah is what a sage learns. Accordingly, the Mishnah contains Torah. It may well be thought to fall into the classification of Torah. But the reason, we recognize, is that authorities whose sayings are found in the Mishnah possess Torah from Sinai. What they say, we cannot overemphasize, is Torah. How do we know it? It is a fact validated by the association of what they say with their own names.

So we miss the real issue when we ask Avot to explain for us the status of the Mishnah, or to provide a theory of a dual Torah. The principal point of insistence—the generative question—before the framers of Avot does not address the status of the Mishnah. And the instrumental status of the Torah, as well as of the Mishnah, lies in the net effect of their composition: the claim that through study of the Torah sages enter God's presence. So study of Torah serves a further goal—that of forming sages. The theory of Avot pertains to the religious standing and consequence of the learning of the sages. To be sure, a secondary effect of that theory endows with the status of revealed truth that which sages say. But then, as we have stressed, it is because they say them, not because they have heard them in an endless chain back to Sinai. The fundament of truth is passed on through sagacity, not through already formulated and carefully memorized truths. That is why the single most important word in Avot is also the most common—the word *says*.

At issue in Avot is not the Torah, but the authority of the sage. It is that standing that transforms a saying into a Torah saying, or to state matters more appropriately, that places a saying into the classification of the Torah. Avot then stands as the first document of the doctrine that the sage embodies the Torah and is a holy man, like Moses "our rabbi," in the likeness and image of God. The beginning is to claim that a saying falls into the category of Torah if a sage says it as Torah. The end will be to view the sage himself as Torah incarnate.

5. THE YERUSHALMI AND THE EMERGENCE OF THE ORAL TORAH

The Mishnah is held in the Talmud of the land of Israel to be equivalent to Scripture (Y. Hor. 3:5). But the Mishnah is not called Torah. Still, once the Mishnah entered the status of Scripture, it would take but a short step to a theory of the Mishnah as part of the revelation at Sinai—hence, oral Torah. In the first Talmud we find the initial glimmerings of an effort to theorize in general, not merely in detail, about how specific teachings of Mishnah relate to specific teachings of Scripture. The citing of scriptural prooftexts for Mishnah propositions, after all, would not have caused much surprise to the framers of the Mishnah; they themselves included such passages, though not often. But what conception of the Torah underlies such initiatives, and how do Yerushalmi sages propose to explain the phenomenon of the Mishnah as a whole? The following passage gives us one statement. It refers to the assertion at M. Hag. 1:8D that the laws on cultic cleanness presented in the Mishnah rest on deep and solid foundations in the Scripture.

Y. HAGIGAH 1:7

[V. A]   The laws of the Sabbath [M. 1:8B]: R. Jonah said R. Hama bar Uqba raised the question [in reference to M. Hag. 1:8D's view that there are many verses of Scripture on cleanness], "And lo, it is written only, 'Nevertheless a spring or a cistern holding water shall be clean; but whatever touches their carcass shall be unclean' [Lev. 11:36]. And from this verse you derive many laws. [So how can M. 8:8D say what it does about many verses for laws of cultic cleanness?]"

[B]   R. Zeira in the name of R. Yohanan: "If a law comes to hand and you do not know its nature, do not discard it for another one, for lo, many laws were stated to Moses at Sinai, and all of them have been embedded in the Mishnah."

The truly striking assertion appears at B. The Mishnah is now claimed to contain statements made by God to Moses. Just how these statements found their way into the Mishnah, and which passages of the Mishnah contain them, we do not know. That is hardly important, given the fundamental assertion at hand. The passage proceeds to a further, and far more consequential, proposition. It asserts that part of the Torah was written down, and part was preserved in memory and transmitted orally. In context, moreover, that distinction must encompass the Mishnah, thus explaining its origin as part of the Torah. Here is a clear and unmistakable expression of the distinction between two forms in which a single Torah was revealed and handed on at Mount Sinai, part in writing, part orally.

While the passage that follows does not make use of the language, "Torah in writing" and "Torah by memory," it does refer to "the written" and "the oral." I believe it fully justified to supply the word *Torah* in brackets. The reader will note, however, that the word *Torah* likewise does not occur at K, L. Only when the passage reaches its climax, at M, does it break down into a number of categories—Scripture, Mishnah, Talmud, laws, lore. It there makes the additional point that everything comes from Moses at Sinai. So the fully articulated theory of two Torahs (not merely one Torah in two forms) does not reach final expression in this passage. But short of explicit allusion to Torah in writing and Torah by memory, which (so far as I am able to discern) we find mainly in the Talmud of Babylonia, the ultimate theory of Torah of formative Judaism is at hand in what follows.

Y. HAGIGAH 1:7

[V. D]   R. Zeirah in the name of R. Eleazar: "'Were I to write for him my laws by ten thousands, they would be regarded as a strange thing' [Hos. 8:12]. Now is the greater part of the Torah written down? [Surely not. The oral part is much greater.] But more abundant are the matters which are derived by exegesis from the written [Torah] than those derived by exegesis from the oral [Torah]."

[E]   And is that so?

[F]   But more cherished are those matters which rest upon the written [Torah] than those which rest upon the oral [Torah].

[J]   R. Haggai in the name of R. Samuel bar Nahman, "Some teachings were handed on orally, and some things were handed on in writing, and we do not know which of them is the more precious. But on the basis of that which is written, 'And the Lord said to Moses, Write these words; in accordance with these words I have made a covenant with you and with Israel' [Ex. 34:27], [we conclude] that the ones which are handed on orally are the more precious."

[K]   R. Yohanan and R. Yudan b. R. Simeon—One said, "If you have kept what is preserved orally and also kept what is in writing, I shall make a covenant with you, and if not, I shall not make a covenant with you."

[L] The other said, "If you have kept what is preserved orally and you have kept what is preserved in writing, you shall receive a reward, and if not, you shall not receive a reward."

[M] [With reference to Deut. 9:10: "And on them was written according to all the words which the Lord spoke with you in the mount,"] said R. Joshua b. Levi, "He could have written, 'On them,' but wrote, 'And on them.' He could have written, 'All,' but wrote, 'According to all.' He could have written, 'Words,' but wrote 'The words.' [These then serve as three encompassing clauses, serving to include] Scripture, Mishnah, Talmud, laws, and lore. Even what an experienced student in the future is going to teach before his master already has been stated to Moses at Sinai."

[N] What is the Scriptural basis for this view?

[O] "There is no remembrance of former things, nor will there be any remembrance of later things yet to happen among those who come after" [Qoh. 1:11].

[P] If someone says, "See, this is a new thing," his fellow will answer him, saying to him, "This has been around before us for a long time."

Here we have absolutely explicit evidence that people believed part of the Torah had been preserved not in writing but orally. Linking that part to the Mishnah remains a matter of implication. But it surely comes fairly close to the surface, when we are told that the Mishnah contains Torah traditions revealed at Sinai. From that view it requires only a small step to the allegation that the Mishnah is part of the Torah, the oral part.

To define the category of the Torah as a source of salvation, as the Yerushalmi states, we can consider a story that explicitly states the proposition that the Torah constitutes a source of salvation. In this story we shall see that because people observed the rules of the Torah, they expected to be saved. And if they did not observe, they accepted their punishment. So the Torah now stands for something more than revelation and life of study, and (it goes without saying) the sage now appears as a holy, not merely a learned, man. This is because his knowledge of the Torah has transformed him. Accordingly, we deal with a category of stories and sayings about the Torah entirely different from what has gone before.

Y. TAANIT 3:8

[II. A] As to Levi ben Sisi: troops came to his town. He took a scroll of the Torah and went up to the roof and said, "Lord of the ages! If a single word of this scroll of the Torah has been nullified [in our town], let them come up against us, and if not, let them go their way."

[B] Forthwith people went looking for the troops but did not find them [because they had gone their way].

[C] A disciple of his did the same thing, and his hand withered, but the troops whet their way.

[D]   A disciple of his disciple did the same thing. His hand did not wither, but they also did not go their way.

[E]   This illustrates the following apothegm: You can't insult an idiot, and dead skin does not feel the scalpel.

What is interesting here is how categories, or taxa (singular: taxon), into which the word *Torah* previously fell have been absorbed and superseded in a new taxon. The Torah is an object: "He took a scroll . . . ." It also constitutes God's revelation to Israel: "If a single word . . . ." The outcome of the revelation is to form an ongoing way of life, embodied in the sage himself: "A disciple of his did the same thing...." The sage plays an intimate part in the supernatural event: "His hand withered...." Now can we categorize this story as a statement that the Torah constitutes a particular object, or a source of divine revelation, or a way of life? Yes and no. The Torah here stands not only for the things we have already catalogued; it represents one more thing which takes in all the others. Torah is a source of salvation. How so? The Torah stands for, or constitutes, the way in which the people Israel saves itself from marauders. This straightforward sense of salvation will not have surprised the author of Deuteronomy.

In the canonical documents up to the Yerushalmi, we look in vain for sayings or stories that fall into such a category. True, we may take for granted that everyone always believed that, in general, Israel would be saved by obedience to the Torah. That claim would not have surprised any Israelite writers, from the first prophets down through the final redactors of the Pentateuch in the time of Ezra and onward through the next 700 years. But, in the rabbinical corpus from the Mishnah forward, the specific and concrete assertion that by taking up the scroll of the Torah and standing on the roof of one's house, confronting God in heaven, a sage could take action against the expected invasion—that kind of claim is not located, so far as I know, in any composition surveyed so far.

Still, we cannot claim that the belief that the Torah in the hands of the sage constituted a source of magical, supernatural, and hence salvific power simply did not flourish prior, let us say, to ca. 400. We cannot show it, hence we do not know it. All we can say with assurance is that no stories containing such a viewpoint appear in any rabbinical document associated with the Mishnah. So what is critical here is not the generalized category—the genus—of conviction that the Torah serves as the source of Israel's salvation. It is the concrete assertion—the speciation of the genus—that in the hands of the sage and under conditions specified, the Torah may be utilized in pressing circumstances as Levi, his disciple, and the disciple of his disciple, used it. That is what is new.

To generalize: This stunningly new usage of Torah found in the Talmud of the Land of Israel emerges from a group of stories not readily classified in our established categories. All of these stories treat the word *Torah* (whether scroll, contents, or act of study) as source and guarantor of salvation. Accordingly, evoking the word *Torah* forms the centerpiece of a theory of Israel's history, on the one side, and an account of the teleology of the entire system, on the other. Torah has indeed ceased to constitute a specific thing or even a category or classification when stories about studying the Torah yield not a judgment as to status (that is, praise for the learned man) but promise for supernatural blessing now and salvation in time to come.

6. FROM TESTAMENT TO TORAH: THE SAGE

With the Yerushalmi, the Torah has left behind the limited classification "testament," "Scripture," and "tradition." The inheritance of ancient Israel now forms merely one component in that much larger, much richer revelation of God to Israel encompassed by the word *Torah*. That shift in meaning, as we noted at the outset, marks the end of the formative age of Judaism. To that final meaning of the word *torah*, everything beyond constituted (mere) commentary. But the commentary too formed part of the Torah, it too was *torah*. And *torah*—that is, Judaism—transcended matters of mere learning. For at stake in *torah*, what was studied in study of the Torah, was God's will for Israel and humanity, God's plan for creation, God's intent for history—that is, in secular language, Judaism.

To the rabbis, the principal salvific deed was to "study Torah," by which they meant memorizing Torah sayings by constant repetition, and, as the Talmud itself amply testifies (for some sages) profound analytic inquiry into the meaning of those sayings. The innovation now is that this act of "study of Torah" imparts supernatural power of a material character. For example, by repeating words of Torah, the sage could ward off the angel of death and accomplish other kinds of miracles as well. So Torah formulas served as incantations. Mastery of Torah transformed the man engaged in Torah learning into a supernatural figure, who could do things ordinary folk could not do. The category of "Torah" had already vastly expanded so that through transformation of the Torah from a concrete thing to a symbol, a Torah scroll, could be compared to a man of Torah, namely, a rabbi. Now, once the principle had been established that salvation would come from keeping God's will in general, as Israelite holy men had insisted for so many centuries, it was a small step for rabbis to identify their particular corpus of learning—namely, the Mishnah and associated sayings—with God's will expressed in Scripture, the universally acknowledged medium of revelation.

The key to the first Talmud's theory of the Torah lies in its conception of the sage, to which that theory is subordinate. Once the sage reaches his full apotheosis as Torah incarnate, then, but only then, the

Torah becomes (also) a source of salvation in the present concrete formulation of the matter. That is why we traced the doctrine of the Torah in the salvific process by elaborate citation of stories about sages, living Torahs, exercising the supernatural power of the Torah, and serving, like the Torah itself, to reveal God's will. Since the sage embodied the Torah and gave the Torah, the Torah naturally came to stand for the principal source of Israel's salvation, not merely a scroll, on the one side, or a source of revelation, on the other.

The history of the symbolization of the Torah proceeds from its removal from the framework of material objects, even from the limitations of its own contents, to its transformation into something quite different and abstract, quite distinct from the document and its teachings. The Torah stands for this something more, specifically, when it comes to be identified with a living person, the sage, and endowed with those particular traits that the sage claimed for himself. Although we cannot say that the process of symbolization leading to the pure abstraction at hand moved in easy stages, we may still point to the stations that had to be passed in sequence. The word *Torah* reached the apologists for the Mishnah in its long-established meanings: Torah scroll, contents of the Torah scroll. But even in the Mishnah itself, these meanings provoked a secondary development, status of Torah as distinct from other (lower) status, hence, Torah teaching in contradistinction to scribal teaching. With that small and simple step, the Torah ceased to denote only a concrete and material thing—a scroll and its contents. It now connoted an abstract matter of status. And once made abstract, the symbol entered a secondary history beyond all limits imposed by the concrete object, including its specific teachings, the Torah scroll.

I believe that Avot stands at the beginning of this process. In the history of the word *Torah* as abstract symbol, a metaphor serving to sort out one abstract status from another regained concrete and material reality of a new order entirely. For the message of Avot, as we saw, was that the Torah served the sage. How so? The Torah indicated who was a sage and who was not. Accordingly, the apology of Avot for the Mishnah was that the Mishnah contained things sages had said. What sages said formed a chain of tradition extending back to Sinai. Hence it was equivalent to the Torah. The upshot is that words of sages enjoyed the status of the Torah. The small step beyond was to claim that what sages said was Torah, as much as what Scripture said was Torah. And, a further small step (and the steps need not have been taken separately or in the order here suggested) moved matters to the position that there were two forms in which the Torah reached Israel: one [Torah] in writing, the other [Torah] handed on orally, in memory. The final step, fully revealed in the Talmud at hand, brought the conception of Torah to its

Bronze lamp, Alexandria, 4th century. (Schloessinger Collection, The Israel Museum, Jerusalem.)

logical conclusion: What the sage said was in the status of the Torah, was Torah, because the sage was Torah incarnate. So the abstract symbol now became concrete and material once more. We recognize the many diverse ways in which the Talmud stated that conviction. Every passage in which knowledge of the Torah yields power over this world and the next, capacity to coerce to the sage's will the natural and supernatural worlds alike, rests upon the same viewpoint.

The first Talmud's theory of the Torah carries us through several stages in the processes of the symbolization of the word *Torah*. First transformed from something material and concrete into something abstract and beyond all metaphor, the word *Torah* finally emerged once more in a concrete aspect, now as the encompassing and universal mode of stating the whole doctrine, all at once, of Judaism in its formative age.

While both the national and the individual dimensions of salvation mark the measure of the word *Torah* in the Babylonian Talmud, the national proves the more interesting, for the notion of private salvation through "Torah" study and practice, of which we hear much, presents no surprise. When, by contrast, we find God saying, "If a man occupies himself with the study of Torah, works of charity, and prays with the community, I account it to him as if he had redeemed me and my children from among the nations of the world" (b. Ber. 8a), we confront a concept beyond the imagination of the framers of Avot and the other compositions of that circle. Still more indicative of the importance for Israel as a whole, imputed to Torah learning, is the view that those who master the Torah do not require protection by this-worldly means. Rabbis need not contribute to the upkeep of the walls of a town, "because rabbis do not require protection" (b. B.B. 8a). Sayings such as these focus, to be sure, upon the individual who has mastered the Torah. But the supernatural power associated with the Torah here is thought to protect not the individual alone, but all Israelites associated with the individual Torah master. So, given the social perspective of our sages, all Israel enjoys salvation through the Torah.

Judaism at the end of its formative age, by the turning of the fifth century, turns out to lay its principal emphases precisely upon those things that the traits of the age and social setting should have led us to expect. The Torah's message as sages present it in the documents of the time speaks of how to attain certainty and authority in a time of profound change. The means lie in the person of the Talmudic sage. Salvation consists in becoming like him. The power to change the world, not merely judge or describe it, was the rabbi's. The power of the rabbi extended backward to Moses' Scripture, forward to the Messiah. He was the link, his word the guarantee. The critical actor of the Judaic system of the dual Torah is the rabbi as authority on earth and intermediary of supernatural power. The rabbi, mediating divine power, yet highly individual, became the center and the focus of the supernatural life of Israel. The rabbi would become Israel's model of sanctification, the Jews' promise of ultimate salvation. That is why from then to nearly now, whatever Judaism there would ever be properly came to be called *rabbinic*. When Israel, God's first love, had succeeded in working its way through the third and last crisis of its formative age, it created as its statement of what it means to be "like God" the figure of the sage, who, for Israel, formed and created worlds—worlds without end.

7. "LIKE GOD . . ."—". . . CREATORS OF WORLDS"

To grasp the meaning of "study of Torah" and, with that critical action, the issues involved in the Judaism of the dual Torah, we turn back to tractate Avot. Specifically, what we wish to find out is the answer to a simple question: when one "studies Torah," what does one actually learn? For here we find the heart and soul of the Judaism of the dual Torah: the contents of the faith, as against its context, upon which we have focused for so long.

TRACTATE AVOT CHAPTER TWO

1. Rabbi says: What is the straight path which a person should choose for himself? Whatever is an ornament to the one who follows it, and an ornament in the view of others. Be meticulous in a small religious duty as in a large one, for you do not know what sort of reward is coming for any of the various religious duties. And reckon with the loss [required] in carrying out a religious duty against the reward for doing it; and the reward for committing a transgression against the loss for doing it. And keep your eye on three things, so you will not come into the clutches of transgression. Know what is above you. An eye which sees, and an ear which hears, and all your actions are written down in a book.

2. Rabban Gamaliel, a son of Rabbi Judah the Patriarch, says: Fitting is learning in Torah along with a craft, for the labor put into the two of them makes one forget sin. And all learning of Torah which is not joined with labor is destined to be null and causes sin. And all who work with the community—let them work with them [the community] for the sake of Heaven. For the merit of the fathers strengthens them, and the righteousness which they do stands forever. And, as for you, I credit you with a great reward, as if you had done [all the work required by the community].

3. Be wary of the government, for they get friendly with a person only for their own convenience. They look like friends when it is to their benefit, but they do not stand by a person when he is in need.

4. He would say: Make His wishes into your own wishes, so that He will make your wishes into His wishes. Put aside your wishes on account of His wishes, so that He will put aside the wishes of other people in favor of your wishes. Hillel says: Do not walk out on the community. And do not have confidence in yourself until the day you die. And do not judge your companion until you are in his place. And do not say anything which cannot be heard, for in the end it will be heard. And do not say: When I have time, I shall study, for you may never have time.

5. He would say: A coarse person will never fear sin, nor will an *am ha-Aretz* ever be pious, nor will a shy person learn, nor will an ignorant person teach, nor will anyone too occupied in business get wise. In a place where there are no individuals, try to be an individual.

6. Also, he saw a skull floating on the water and said to it [in Aramaic]: Because you drowned others, they drowned you, and in the end those who drowned you will be drowned.

7. He would say: Lots of meat, lots of worms; lots of property, lots of worries; lots of women, lots of witchcraft; lots of slave girls, lots of lust; lots of slave boys, lots of robbery. Lots of Torah, lots of life; lots of discipleship, lots of wisdom; lots of counsel, lots of understanding; lots of righteousness, lots of peace. [If] one has gotten a good name, he has gotten it for himself. [If] he has gotten teachings of Torah, he has gotten himself life eternal.

8. Rabban Yohanan ben Zakkai received [the Torah] from Hillel and Shammai. He would say: If you have learned much Torah, do not puff yourself up on that account, for it was for that purpose that you were created. He had five disciples, and these are they: Rabbi Eliezer ben Hyrcanus, Rabbi Joshua ben Hananiah, Rabbi Yosé the Priest, Rabbi Simeon ben Nethanel, and Rabbi Eleazar ben Arakh.

He would list their good qualities:

Rabbi Eliezer ben Hyrcanus—a plastered well, which does not lose a drop of water.

Rabbi Joshua—happy is the one who gave birth to him.

Rabbi Yosé—a pious man.

Rabbi Simeon ben Nethanel—a man who fears sin.

Rabbi Eleazar ben Arakh—a surging spring.

He would say: If all the sages of Israel were on one side of the scale, and Rabbi Eliezer ben Hyrcanus were on the other, he would outweigh all of them.

Abba Saul says in his name: If all of the sages of Israel were on one side of the scale, and Rabbi Eliezer ben Hyrcanus was also with them, and Rabbi Eleazar [ben Arakh] were on the other side, he would outweigh all of them.

9. He said to them: Go and see what is the straight path to which someone should stick.

Rabbi Eliezer says: A generous spirit.

Rabbi Joshua says: A good friend.

Rabbi Yosé says: A good neighbor.

Rabbi Simeon says: Foresight.

Rabbi Eleazar says: Good will.

He said to them: I prefer the opinion of Rabbi Eleazar ben Arakh, because in what he says is included everything you say.

He said to them: Go out and see what is the bad road, which someone should avoid.

Rabbi Eliezer says: Envy.

Rabbi Joshua says: A bad friend.

Rabbi Yosé says: A bad neighbor.

Rabbi Simeon says: A loan. (All the same is a loan owed to a human being and a loan owed to the Omnipresent, the blessed, as it is said, *The wicked borrows and does not pay back, but the righteous person deals graciously and hands over [what is owed].*) [Ps. 37:21].

Rabbi Eleazar says: Ill will.

He said to them: I prefer the opinion of Rabbi Eleazar ben Arakh, because in what he says is included everything you say.

10. They [each] said three things.

Rabbi Eliezer says: Let the respect owing to your companion be as precious to you as the respect owing to yourself. And don't be easy to anger. And repent one day before you die. And warm yourself by the fire of the sages, but be careful of their coals, so you don't get burned—for their bite is the bite of a fox, and their sting is the sting of a scorpion, and their hiss is like the hiss of a snake, and everything they say is like fiery coals.

11. Rabbi Joshua says: Envy, desire of bad things, and hatred for people push a person out of the world.

12. Rabbi Yosé says: Let your companion's money be as precious to you as your own. And get yourself ready to learn Torah, for it does not come as an inheritance to you. And may everything you do be for the sake of Heaven.

13. Rabbi Simeon says: Be meticulous about the recitation of the *Shema* and the Prayer. And when you pray, don't treat your praying as a matter of routine; but let it be a [plea for] mercy and supplication before the Omnipresent, the blessed, as it is said, *For He is gracious*

and full of compassion, slow to anger and full of mercy, and repents of the evil. And never be evil in your own eyes. [Joel 2:13].

14. Rabbi Eleazar says: Be constant in learning of Torah; And know what to reply to an Epicurean; And know before whom you work, for your employer can be depended upon to pay your wages for what you do.

15. Rabbi Tarfon says: The day is short, the work formidable, the workers lazy, the wages high, the employer impatient.

16. He would say: It's not your job to finish the work, but you are not free to walk away from it. If you have learned much Torah, they will give you a good reward. And your employer can be depended upon to pay your wages for what you do. And know what sort of reward is going to be given to the righteous in the coming time.

The sage as model, as humanity "in our image, after our likeness," was one who, like God, creates worlds. The sage talks about humble things, human things. At stake is "the right path," and "the wrong path." The lessons of the Torah address humanity at large, not Israel in particular, because wisdom is wisdom and right is right. The study of Torah leads to lessons to tell us to earn an honest living and to study the Torah, not to use the latter as a spade with which to dig. The counsel to make God's will our will has already struck us for its political savvy. But we see it as a powerful religious emotion in its own right. It is the aspect of God with which humanity can identify, the trait of God that humanity can emulate. That teaching imparts to attitude a transcendent importance, and, of course, the one thing that humanity can shape is attitude. No one controls that but the individual.

The most striking trait imputed to Torah study is the matched set attributed to Yohanan ben Zakkai. Do not take pride in Torah study, because that is what you were created to do. In common language, to be a human being means to study the Torah. In this context, to study the Torah means *to receive God's revelation and to do it.* And, not surprisingly, at the heart of God's Torah to humanity is the attitude of humanity: good will, a spirit of generosity, conciliation: loving one's neighbor as oneself, translated into concrete and specific terms by Yohanan's disciples. That is the whole Torah, all of it. All the rest is commentary. But commentary is Torah too. The task of the sage, then is so to live as to provide, in heart and soul, a commentary on the text of the Torah: This is what it means to be "like God," and, therefore, this is what God wants of me in the here and now:

> But the serpent said to the woman, "You will not die, for God knows that when you eat of it your eyes will be opened and you will be like God . . ."

Genesis 3:5

> "...to be like God..." [means] *creator of worlds*

Rashi (R. Solomon Isaac, 1040–1105)

what we do when we study a religion

1. TO STUDY A RELIGION IS TO COMPARE RELIGIONS: TOWARD THE COMPARATIVE STUDY OF JUDAISMS

We have learned much about the Judaism of the dual Torah in its formative áge. But until we have perspective on what we have learned, we shall not be able to analyze and interpret our findings. And if we wish to understand, not merely describe, we must analyze and interpret. To analyze, moreover, requires that we compare, for to seek the distinguishing traits of something we wish to study, we have to know what traits matter and what indicate nothing beyond themselves. That inquiry requires us to compare two species of the same genus, to find out in what way they are alike, so that we may identify and explain the points of difference. That exercise of comparison is necessary for all work of analysis and explanation.

In the case of the Judaism of the dual Torah, moreover, comparison to another Judaic system is made all the more necessary by the very familiarity of the Judaism under study. The principal documents of the Judaism of the dual Torah form the common heritage of all Judaisms today. The world view characterizes Orthodox, Reform, Conservative, and Reconstructionist Judaisms of our own time. It furthermore continues in its essentially received formulation among Judaic communities in the State of Israel and in the United States and Europe, unmediated by the revisions of nineteenth- and twentieth-century experience in philosophy and history, for instance. The way of life of the Judaism of the dual Torah, with its emphasis on study of the Torah and performance of the religious duties and also of acts of grace, with its expression in the holy way of life affecting food and the use of one's time and the sanctification of days, circumcision, the Sabbath, the dietary rules, and on and on—that way of life is a living reality. But we perceive it as a given, the way things naturally are, and not as a set of choices that people made in order to cope with urgent questions and to discover self-evidently valid answers to those questions. So long, so to speak, as we imagine we have already heard what these texts are saying, we have not yet really understood them in all their power and majesty as human responses to difficult circumstances.

Accordingly, it is difficult for us to imagine a world in which the Judaism of the dual Torah, once in being, faced competition and therefore constituted one choice among many that Jews faced. If what is truly original and epoch-making appears to us routine and predictable, then we clearly do not fully grasp what is new and remarkable in what has become accepted and successful. On that account, comparison is all the more necessary, to help us see the Judaism of the dual Torah as a persuasive and new force, not as something hallowed by age and everywhere accepted as the norm. For that purpose we address a different Judaism of the same age as the one at hand, a Judaism for which the evidence, moreover, is not in writing and in words, but in art on synagogue walls.

2. THE JUDAISM OF THE DUAL TORAH AND THE JUDAISM OF ASTRAL ASCENT

Most ancient synagogues, both in the land of Israel and abroad, have important decorations on their walls. The decorations turn up fairly consistently. Some symbols recur nearly everywhere. Other symbols never make an appearance at all. A *shofar*, a *lulab* and *ethrog*, a *menorah*, all of them Jewish in origin, but also such pagan symbols as a Zodiac, with symbols difficult to find in Judaic written sources—all of these form part of the absolutely fixed symbolic vocabulary of the synagogues of late antiquity. By contrast, symbols of other elements of the calendar year, on the one side, and of the Temple, at least as important as those that we do find, never make an appearance. So the comparative study of Judaisms requires us to compare the symbolic vocabulary of one Judaism with that of some other. And we have also to bring into alignment the symbols of a Judaism with those same symbols in some other religious system altogether.

Obviously, a vast number of pagan symbols proved useless to Judaic synagogue artists. It follows that the artists of the synagogues spoke through a certain set of symbols and ignored other available ones. That simple fact makes it highly likely that the symbols they did use meant something to them, represented a set of choices, delivered a message important to the people who worshipped in these synagogues on the walls of which these particular symbols made their appearance.

In *The Sacred Portal, A Primary Symbol in Ancient Judaic Art,* Bernard Goldman addresses one of the most important problems in the study of ancient Judaism. He confronts a synagogue and its art. His purpose is to deal not with symbols in the abstract but with the meaning of symbols in one particular setting. That is what makes his book important. Among the studies of symbolism, only a few concentrate on how things are put together into a single symbolic system—a "Judaism," so to speak—and Goldman is one of those few.

He takes up the mosaic floor at the Beth Alpha synagogue, and he deals with the two artists who signed the mosaics, Jews named Marianos and Hanina. He concentrates on the portal motif and asks such questions as, What gave this work of art its character? Why does it carry this particular set of motifs? What are the sources of the symbols? How are they used? At Beth Alpha the mosaic dominates all, and it is the portal, in particular, that the mosaic artists choose as their focus.

He deals with these questions: What does this doorway stand for? Why do Jewish worshippers, walking through the doorway, regard the art as important? Goldman explains that the doorway stands for transformation: "It is the icon of metamorphosis and revelation . . . the moment of rebirth and regeneration." So the synagogue meant to provide the Jewish worshippers with the experience of transformation. That is an experience for which we look in vain in the siddur we have received from antiquity: It is a different Judaism from the one we know. So it would seem. The experience of the Judaic system of Beth Alpha is one of an astral ascent, from earth to heaven and to God in the heights.

Who were the philosophers who chose this symbol? We know their names: "May the craftsmen who carried out this work, Marianos and his son Hanina, be held in remembrance." But we cannot assume that only the named artists found the art meaningful. To the contrary, the art is public. An entire community revered it, agreed with its values. The fact that the synagogue was dominated by the mosaic tells us that, at the time of the mosaic—in the sixth century, around 518–527, about a century after the Talmud of the land of Israel had been closed but about a century before the Talmud of Babylonia would be closed, the members of the synagogue renovated their building. They built the new floor at that time. About three generations later, around the early seventh century, the building was destroyed, probably suddenly. The floor was preserved until, with the return of Israel to the land of Israel, Jewish archaeologists found and dug it up and preserved it for a new generation.

What are the stages of the transformation of Beth Alpha? These tell us the stages of the astral ascent. We begin with

1. the Akedah, Abraham's raising his knife in his uplifted arm to kill his son Isaac, then (the finger of) God intervenes and saves the youth. In the middle is
2. the sun, Helios, in the center of the zodiac. In the third panel, as we proceed inward, is
3. a building facade—a heavenly temple.

So there we have it—three stages in the transformation, whatever these stages can have meant. We move from the binding of Isaac, to the level of heaven represented by the sun, and then beyond to a temple. Along with the portal of this temple are candelabra, birds, lions, and what Goldman calls "ritual equipment." Goldman takes as his task the systematic explanation of the symbolism of the synagogue. He works his way through the meanings associated with

1. the *akedah*
2. the heavenly portal (the zodiac)
3. the altar and the heavenly palace.

The astral ascent symbolized by the zodiac is given concrete and particular meaning for Israel, the Jewish people, by reference to the received stories of Scripture and the symbolism of the Temple. But the religious experience afforded by this Judaism, the urgent questions raised by its—clearly very numerous—devotees and the self-evidently valid answers this Judaism provided, these issues of description, analysis, and interpretation await attention. For our purposes it suffices to note that the Judaism of the dual Torah took shape in an age when other Jews, numerous in the synagogues, treated as urgent quite different questions and responded to the self-evident (to them) truth of answers of a clearly different sort. Beyond that statement, at this point, we do not have to go.

Goldman insists that the mosaic played an integral part in the religious and imaginative life of the Jews of the synagogue. He does not reduce the symbols to mere decoration, and he does not dismiss the art as a sign that at hand are Jews who (invoking a very inappropriate anachronism) were somehow "assimilated" or "syncretistic" or "less loyal to the Torah" than those who did not use art and symbolism, including the representation of the human form as well as of pagan objects, in synagogue decoration. Indeed, so few synagogues have appeared out of late antiquity without decoration such as that before us that we should have to wonder who was normative; and who was not. Decorating synagogues was normative, not doing so was not really "orthodox"—in that context.

And that is the fact, despite the position of the two Talmuds that there are many kinds of decoration that synagogues should not have. Talmudic Rabbis at best tolerated this kind of art; they did not provide the motivating force for creating it.

Goldman follows in the great tradition of Erwin R. Goodenough, who, in his *Jewish Symbols in the Greco Roman Period* (Princeton, 1953–1966) I–XIII, pioneered in the interpretation of the Judaism represented by synagogue art in antiquity. Goodenough asked a simple question: Who stands behind this art? As just noted, we should look vainly in the circles in which Talmudic literature developed for the origins of the various symbols and ideas of Hellenistic Judaism we find on synagogue walls. So the synagogues we have at hand do not testify to the values or the laws of the rabbis whose views we have in the two Talmuds. It follows that evidences of the use of the pagan inheritance of ancient civilization for the specifically Jewish purposes derives from Jews whose legacy is not recorded in the pages of the Talmud.

It was Goodenough who first took that fact seriously and did not try to explain it away. His first question is, If the rabbis whose writings we possess did not lead people to use the symbols at hand, then who did? If, as Goodenough contends, not all Jews (perhaps not even many Jews) were under the hegemony of the rabbis of the Talmud, who did not lead the way in the utilization of pagan symbols in synagogue decoration, then what shall we think if we discover substantial, identifiably Jewish purposes of forms we should expect to uncover not in a Jewish setting, but rather in a pagan one?

One conclusion would render these finds insignificant. Illegal, symbolic representations of lions, eagles, masks, and victory wreaths, not to mention the Zodiac and other astral symbols, were made for merely ornamental purposes, and while "the rabbis" may not have approved of them, they had to "reckon with reality" and "accepted" them. That view was commonly expressed but never demonstrated. But it is difficult to agree that the handful of symbolic objects so carefully chosen from a great variety of available symbols, so frequently repeated at Dura, Randanini, Beth Alpha, Hammam Lif, and elsewhere, used to the exclusion of many other symbols and so sloppily drawn that no ornamental artist could have done them, constituted mere decoration. Furthermore, it begs the question to say that these symbols were "merely" ornamental: Why specifically these symbols and *no others?* Why in these settings?

Two extreme positions present themselves. One maintains that a "symbol" is perpetually symbolic, retaining its emotive value forever and everywhere. The other contends that symbols (in this sense, representations of real things) are never more than "mere" ornament. What is meant by "mere ornament"? What other instances of wholly meaningless decoration attached to other places of worship and burial, which in antiquity were normally adorned with meaningful and evocative designs, do we have? Those who reject Goodenough's and

Goldman's insistence that symbols usually bear meaning do not trouble themselves with such questions as these. Rather, Goodenough's critics asked where and how we know that a symbol is symbolic, as though Goodenough himself did not address that question. Goodenough concludes:

> In these synagogues certainly was a type of ornament, using animals, human figures, and even pagan deities, in the round, in deep relief, or in mosaic, which was in sharp distinction to what was proper for Judaism.... The ornament we are studying is an interim ornament, used only after the fall of Jerusalem and before the completion or reception of the Talmud. The return to the old standards, apparently a return to the halakhic or legal Judaism that the rabbis advocated and represented in the dual Torah, is dramatically attested by the destruction, obviously by Jews themselves, of the decorative abominations, and only for the abominations, in these synagogues. Only when a synagogue was abandoned as at Dura ... are the original effects preserved or the devastations indiscriminate.

The decoration in these synagogues must have seemed more than merely decorative to those who destroyed them so discriminatingly. Goodenough summarizes the consequences of his evidence as follows (*Jewish Symbols in the Graeco-Roman Period,* vol. II, p. 295):

> The picture we have got of this Judaism is that of a group still intensely loyal to Yao Sabaoth, a group which buried its dead and built its synagogues with a marked sense that it was a peculiar people in the eyes of God, but which accepted the best of paganism (including its most potent charms) as focusing in, finding its meaning in, the supreme Yao Sabaoth. In contrast to this, the Judaism of the rabbis was a Judaism which rejected all of the pagan religious world (all that it could).... Theirs was the method of exclusion, not inclusion.

Goodenough argues that the written documents, particularly the Talmudic ones, do not suffice to interpret symbols so utterly alien to their spirit, and in any case, so rarely discussed in them. Furthermore, even where some of the same symbols are mentioned in the Bible or Talmud and inscribed on graves or synagogues, it is not always obvious that the biblical antecedents or Talmudic references engage the mind of the artist. Why not? Because the artists follow the conventions of Hellenistic art, and not only Hellenistic art, but the conventions of the artists who decorated cultic objects and places in the same locale in which, in the Jewish settings, the symbols have turned up.

Goodenough asks for a general theory to make sense of all the evidence—something no one gives—and asks (*Symbols,* vol. IV, p. 10) the following:

> Where are we to find the moving cause in the taking over of images, and with what objective were they taken over? It seems to me that the motive for borrowing pagan art and integrating it into Judaism throughout the Roman world can be discovered only by analyzing the art itself.

An interpretive method needs to be devised. Goodenough succinctly defines this method:

> The first step . . . must be to assemble . . . the great body of evidence available . . . which, when viewed as a whole, demands interpretation as a whole since it is so amazingly homogeneous for all parts of the Empire. The second step is to recognize that we must first determine what this art means in itself, before we begin to apply to it as proof texts any possible unrelated statements of the Bible or the Talmud. That these artifacts are unrelated to proof texts is a statement which one can no more make at the outset than one can begin with the assumption of most of my predecessors, that if the symbols had meaning for Jews, that meaning must be found by correlating them with Talmudic and biblical phrases . . .

What is the method that will lead us within the Judaism represented by the art of the synagogue of late antiquity—and not by the writings of the sages of the Judaism of the dual Torah? The problem here is to explain how Goodenough determines what this art means in itself. Goodenough begins by asking (*Symbols*, vol. IV, p. 27):

> Admitting that the Jews would not have remained Jews if they had used these images in pagan ways and with pagan explanations, do the remains indicate a symbolic adaptation of pagan figures to Judaism or merely an urge to decoration?

Goodenough defines a symbol as "an image or design with a significance to one who uses it quite beyond its manifest content . . . an object or a pattern which, whatever the reason may be, operates upon men and causes effect in the viewer beyond mere recognition of what is literally presented in the given form." Goodenough emphasizes that most important thought is in "this world of the suggestive connotative meaning of words, objects, sounds, and forms . . . ." He adds (IV, p. 33) that in religion, a symbol conveys not only meaning, but also "power or value." Further, some symbols move from religion to religion, preserving the same "value" while acquiring a new explanation. In the long history of Judaism, religious "symbols" in the form of actions or prohibitions certainly endure through many varied settings, all the while acquiring new explanations and discarding old ones, and perpetually retaining religious "force" or value or (in more modern terms) "meaning." Hence, Goodenough writes (*Symbols*, vol. IV, p. 36):

> Indeed when the religious symbols borrowed by Jews in those years are put together, it becomes clear that the ensemble is not merely a "picture book without text," but reflect a lingua franca that had been taken into most of the religions of the day, for the same symbols were used in association with Dionysius, Mithra, Osiris, the Etruscan gods, Sabazisus, Attis, and a host of others, as well as by Christianity later. It was a symbolic language, a direct language of values, however, not a language of denotation.

Goodenough is far from suggesting the presence of a pervasive syncretism. Rather, he points to what he regards as pervasive religious values applied quite parochially by various groups, including some Jews to the worship of their particular "Most High God." These values, while connotative and not denotative, may nonetheless be recovered and articulated in some measure by the historian who makes use of the insights of recent students of psychology and symbolism:

> The hypothesis on which I am working . . . is that in taking over the symbols, while discarding the myths and explanations of the pagans, Jews and Christians admitted, indeed confirmed, a continuity of religious experience which it is most important to be able to identify . . . for an understanding of man, the phenomenon of a continuity of religious experience or values would have much more significance than that of discontinuous explanations (*Symbols*, vol. IV, p. 42).

At this point Goodenough argues that the symbols under consideration were more than merely space fillers. Since this matter is crucial to his argument, as well as to Goldman's, let us note his reasons, with appropriate emphasis. All of them apply equally to the work at hand.

1. They were all *living* symbols in surrounding culture.
2. The vocabulary of symbols is extremely limited, on all the artifacts not more than a score of designs appearing in sum, and thus highly selected.
3. The symbols were frequently not the work of an ornamental artist at all.
4. The Jewish and "pagan" symbols are mixed on the same graves, so that if the menorah is accepted as "having value," then the peacock or wreath of victory ought also to have "had value."
5. The symbols are found in highly public places, such as synagogues and cemeteries, and not merely on the private and personal possessions of individuals, such as amulets or charms.

Enough has been said to make the simple point important for the method of the study of a Judaism, or of any religious system. We now realize that the synagogue walls testify to a system different from the one we know from the writings of the sages. We realize that the sages' Judaism of the dual Torah, expressed through words, represented one set of choices; and the synagogue artists' Judaism of an astral ascent, expressed through the use of art on the walls of the synagogue to convey an experience beyond this world, represented a different set of choices. When we can show the points of congruence and commonality that bring the one Judaism into contact with the other, we may be able to speak of not simply Judaisms, but Judaism. But that task lies beyond the limits of this book for it requires that we speak not only of some Judaisms but all of them, and it demands that we address not only ancient times but our own day as well.

3. WHAT WE STUDY WHEN WE ANALYZE A RELIGION—JUDAISM, FOR EXAMPLE

Now that we have completed our study of the formation of the Judaism of the dual Torah, the history, in its initial period, of one of the two formative religious traditions of the West, let us turn back and see what we have done. For if the methods I have followed work, then you can use them in studying other systems, both religious and otherwise, and in relating those systems to the life and society of the people who produced them. Judaism is a religion, and therefore a case, an example of religion in general. Methods that prove illuminating in the study of one religion should apply also when we study other religions—and religion. The purpose of studying religions is to define religion, and, in the academic setting, the definition of religion must encompass all religions equally and on the same plane of value and meaning. That definition, of course, will not serve theological purposes, but it should help us to understand the settings in which human beings work out their religious lives, and—in a this-worldly sense—what they do when they do so. So let us go back over the case of Judaism and derive lessons that will help us in other cases.

We begin with creation, with the fall of Adam and Eve, when humanity became, within the biblical narrative, what it is. Guided by Scripture, we define humanity, and therefore also religion.

The snake defines what it means for humanity to eat of the fruit of the tree of knowledge and so to become "like God." For our purpose, the serpentine definition provides a good working hypothesis on the definition of religion. Humanity in society, having tasted knowledge, creates worlds. In the serpent's view, that is what it means to be like God. As Rashi, the greatest Jewish commentator to Scripture, explains, for humanity to be "like God" is to be creators of worlds. To be human (in the view of Judaism as Rashi conveys it), therefore, is to have the power to make worlds.

This book has explained the beginnings of that world-creating religion, Judaism, that for 2,000 years has explained to Jews what it means to be a human being. Specifically, we have found out where that Judaism took shape, the particular set of urgent questions it addressed, the distinctive program of self-evidently accurate answers it gave to those questions, and why, for nearly the entire history of Western civilization, Judaism endured among the very people to whom it meant to speak: Israel, the Jewish people. Judaism began with the Hebrew Scriptures, the Old Testament; hence it started *from testament*. It reached its full expression in the single word *Torah*, which stands for God's whole and complete revelation to Israel, the Jewish people; thus, *to Torah*. When we explain the journey from testament to Torah, we account for the beginning of Judaism as one of the formative religious systems of Western civilization.

Judaism is a religion, a world-creating system of behavior and belief that defines the life of a distinctive group of people. To understand that definition of any religion, including Judaism, we want to know what we mean by a "world-creating system." Only then shall we understand the limits, the boundaries, of the world created by Judaism.

Let us start back with the conception of a religious system, since, as we now realize, Judaism falls into the classification of "religious system." What it means to create a world is to make a complete and encompassing system to explain how things are and what they mean. "How things are" represents a set of concerns that a group finds urgent, and the explanation consists of a set of self-evident truths that make sense of the world framed by those pressing questions. We now realize that Judaism began with self-evidently true answers to critical and pressing questions. It explained the life of the group, accounting for the world confronting that group. It follows that a system addresses the profound questions shared among a group of people and imparts to the traits of that group—how they conduct their lives together—meaning and enduring order.

That is how, in creating worlds, humanity is like God. The systems that humanity makes ordinarily, though not always, have invoked heaven and earth to explain the social world formed by a group. So world-creating systems very commonly speak of God and the sacred side of things; hence they constitute statements of a religious character. A religion accounts for the life of a social group by systematically explaining the distinctive way of life of that group through a cogent account of heaven and earth, humanity and divinity, and how these come together in the here and now. The components of a religion therefore encompass

1. a world view—the explanation—and
2. the way of life—what is explained—of
3. a distinctive social, and therefore also political, entity.

A religion confronts urgent questions, those of who we are and why we behave as we do, and presents compelling and self-evidently correct answers.

This book has introduced a family of religions out of ancient times, from 500 B.C. to A.D. 600, that share a number of distinctive traits and has explained how that family—"Judaism(s)"—ultimately produced a single definitive and normative account, a single system to supplant and predominate over all the prior and competing ones. That family of religions in the beginning was made up of diverse Judaisms, but the single Judaism that emerged from the formative age is the one that predominated from the beginnings of Western civilization in late antiquity to modern times. We have traced the formation of that Judaic system here in three stages,

from the first layer, constituted by the Five Books of Moses, ca. 500 B.C.,
to the second, represented by the Mishnah, ca. A.D. 200, and
the third, attested by the Yerushalmi, also called the Talmud of the land of
Israel, and two great commentaries to books of Moses, Genesis Rabbah and
Leviticus Rabbah, ca. A.D. 400–450.

We have delineated how, through responses to three critical
turnings in the history of Israel, the Jewish people, that single Judaism
came to full and rich expression and why it succeeded for nearly the entire
history of the West in constituting the one and normative Judaism.

4. THE ECOLOGY OF A RELIGION—A JUDAISM, FOR INSTANCE

A religious system provides self-evidently true answers to questions
people must ask. Those questions, those matters of concern or profound
resentment, derive from the social world in which a group makes its life.
So when we study a religious system, we want in particular to know about
the relationship between two things:

1. the ideas people hold and the way of life that expresses and is explained by
   those ideas, and
2. the world in which that group makes its life.

We want to know about the interplay between society and scripture
(meaning, the written-down ideas and prescriptions for everyday life),
system and setting, between the context of a group and the contents of that
group's religious system. In asking that question, we turn to the
perspective of ecology. In particular, we propose to study the ecology of a
religion, with Judaism as our example.
    Let us therefore define ecology and then revert to the ecology of a
religion—Judaism in our instance. *Ecology* is a branch of science concerned
with the interrelationships of organisms and their environments. By
"ecology of" is meant the study of the interrelationship between a
particular, religious way of viewing the world and living life, and the
historical, social, and especially political situation of the people who
view the world and live life in accord with the teachings of their
religion. The Jewish people form a very small group, spread over many
countries.

One fact of their natural environment is that they form a distinct group in
diverse societies.

A second is that they constitute solely a community of fate and, for many, of
faith, in that they have few shared social or cultural traits.

A third is that they do not form a single political entity.

A fourth is that they look back upon a very long, and in some ways
exceptionally painful, history.

A world view suited to the Jews' social ecology must make sense of their unimportance and explain their importance. It must explain the continuing life of the group and persuade people that their forming a distinct and distinctive community is important and worth carrying on. The interplay between the political, social, and historical life of the Jews and their conceptions of themselves in this world and the next—that is, their world view, contained in their canon, their way of life, explained by the teleology of the system, and the symbolic structure that encompasses the two and stands for the whole all at once and all together—these define the focus for the inquiry into the ecology of the religion at hand—that is, the ecology of Judaism.

5. A RELIGIOUS SYSTEM IN ITS SETTING

The ancient world—ca. 500 B.C. to A.D. 500—knew many Judaisms but, as we have noted, in the end bequeathed to the West only one, the Judaism of the dual Torah. Our task has been not only to describe a fair sample of the diverse Judaisms that flourished in the period at hand, but also to explain why one in particular succeeded while the others disappeared. That is to say, why did one system serve and so survive, while other systems lost that status of self-evidence for the group that they addressed? Let us now consider how we have described a religious system in its setting, a particular Judaism.

In describing a system, we see it whole and complete, but also all by itself. What we examine is

1. the setting, hence the urgent questions,
2. the evidence out of which to reconstruct the system, hence the scriptures and material artifacts, and
3. the system that is at hand. The simplest facts of history define the setting of a system.

We have looked only at obvious things, events everyone had to have known, facts of social existence every person must acknowledge. So when we propose the facts that constitute the definitive setting, we look for simple things. Each system defines its evidence for us—whether the books of the dual Torah or the art of the synagogue walls. A system specifies the type of holy object, whether a book or a building, and then tells us which particular example of that type matters: the holy building—the Temple in Jerusalem, for example; the holy books—the official and authoritative writings of the canon of the system, for example; or the holy works of art and the sacred objects and the symbols that these stand for—the zodiac, for example. All these in their settings respectively constitute, in a broad sense, the "scripture," the definitive canon of the system. As to describing the system, we have the simple task of finding the questions and defining the answers.

But the main thing is to see things whole, complete, and as a cogent statement, a system comprising a way of life, a world view, and a social group to give reality to both. These we see in all their coherence. But that means to see systems one by one and all by themselves, each as a single and singular statement, again, as a distinct and distinctive system. The alternative is to see as a single group—one Judaism—what are in fact elements of diverse systems or Judaisms. Then we combine systems that originally stood on their own, each facing its society.

We have avoided the confusion of thinking that all Judaisms really constituted one Judaism, just as historians of religion, when they come to study Christianity, will sidestep the question of how all Christianities really are one Christianity. That theological question demands a theological answer, and historians of religion have nothing to contribute. That is, we should not allow ourselves to confuse one thing with something—everything—else. If we do, we lose sight of the distinctive and individual character of a system, its standing as one Judaism among several. We miss the particular questions it asked, the distinctive answers it supplied as self-evidently true for its society. Rather, we treat as one and the same a whole variety of Judaic systems or Judaisms, imputing connections where there is none.

A system seen as it flourished—even for a brief span of time—served its society. *At that moment, it had no past and defined its own future.* At that moment, that system did not stand in linear relationship to a past. Nor did it form part of an incremental process leading beyond itself. Rather, it constituted, on its own, one complete, whole, entirely sufficient Judaism: world view, way of life, for (an) Israel, a social group. No system recapitulates any other. That is, none in the mind of its participants covered the same ground as some other. Each was unique: the truth. But all systems confronted the same social situation that characterized the Jews as a group. Every system had to answer essentially the same questions, though each did so in its own way. All systems sorted out those same facts of ecology—the natural, that is, the political, situation of the Jewish people.

Let me frame these propositions as generalizations or "laws" of religion:

1. *No religious system recapitulates any other.*
2. *All religious systems within a given social and political setting recapitulate the same resentments.*

The first of the two rules simply says that each system stands on its own and therefore has to be examined ecologically, as a complete and cogent response to a particular setting.

How a system began, where, when, and why people made it up or discovered it—these questions cannot be answered on the basis of the evidence we have, and they are also the wrong questions. For what matters is not where a system came from but how it works when it works. That is the center of the problem of describing a system and making sense of it, of interpreting. So in its moment of self-evidence—however brief—a system has no past and contemplates no future. At that moment a system does not derive from some other, nor does it stand behind one to come: It recapitulates no other system.

The second of the two rules spells out what links a family of systems, (a set of Judaisms) and makes of the species (Judaisms) one genus (Judaism). When we know those everyday questions that demanded answers—questions of politics, of social standing and status—we discover that any Judaism had to take up a certain few questions. But each Judaism framed its own answers to those questions, answers that proved self-evidently true—that is, appropriate and beyond all argument for the group at hand. To analyze a set of Judaic systems, then, we should compare and contrast the list of urgent questions asked by all of them and the program of self-evidently valid answers—expressed in belief and behavior—proposed by each.

This comparison of systems, of Judaisms, then forms the first step in the larger comparison of religions—religious systems, in our terminology—that allows us to reach a level of generalization about the nature of not religions, but religion. When we attain that elevation from which we may see the landscape—the ecology not of religions, but of religion—we shall find out what the serpent meant and whether or not the serpent was right about humanity: creators of worlds indeed!

6. HOW TO STUDY A RELIGION, IN THE CASE OF A JUDAISM: SETTING, SCRIPTURE, SYSTEM

From these rather abstract statements of method, let us turn to review how we have carried out the particular task at hand. We required two things. First, we wanted to know the overall characteristics of the Judaic systems at hand. That information is simple.

1. From the building of the Temple of Jerusalem and the formation of the Hebrew Scriptures in 500 B.C. to A.D. 70, when the Temple was destroyed, the Jews of the Land of Israel (also Palestine, the Holy Land) coalesced in a variety of Judaic systems, or Judaisms. But among them, the one that was normative was the Judaism of the Five Books of Moses: Genesis, Exodus, Leviticus, Numbers, and Deuteronomy. That Judaism came into being in the aftermath of the destruction of the first Temple in 586 B.C.

2. From 70 to 312, a Judaic system which lay stress on the sanctification of Israel, the Jewish people, came into being in the aftermath of the destruction of the second Temple.

3. From 312, the year in which Constantine, the Roman Emperor, accorded to Christianity the status of a licit religion, to the end of the fourth century, Christianity gained control of the politics and culture of the Roman Empire. In the aftermath of that crisis, Judaic writings of the period set forth a Judaic system which joined to the emphasis on the sanctification of Israel a message of salvation as well. That system, resting on the belief of an oral and written Torah—with the oral Torah telling the story of sanctification, and the written one, as read by the rabbis or sages, telling the story of salvation—came to define "Judaism—that is, to constitute the single normative system that predominated from the ancient world to our own times.

Second, we wanted to to specify the rules of procedure, to be followed in the description of each Judaism among the Judaisms of the formative age under study. These, it is clear, required attention to

1. setting,
2. scripture, in the sense of pertinent evidence, and
3. consequent system and its definition of urgent questions and self-evidently true answers.

In terms just now worked out, we wanted to know

1. what particular "resentment," urgent question, captured the social imagination of a particular group, and how, described
2. through the evidence now in our hand,
3. the group's Judaic system responded to that inescapable question.

If this mode of description serves, then students should be able to construct their own theory of the ecology of a Judaism, *or of any other religious system,* by the procedures we have explored in the pages of this book. In this way the study of the passage from testament to Torah will teach us lessons that will serve in the study of other passages in the religious history of humanity. If this book succeeds, it will enhance students' understanding of the world by showing them how to cope with difference within a coherent group—and beyond. Since all humanity will form a single social entity in the world of the twenty-first century facing students of today, the lessons of how to study a religious system may prove relevant to a world that the sages of the Judaism of the dual Torah could not have imagined—and yet to which, under the aspect of eternity, they then spoke and continue now to speak.

Glossary

Am Haares An ordinary person; not a person who observes the cultic tithing and purity laws, but who eats ordinary food without regard to the purity laws in the book of Leviticus. Those rules were observed by priests in the Temple, and by certain people, everywhere, even outside of the holy place. Those people, who wished to make themselves holy as though they were Temple priests, were called Pharisees.

Apothegm A wise saying, nicely framed.

Apotheosis Appearance of God.

Avot, Pirke Avot Mishnah tractate Avot, "the Founders," or "the Fathers," contains sayings attributed to sages from Moses at Sinai through the names of authorities who flourished in the third century.

Bavli The Talmud of Babylonia, consisting of the Mishnah and the extensive commentary on the Mishnah produced by the sages in Babylonia (present-day Iraq, then part of the Iranian empire) between the third and the seventh centuries A.D. The Bavli serves thirty-seven of the Mishnah's sixty-two tractates.

Covenantal Nomism The belief that God's covenant with Israel, the people, is carried out in part through observing the Torah that God has revealed, including the concrete actions God has commanded Israel to do, such as loving one's neighbor and observing certain rites of sanctification, including circumcision, the Ten Commandments, which encompass the moral and religious actions.

Doxology Praise of God.

Eisegesis The interpretation of Scripture or a holy book in which meanings not necessarily present in the mind of the original author are imputed to the text; reading meaning into a text which is not there to begin with.

Eschatology Theory of the end of time; what will happen when history is over.

Essenes A community of Jews who believed in living their everyday lives in a state of sanctification like Temple priests, and who formed a monastic community; the community expected history to come to an end in a final war, after which that community would constitute the remnant of Israel, God's people.

Ethnarchs Rulers of the Jewish communities in other parts of the world, besides the land of Israel.

Ethrog A kind of citron, used for the observance of the Festival of Tabernacles (Sukkot).

Exegesis Interpretation of a text; amplifying the sense and meaning of a text.

Gospels The New Testament books about the life of Jesus: Matthew, Mark, Luke, and John.

Hakhamim Sages (singular: Hakham).

Hasmoneans Rulers of the Jews from ca. 165 to 60 B.C., who fought a war against the Syrian-Greek rulers and with Rome helped achieve independence; also called Maccabees, their original victory is celebrated by the Jewish festival of Hanukkah. Their dynasty came to an end when the Romans put a client-king, Herod, on the throne in their place.

Haverim Fellows of a group of Jews who observed the purity laws when eating everyday meals.

Havurah A group formed by haverim (above).

Levites, levitical The book of Leviticus dictates laws about the conduct of the Temple and its offerings, indicating what animals are to be offered up, under what conditions, and by whom. These laws are called "levitical," from the caste of Levites, who served in the Temple along with the priests.

Lulab A palm branch that is carried and shaken on the festival of Tabernacles (Sukkot).

Maasim Tovim Good deeds.

Maccabees See Hasmoneans.

Mamzer A person whose parents under the law of Judaism are permanently ineligible to marry.

Menorah A candelabrum.

Midrash Philosophical law code, produced in ca. A.D. 200, by Judah the Patriarch, ruler of the Jews of the land of Israel; in six divisions, comprising sixty-two tractates, plus tractate Avot, added ca A.D. 250.

Mitzvot Religious duties; commandments of God to Israel, the Jewish people.

Pentateuch The Five Books of Moses: Genesis, Exodus, Leviticus, Numbers, Deuteronomy.

Pharisees, Pharisaism A group of Jews in the land of Israel who in the second and first centuries were active in the politics of the Hasmonean court; sources that refer to them at that time assign them certain philosophical beliefs. In the first century A.D., sources that speak of the Pharisees know them as a group of people active in politics, but who also are characterized by stricter-than-common observance of the laws of tithing and cultic cleanness; hence, a group of people who eat food together, and apart from outsiders; an eating club.

Prophets   Joshua, Judges, Samuel, Kings, Isaiah, Jeremiah, Ezekiel, and the twelve smaller books of prophets comprise the Hebrew Scriptures' section called "Prophets."

Sadducees   A group of Jews of the time of the Pharisees—second century B.C. through the first century A.D. Described as holding certain philosophical views and forming a political party, the Sadducees left behind no writings of their own, and we know virtually nothing about them beyond a few scattered references.

Samaritans   A group of Jews who descended from those who had not gone into exile in the time of the destruction of the First Temple, 586 B.C., but had remained in the land.

Sanhedrin   Name for the Jewish internal administration in the land of Israel in the first century, during which time the Romans governed the country as part of their larger empire.

Scriptures (Hebrew, Mosaic)   The Hebrew Scriptures correspond, in Judaism, to what Christians know as the "Old Testament."

Shekel   A coin.

Schofar   A ram's horn, sounded on the New Moon, the New Year, and in times of trouble.

Talmud   There are two Talmuds—the Talmud of the land of Israel (Yerushalmi), ca. A.D. 400, and the Talmud of Babylonia (Bavli), ca A.D. 600. Both serve as amplifications of passages of the Mishnah. The Yerushalmi covers thirty-nine tractates in four divisions, the Bavli, thirty-seven in four divisions, with the Yerushalmi and Bavli covering three divisions in common—those on holy seasons, family law and women, and civil law and damages. The Yerushalmi, in addition, treats agricultural law, which the Bavli does not touch (since the agricultural law applied only to the holy land, and the Bavli was produced outside of the holy land). The Bavli covers the laws governing the everyday conduct of the Temple and the support and maintenance of the Temple buildings.

Teleology   Doctrine of the purpose or goal of things.

Tithing, tithe (n)   Giving a tenth of one's crop or income for God's purposes.

Torah   Revelation; God's revealed will for the world and for Israel, the Jewish people, contained in the Five Books of Moses. The word then covered the whole of Scripture; ultimately extended to the writings of the sages of late antiquity; finally became synonymous with Judaism.

Torah Shebeal Peh   The Torah that is preserved through oral formulation and memorization, hence the oral, or memorized Torah. This refers specifically to the teachings finally recorded in the writings of the ancient sages, beginning with the Mishnah and the two Talmuds, covering also the sages' exegeses of Scripture, called Midrashim.

Torah Shebikhtav   The written Torah, corresponding to the Hebrew Scriptures or "Old Testament."

Tosefta   A collection of supplements to the Mishnah, teachings deriving in part from the period of the Mishnah, but not included in that document; these are preserved in the Tosefta, along with amplifications of Mishnah teachings and citations and commentaries of Mishnah sentences.

Writings   The Scriptures are presented in the tripartite division into Torah, the Pentateuch or Five Books of Moses, Prophets, and Writings. The Writings include Psalms, Proverbs, Job, Qohelet or Ecclesiastes, Esther, Lamentations, Ruth, Jonah, and Chronicles, and the like.

Yerushalmi   The Talmud of the land of Israel. See Talmud.

BIBLIOGRAPHY

This book presents in a nutshell the results of a sizable number of my other books. This bibliography refers readers to these other works, each of which contains an extensive bibliography on its topic.

Chapter 1

"To See Ourselves as Others See Us." Jews, Christians, "Others" in Late Antiquity. [Edited with Ernest S. Frerichs] Chico, 1985: Scholars Press. Studies in the Humanities.

Judaic Perspectives on Ancient Israel. Philadelphia, 1986: Fortress Press. [Edited with Baruch A. Levine and Ernest S. Frerichs.]

Judaisms and their Messiahs in the Beginning of Christianity. New York, 1986: Cambridge University Press. [Edited with William Scott Green, Jonathan Z. Smith, and Ernest S. Frerichs.]

Chapter 2

This chapter is taken from the following title, with only minor revisions: *Judaism in the Beginning of Christianity.* Philadelphia, 1983: Fortress.

A Life of Yohanan ben Zakkai. Leiden, 1962: Brill. Awarded the Abraham Berliner Prize in Jewish History, Jewish Theological Seminary of America, 1962. Second edition, completely revised, 1970.

Development of a Legend. Studies on the Traditions Concerning Yohanan ben Zakkai. Leiden, 1970: Brill.

The Rabbinic Traditions about the Pharisees before 70. Leiden, 1971: Brill. I–III.

Das pharisaeische und talmudische Judentum. Tuebingen, 1984: J.C.B. Mohr (Paul Siebeck). Edited by Hermann Lichtenberger. Foreword by Martin Hengel. Italian translation underway.

Eliezer ben Hyrcanus. The Tradition and the Man. Leiden, 1973: Brill. I–II.

The Pharisees. Rabbinic Perspectives. New York, 1985: Ktav Publishing House. Reprise of *Rabbinic Traditions about the Pharisees before 70.* I–III.

From Politics to Piety. The Emergence of Pharisaic Judaism. Englewood Cliffs, N.J., 1973: Prentice-Hall. Second printing, New York, 1978: Ktav. Japanese translation: Tokyo, 1985: Kyo Bun Kwan.

(Ed.) *Goodenough's Jewish Symbols. An Abridged Edition.* Princeton, 1986: Princeton University Press.

Early Rabbinic Judaism. Historical Studies in Religion, Literature, and Art. Leiden, 1975: Brill.

First Century Judaism in Crisis. Yohanan ben Zakkai and the Renaissance of Torah. Nashville, 1975: Abingdon. Second printing, N.Y., 1981: Ktav.

Chapter 3

The Mishnah

Invitation to the Talmud. A Teaching Book. New York, 1973: Harper & Row. Second printing, 1974. Paperback edition, 1975. Reprinted, 1982. Second edition, completely revised, San Francisco, 1984: Harper & Row. Japanese translation, Tokyo, 1986: Yamamoto Shoten. Covers Mishnah, Tosefta, Yerushalmi, and Bavli.

(Ed.) *The Modern Study of the Mishnah.* Leiden, 1973: Brill.

A History of the Mishnaic Law of Purities. Leiden, 1974–1977: Brill. I–XXII.

A History of the Mishnaic Law of Holy Things. Leiden, 1979: Brill. I–VI.

Form Analysis and Exegesis: A Fresh Approach to the Interpretation of Mishnah. Minneapolis, 1980: University of Minnesota Press.

A History of the Mishnaic Law of Women. Leiden, 1979–1980: Brill. I–V.

A History of the Mishnaic Law of Appointed Times. Leiden, 1981–1983: Brill. I–V.

A History of the Mishnaic Law of Damages. Leiden, 1983–1985: Brill. I–V.

The Mishnah. A New Translation. New Haven and London, 1986: Yale University Press.

The Mishnah and the Tosefta. Formal and Redactional Relationships. Atlanta, 1987: Scholars Press for Brown Judaic Studies.

Judaism. The Evidence of the Mishnah. Chicago, 1981: University of Chicago Press. Paperback edition, 1984. Choice, "Outstanding academic book list 1982–1983." Second printing, 1985. Hebrew translation: Tel Aviv, 1986: Sifriat Poalim. Italian translation: Casale Monferrato, 1987: Editrice Marietti

Ancient Israel after Catastrophe. The Religious World-View of the Mishnah. The Richard Lectures for 1982. Charlottesville, 1983: The University Press of Virginia.

From Mishnah to Scripture. The Problem of the Unattributed Saying. Chico, 1984: Scholars Press for Brown Judaic Studies. Reprise and reworking of materials in *A History of the Mishnaic Law of Purities.*

In Search of Talmudic Biography. The Problem of the Attributed Saying. Chico, 1984: Scholars Press for Brown Judaic Studies. Reprise and reworking of materials in *Eliezer ben Hyrcanus. The Tradition and the Man.*

The Memorized Torah. The Mnemonic System of the Mishnah. Chico, 1985: Scholars Press for Brown Judaic Studies. Reprise and reworking of materials in *Rabbinic Traditions about the Pharisees before 70* I and III, and *A History of the Mishnaic Law of Purities* XXI.

Judaism: The First Two Centuries. Abbreviated version of *Judaism: The Evidence of the Mishnah.* Chicago, 1987: University of Chicago Press.

(Ed.) *The Formation of the Babylonian Talmud. Studies on the Achievements of Late Nineteenth and Twentieth Century Historical and Literary-Critical Research.* Leiden, 1970: Brill.

(Ed.) *The Modern Study of the Mishnah.* Leiden, 1973: Brill.

Form Analysis and Exegesis: A Fresh Approach to the Interpretation of Mishnah. Minneapolis, 1980: University of Minnesota Press.

The Tosefta

The Tosefta. Translated from the Hebrew. New York, 1977–1980: Ktav. II–VI.
The Tosefta: Its Structure and its Sources. Atlanta, 1986: Scholars Press for Brown Judaic Studies.

Tractate Avot

Torah from Our Sages: Pirke Avot. A New American Translation and Explanation. Chappaqua, 1983: Rossel. Paperback edition: 1986.

Chapter 4

Judaism in the Matrix of Christianity. Philadelphia, 1986: Fortress Press.
Judaism and Christianity in the Age of Constantine. History, Messiah, Israel, and the Initial Confrontation. Chicago, 1987: University of Chicago Press.
The Death and Birth of Judaism. From Self-Evidence to Self-Consciousness in Modern Times. New York, 1987: Basic Books.

The Yerushalmi

The Talmud of the Land of Israel. A Preliminary Translation and Explanation. Chicago: The University of Chicago Press: 1982–1989. IX–XII, XIV–XV, XVII–XXXV.
(Ed.) *In the Margins of the Yerushalmi. Notes on the English Translation.* Chico, 1983: Scholars Press for Brown Judaic Studies.
The Talmud of the Land of Israel. A Preliminary Translation and Explanation. Chicago: The University of Chicago Press: 1983.
Judaism in Society: The Evidence of the Yerushalmi. Toward the Natural History of a Religion. Chicago, 1983: The University of Chicago Press. Choice, "Outstanding Academic Book List, 1984–1985."
Our Sages, God, and Israel. An Anthology of the Yerushalmi. Chappaqua, 1984: Rossel.

The Bavli and the Jews and Judaism in Babylonia

A History of the Jews in Babylonia. Leiden: Brill, 1965–1970. I–V.
Talmudic Judaism in Sasanian Babylonia. Essays and Studies. Leiden, 1976: Brill.
Aphrahat and Judaism. The Christian Jewish Argument in Fourth Century Iran. Leiden, 1971: Brill.
(Ed.) *The Formation of the Babylonian Talmud. Studies on the Achievements of Late Nineteenth and Twentieth Century Historical and Literary-Critical Research.* Leiden, 1970: Brill.
The Talmud of Babylonia. An American Translation. Chico, 1984–1985: Scholars Press for Brown Judaic Studies.
Judaism: The Classical Statement. The Evidence of the Bavli. Chicago, 1986: University of Chicago Press.
Israel and Iran in Talmudic Times. A Political History. Lanham, 1986: University Press of America Studies in Judaism Series. Condensation of materials in *A History of the Jews in Babylonia* II–V, parts of chapter one of each volume.
Judaism, Christianity, and Zoroastrianism in Talmudic Babylonia. Lanham, 1986: University Press of America Studies in Judaism Series. Condensation of materials in *A History of the Jews in Babylonia* II–V, parts of chapter one of each volume and of *Aphrahat and Judaism.*

Israel's Politics in Sasanian Iran. Jewish Self-Government in Talmudic Times. Lanham, 1986: University Press of America Studies in Judaism Series. Condensation of materials in *A History of the Jews in Babylonia* II–V, parts of chapter two of each volume.

Genesis Rabbah

Genesis Rabbah. The Judaic Commentary on Genesis. A New American Translation. Atlanta, 1985: Scholars Press for Brown Judaic Studies. I–III.

Reading Scriptures: An Introduction to Rabbinic Midrash. With special reference to Genesis Rabbah. Chappaqua, 1986: Rossel.

Genesis and Judaism: The Perspective of Genesis Rabbah. An Analytical Anthology. Atlanta, 1986: Scholars Press for Brown Judaic Studies.

Leviticus Rabbah

Judaism and Scripture: The Evidence of Leviticus Rabbah. Chicago, 1985: The University of Chicago Press.

The Integrity of Leviticus Rabbah. The Problem of the Autonomy of a Rabbinic Document. Chico, 1985: Scholars Press for Brown Judaic Studies.

Comparative Midrash: The Plan and Program of Genesis Rabbah and Leviticus Rabbah. Atlanta, 1986: Scholars Press for Brown Judaic Studies.

Canon and Connection: Judaism and Intertextuality. Lanham, 1986: University Press of America.

Other Compilations of Rabbinic Exegeses of Scripture

Sifra. The Judaic Commentary on Leviticus. A New Translation. The Leper. Leviticus 13:1–14:57. Chico, 1985: Scholars Press for Brown Judaic Studies. Based on the translation of *Sifra Parashiyyot Negaim* and *Mesora* in *A History of the Mishnaic Law of Purities. VI. Negaim. Sifra.* [With a section by Roger Brooks.]

Sifré to Numbers. An American Translation. I–II. Lanham, 1986: University Press of America Studies in Judaism series.

Chapter 5

Vanquished Nation, Broken Spirit. The Virtues of the Heart in Formative Judaism. New York, 1986: Cambridge University Press.

Chapter 6

The Foundations of Judaism. Method, Teleology, Doctrine. Philadelphia, 1983–1985: Fortress Press. I–III.

The Oral Torah. The Sacred Books of Judaism. An Introduction. San Francisco, 1985: Harper & Row. Paperback: 1987. Bnai Brith Jewish Book Club Selection, 1986.

(Ed.) *Understanding Jewish Theology. Classical Themes and Modern Perspectives.* New York, 1973: Ktav. To date, three printings.

(Ed.) *Understanding Rabbinic Judaism. From Talmudic to Modern Times.* New York, 1974: Ktav. Second printing, 1977; fourth printing, 1985.

(Ed.) *Religions in Antiquity. Essays in Memory of Erwin Ramsdell Goodenough.* Leiden, 1968: Brill. Supplements to Numen. Vol XIV. Second printing, 1970; third printing, 1972.

(Ed.) *Christianity, Judaism, and Other Greco-Roman Cults. Studies for Morton Smith at Sixty.* Leiden, 1975: Brill.

The Way of Torah. An Introduction to Judaism. Encino, 1970: Dickenson Publishing Co. In *Living Religion of Man* Series, edited by Frederick Streng. Second printing, 1971; third printing, 1971.; second edition, revised, 1973; third printing, 1976; third edition, thoroughly revised, Belmont: 1979: Wadsworth Publishing Co.; third printing, 1980;

fourth printing, 1982; fifth printing, 1983; sixth printing, 1985; fourth edition, thoroughly revised, planned for 1987.

(Ed.) *Life of Torah. Readings in the Jewish Religious Experience.* Encino, 1974: Dickenson Publishing Co. Third printing, Belmont, 1980: Wadsworth. Sixth printing, 1984.

There We Sat Down. Talmudic Judaism in the Making. Nashville, 1972: Abingdon. Second printing, New York, 1978: Ktav.

Between Time and Eternity. The Essentials of Judaism. Encino, 1976: Dickenson Publishing Co. Fifth printing, Belmont, 1983: Wadsworth.

Epilogue on Method

(Ed.) *The New Humanities and Academic Disciplines. The Case of Jewish Studies.* Madison, 1984: University of Wisconsin Press.

The Academic Study of Judaism. Essays and Reflections. New York, 1975: Ktav. Second printing, Chico, 1982: Scholars Press for Brown Judaic Studies.

The Academic Study of Judaism. Second Series. New York, 1977: Ktav.

The Academic Study of Judaism. Third Series. Three Contexts of Jewish Learning. New York, 1980: Ktav.

(Ed.) *Take Judaism, for Example. Studies toward the Comparison of Religions.* Chicago, 1983: University of Chicago Press.

(Ed.) *The Study of Ancient Judaism.* New York, 1981: Ktav. I–II.

Judaism in the American Humanities. Chico, 1981: Scholars Press for Brown Judaic Studies.

Judaism in the American Humanities. Second Series. Jewish Studies and the New Humanities. Chico, 1983: Scholars Press for Brown Judaic Studies.

Method and Meaning in Ancient Judaism. Missoula, 1979: Scholars Press for Brown Judaic Studies. Second printing, 1983.

Method and Meaning in Ancient Judaism. Second Series. Chico, 1980: Scholars Press for Brown Judaic Studies.

Method and Meaning in Ancient Judaism. Third Series. Chico, 1980: Scholars Press for Brown Judaic Studies.

Ancient Judaism. Disputes and Debates. Chico, 1984: Scholars Press for Brown Judaic Studies.

The Public Side of Learning. The Political Consequences of Scholarship in the Context of Judaism. Chico, 1985: Scholars Press for the American Academy of Religion *Studies in Religion* Series.

Reading and Believing: Ancient Judaism and Contemporary Gullibility. Atlanta, 1986: Scholars Press for Brown Judaic Studies.

Ancient Judaism and Modern Category-Formation. "Judaism," "Midrash," "Messianism," and Canon in the Past Quarter-Century. Lanham, 1986: University Press of America *Studies in Judaism* Series.

Formative Judaism. Religious, Historical, and Literary Studies. First Series. Chico, 1982: Scholars Press for Brown Judaic Studies.

Formative Judaism. Religious, Historical, and Literary Studies. Second Series. Chico, 1983: Scholars Press for Brown Judaic Studies.

Formative Judaism. Religious, Historical, and Literary Studies. Third Series. Torah, Pharisees, and Rabbis. Chico, 1983: Scholars Press for Brown Judaic Studies.

Formative Judaism. Religious, Historical, and Literary Studies. Fourth Series. Problems of Classification and Composition. Chico, 1984: Scholars Press for Brown Judaic Studies.

Formative Judaism. Religious, Historical, and Literary Studies. Fifth Series. Revisioning the Written Records of a Nascent Religion. Chico, 1985: Scholars Press for Brown Judaic Studies.

Major Trends in Formative Judaism. First Series. Society and Symbol in Political Crisis. Chico, 1983: Scholars Press for Brown Judaic Studies.

Major Trends in Formative Judaism. Second Series. Texts, Contents, and Contexts. Chico, 1984: Scholars Press for Brown Judaic Studies.

Major Trends in Formative Judaism. Third Series. The Three Stages in the Formation of Judaism. Chico, 1985: Scholars Press for Brown Judaic Studies. Italian translation: Casale Monferrato, 1988: Editrice Marietti

The Religious Study of Judaism. Description, Analysis, Interpretation. Volume One. Lanham, 1986: University Press of America *Studies in Judaism* Series.

The Religious Study of Judaism. Description, Analysis, Interpretation. Volume Two. *The Centrality of Context.* Lanham, 1986: University Press of America *Studies in Judaism* Series.

The Religious Study of Judaism. Volume III. *Debates on Method, Reports of Results.* Lanham, 1986: University Press of America *Studies in Judaism* Series.

Index

index to biblical and talmudic references